T0301624

Institutions in Crisis

NEW THINKING IN POLITICAL ECONOMY

Series Editor: Peter J. Boettke, *George Mason University, USA*

New Thinking in Political Economy aims to encourage scholarship in the intersection of the disciplines of politics, philosophy and economics. It has the ambitious purpose of reinvigorating political economy as a progressive force for understanding social and economic change.

The series is an important forum for the publication of new work analysing the social world from a multidisciplinary perspective. With increased specialization (and professionalization) within universities, interdisciplinary work has become increasingly uncommon. Indeed, during the 20th century, the process of disciplinary specialization reduced the intersection between economics, philosophy and politics and impoverished our understanding of society. Modern economics in particular has become increasingly mathematical and largely ignores the role of institutions and the contribution of moral philosophy and politics.

New Thinking in Political Economy will stimulate new work that combines technical knowledge provided by the 'dismal science' and the wisdom gleaned from the serious study of the 'worldly philosophy'. The series will reinvigorate our understanding of the social world by encouraging a multidisciplinary approach to the challenges confronting society in the new century.

Recent titles in the series include:

Media, Development, and Institutional Change
Christopher J. Coyne and Peter T. Leeson

The Economics of Ignorance and Coordination
Subjectivism and the Austrian School of Economics
Thierry Aimar

Socialism, Economic Calculation and Entrepreneurship
Jesús Huerta de Soto

The Political Economy of Hurricane Katrina and Community Rebound
Edited by Emily Chamlee-Wright and Virgil Henry Storr

Robust Political Economy
Classical Liberalism and the Future of Public Policy
Mark Pennington

Good Governance in the 21st Century
Conflict, Institutional Change, and Development in the Era of Globalization
Edited by Joachim Ahrens, Rolf Caspers and Janina Weingarth

Institutions in Crisis
European Perspectives on the Recession
Edited by David Howden

Institutions in Crisis

European Perspectives on the Recession

Edited by

David Howden

Saint Louis University, Madrid, Spain

NEW THINKING IN POLITICAL ECONOMY

Edward Elgar

Cheltenham, UK • Northampton, MA, USA

Published by
Edward Elgar Publishing Limited
The Lypiatts
15 Lansdown Road
Cheltenham
Glos GL50 2JA
UK

Edward Elgar Publishing, Inc.
William Pratt House
9 Dewey Court
Northampton
Massachusetts 01060
USA

A catalogue record for this book
is available from the British Library

Library of Congress Control Number: 2011926266

ISBN 978 0 85793 211 2

Typeset by Servis Filmsetting Ltd, Stockport, Cheshire
Printed and bound by MPG Books Group, UK

Contents

Figures

Tables

Contributors

Maria Alvarado is Professor of Accounting at Rey Juan Carlos University, Madrid, Spain.

Philipp Bagus is Professor of Economics at Rey Juan Carlos University, Madrid, Spain.

Anthony J. Evans is Associate Professor of Economics at ESCP Europe Business School, London, England.

Gabriel A. Giménez-Roche is Professor and Chair of the Economics Department at the Champagne School of Management, Troyes, France, and Maître de Conférences at the Paris Institute of Political Science.

David Howden is Chair of the Division of Business and Social Sciences and Assistant Professor of Economics at St Louis University, at their Madrid campus, Madrid, Spain.

Jesús Huerta de Soto is Professor of Economics at the University Rey Juan Carlos, Madrid, Spain.

Jörg Guido Hülsmann is Professor of Economics at the University of Angers, Angers, France.

Malte Tobias Kähler is a management consultant for Steria Mummert Consulting AG.

Laura Muro is Assistant Professor of Accounting at St Louis University, at their Madrid campus, Madrid, Spain.

Brian Ó Caithnia is Adjunct Professor of Economics at Syracuse University, Madrid, Spain.

Jiří Schwarz teaches Institutional Economics at Charles University, Prague, and serves as an advisor to the Czech National Bank Board.

Josef Šíma is Professor of Economics and President of CEVRO Institute (School of Legal and Social Studies), Prague, Czech Republic.

Kirk Lee Tennant is Assistant Professor of Business at St Louis University, at their Madrid campus, Madrid, Spain.

Fernando Ulrich holds a Master's in Economics from the University Rey Juan Carlos in Madrid, Spain, and works in investment banking at Voga Capital in Brazil.

Antonio Zanella is a PhD candidate in Economics at Rey Juan Carlos University, Madrid, Spain.

Foreword

Jesús Huerta de Soto

The crisis that erupted in Europe in late 2008 and the accompanying recession that continues to this day have exposed the unsustainable situation the European Union has long promoted. What has been lost on commentators and economists alike is that the current problems have very little to do with the present state of affairs. This financial crisis began the moment that the market, which is a dynamically efficient process (Huerta de Soto, 2010c, pp. 1–30), discovered the true errors of its past.

Banks in particular realized that the loans granted throughout the boom were only backed by a smaller fraction of the asset values than they previously thought. Bank liabilities, primarily the deposits created during the boom, retained their value throughout the collapse. The specific characteristics of bank demand deposits, characteristics that they share with physical cash – that they are available continuously on demand and at par value – retained their value while the assets backing these liabilities quickly lost value. The resultant widespread illiquidity and eventual insolvencies were not the cause of the recession, but were some of its most important and early symptoms (Huerta de Soto, 2010a). Understanding the root causes to the crisis, and more importantly that the current recession is a necessary consequence of these causes, is essential to exiting the situation as quickly and painlessly as possible.

Indeed, a situation where a general cluster of entrepreneurial errors occurs, much like the present situation, can only arise through a general disruption to the common bond between all market transactions: money. The Austrian theory of economic cycles, as most fully propounded by Friedrich Hayek (1931) and Ludwig von Mises ([1949] 1998), describes much of the current imbalances in need of correction. The theory is, however, only a special and specific case of the more general theory of the impossibility of calculation under socialism, discovered and explained by Mises (1951).

Explaining why entrepreneurs fall prey to the false signals caused by artificially low interest rates is one area where the Austrian theory of the business cycle has traditionally been weakest. Several critiques have taken aim at the supposed irrationality that entrepreneurs must be assumed to exercise in order continually to fail to understand that the interest rate as controlled by a central bank is not necessarily indicative of that set by social time preference (see, for example, Cowen, 1997; Wagner, 1999; Yeager, 1997). Some of my own work, as well as that of my students, has shown that even if entrepreneurs understand that the credit expansion is not sustainable, they are forced to participate via a 'prisoner's dilemma' situation (Huerta de Soto, 2009, pp. 664–71; Howden, 2010). Not partaking in the boom sacrifices market share and profit to those firms that do partake. Participation in a boom must be undertaken lest other less prudent companies participate successfully and push the more prudent out of business.

In this current book, Gabriel A. Giménez-Roche expands on the analysis of entrepreneurial error, and delves into the particular avenues where entrepreneurs see their plans disrupted during the boom. Financial intermediaries, despite having erred during the past decade and facilitating the current recession, do serve an instrumental role in the market. By connecting entrepreneurs with access to capital and other resources to those with the money capital necessary to put their plans into action, the financial entrepreneur is ultimately responsible for much of the plan coordination in the modern economy. Giménez-Roche outlines in great detail how the financial entrepreneur leads others into error as they are provided with false interest rate signals coupled with an artificially high supply of credit. Indeed, by furthering the work of Hülsmann (1998) he demonstrates how an analysis of entrepreneurship that incorporates both the social and institutional structures of the market exposes the illusory signals that the fractional reserve banking system provides. It is only when we view the market through the entrepreneur's compromised spectacles that we can gain understanding of how they err under such conditions.

While expansion of money and credit by the European Central Bank (ECB) has been somewhat less irresponsible than America's Federal Reserve system, it has not been entirely free of errors.[1] Indeed, during the early stages of the lead-up to and formation of the European Monetary Union (EMU) many countries previously notorious for their loose credit policies were tamed as part of the convergence criteria. Only several countries in Europe's periphery – the now infamous PIIGS of Portugal, Ireland, Italy, Greece and Spain – continued to be immersed with considerable credit expansion after the convergence process subsided. Understanding how high-inflation periphery countries experienced such high expansion credit rates goes far in understanding how the boom reached such dizzying heights. In 2006 the Spanish economy, for example, built 700,000 new homes – more than the total built in Germany, France and the United

Kingdom combined. Today more than 1 million of these homes are empty – more than the total for the whole of the US, a country with almost eight times the population.[2]

While the ECB for the most part pursued a tight money policy when viewing the Eurozone as a whole, the crisis of 2008 changed the situation dramatically. Credit expansion was still not pursued to the same extent as with the Federal Reserve's quantitative easing programs (QEI, and now QEII), but there was a severe reduction in collateral requirements on its refinancing operations. As Philipp Bagus and David Howden (2009a; 2009b) have demonstrated, the ECB continually altered its scope of accepted collateral to maintain lending operations to illiquid European nations. Each time a Eurozone member state had its credit rating cut over the previous two years the ECB responded by altering its acceptable loan collateral to accommodate these 'misfortunate' countries.

While these inflationary policies over the last decade brought on vast and evident entrepreneurial malinvestments, there is a more pressing problem now becoming apparent. Real economic growth did occur in the Eurozone over the past ten years. Unfortunately the inflationary malinvestments make it incredibly difficult to identify what Europeans did right, while shifting the focus to what was evidently done wrong.

Anthony Evans's contribution to the current volume assesses what was right and what was wrong in Ireland. One of the largest problems with the current recalculation is discerning what was and is misallocated capital. Although we know that there were many entrepreneurial mistakes incurred in the past, we also know that not every single entrepreneurial decision was misguided. Ireland underwent a boom due to real causes in the late 1990s and early part of the 21st century. Unfortunately, while some forms of growth were real, much was also fueled by an expansion of money and credit, which grew at rates many multiples faster than in the core of Europe.

The recognition of such prior malinvested capital can lead to surprisingly swift adjustments. For example, once Spanish economic agents realized the errors previously induced by the inflationary policy pursued by the ECB the adjustment was relatively swift. In less than a year more than 150,000 companies disappeared, mainly related to the housing sector, and almost 5 million workers previously employed in the wrong sectors were laid off. While the current economic situation in Spain today looks quite bleak, the shedding of these erroneous investments was a necessary step before commencing a period of economic growth. Prolonging these malinvestments in unprofitable industries, much as is happening today in many bailed-out areas of the European economy, serves no purpose other than to lengthen the difficult time necessary to be endured before recovery can commence.

When we compare the level of credit expansion with the volume of malinvestment produced from it, we would be inclined to state that this particular business cycle will be less severe in the Eurozone than in the US. While this may be true for the root causes of the bust, the current after-shocks of the crisis are being bred asymmetrically across the Eurozone's member states. In particular, while the core mostly muddles through today's recession at marginally higher unemployment rates and below-trend GDP growth, much of the periphery witnesses soaring unemployment rates, government deficits and debt.

David Howden looks into this asymmetry, and particularly at its effects in the labor market. Europe has always been 'victim' to a high long-run unemployment rate, at least by American standards. Despite these seemingly high average unemployment rates, throughout most of the post-war period the European economies have enjoyed prosperity in terms of productivity and growth on a par with their Anglo counterparts. Part of the reason for the current high unemployment rates is also the reason for the maintained performance during the post-war period. Highly regulated European economies, especially in Southern Europe, have seen their labor forces exit the official (taxpaying) sectors and enter into the grey, or shadow economy (non-taxpaying). This increase in regulation was sufficient to lead an entrepreneurial exodus from the formal economy, but it has been only partially successful in completely breaking the European entrepreneurial spirit. The shadow economy, which reaches as high as 25 percent of the official GDP in some Southern European countries, continues to flourish as increased regulation and increased taxes drive entrepreneurs from the more comfortable and legal formal economy.

In fact, while unemployment as reported has been strikingly high in many Southern European countries, the very construction of the unemployment figures masks the true situation of these blighted economies. Spain, which has 20 percent of its labor force out of work, has a sizable underground economy that employs hundreds of thousands of workers. The 20 percent unemployment rate is not necessarily a concern for many employees, who are able to find waged employment in the informal sector. There is no doubt that conditions, wages and benefits are much lower with informal work, but it would be a misnomer to pronounce these laborers as being 'unemployed'. These unemployed workers have exacerbated already tenuous fiscal positions, as they represent workers typically enrolled in some type of unemployment benefits program but not contributing to the system that funds it.

On their own, such conditions would only represent a misuse of resources. Today, however, they are indicative of a broader problem afflicting European countries to varying degrees as they search for recovery. Labor rigidities in the form of high unemployment benefits and stringent employment laws restrict the ease to which misallocated laborers can be reallocated. Despite promising freedom of mobility within the European Union, heavily regulated labor markets form an implicit barrier to entry for most laborers regardless of their country of origin.

Yet, while loose credit conditions have worsened an already problematic European labor market, they are only incomplete explanations for why the crisis was as extreme as it was, and why the present recession has persisted for as long as it has.

The acceptance of international accounting standards (IAS) and the incorporation of them into law in many European countries has abandoned the traditional principle of prudence that accounting abided by. As the historical cost accounting was replaced by 'fair value' assessments for balance sheet assets, particularly financial assets, an illusion of wealth drove firms to take on ever-riskier positions. This turned into a feedback loop, as rising financial asset values ballooned firms' balance sheets, thus allowing them to take on ever-increasing amounts of liabilities. The shift away from prudent accounting rules acted in a pro-cyclical manner. During prosperous times a false 'wealth effect' increased risk taking. As financial asset values dried up, a feedback loop commenced that required firms to recapitalize their balance sheets, leading to shifts out of newly risky (i.e. deflating) assets and into 'safer' assets – traditionally thought to be government debt. María Alvarado, Laura Muro and Kirk Lee Tennant's contribution to this volume explains the effects of these accounting rule changes on firms, and specifically what macro-events resulted from the shift from tradition to the unknown (and untested).

Similarly, Antonio Zanella probes into insurance regulations, specifically the Solvency Accords governing the capital requirements of the European insurance industry. While the European Commission functions as the ultimate regulator for industries within its jurisdiction, few have questioned whether a stark conflict of interest exists between the regulations that businesses are subjected to and the welfare of the greater European project. Indeed, prior to the current recession there was little reason to believe that there was any such conflict.

In response to increasing pressure on Eurozone sovereign debt starting in 2008 the insurance industry has been subject to more stringent capital requirements. Although higher capital ratios must be increased across the board, the asset-specific capital ratios have been altered to provide more favorable incentives for the insurance industry to hold sovereign debt. As the insurance industry currently holds in excess of €2.5 trillion in fixed income securities out of over €6.5 trillion of total assets, it is a sizable increase in funding to troubled governments. The result has been a continued deterioration of the insurance industry's balance sheet, as increasing levels of risky government debt are taken on just to satisfy the regulators who are also the originators of these risky assets. A more severe repercussion has been yield compression, which has allowed unsustainable government finances to persist. By legislating an artificially increased demand for sovereign debt through the not insubstantial insurance asset market, several European countries have found willing buyers for their debt that would normally be purchased only with some reluctance. This decreased cost of borrowing has allowed, in turn, sustained budget deficits to reach a breaking point – one that is becoming all too obvious today.

As European regulators are only concerned with risk-weighted assets, and not total leverage, there were no red flags raised by financial institutions overleveraging their balance sheets. Lulled into complacency that the Solvency and Basel Accords would adequately define the necessary capital to mitigate illiquidity-induced losses, the financial system continued overextending itself. This past trend has not been rectified; the financial system still finds itself needing to adequately meet a risk-weighted capital level – one for which the actual weights of the different asset classes are skewed from where reality (and prudence) would suggest they should be. Sovereign debt has proven itself to be anything but 'risk free' over the past two years. Yet such fixed income securities still enjoy a prized place atop the risk-classification ladder as the safest, and hence least capitalized, asset class.

While one of Zanella's conclusions is that the European insurance market artificially sustains the sovereign debt market, Philipp Bagus peers into the structure of the European Central Bank's refinancing operations to show a similar effect. By backing its balance sheet with European sovereign debt, structural support for government deficits was built into the ECB from its very inception. The bailout that has been explicitly given to some countries is only a special example of the implicit bailout that has been ongoing in the Eurozone for a decade. As the ECB exchanged Euro funding for sovereign debt collateral, an increased demand for Eurozone government debt was created. Countries were effectively rewarded for increasing their debt loads.

More troubling was that the countries that took on the largest debt-financing schemes gained at the expense of the more prudent. As the ECB effectively monetized a large portion of all Eurozone government debts, the effect of this monetization – price inflation – spread throughout all of the countries using the common currency. Highly indebted peripheral European countries saw the real value of their debts reduced through inflation, while their more prudent core European counterparts bore the costs of this increased inflation. In essence, the core has been giving implicit aid to the periphery for over a decade.

Unfortunately a lack of logic has swept the European continent. The drive for market liberalizations spawned a prosperous epoch throughout the late 1990s and 2000s. This causal connection has been seemingly forgotten as policymakers – both of the individual member states and the centralized European Commission – clamor for increasing interventions. A crisis brought on by an excess of government spending and deficits is now, according to prevailing Keynesian theories, going to be resolved via additional doses of government spending and deficits.

Fernando Ulrich exposes some of the myths of these government spending programs. Indeed, while short-term gains may be realized by these 'make work' projects, three conditions will lead to longer-term problems. First, as governments turn to deficit financing to fund these projects, we see the crowding-out effect via reduced private investment. Indeed, in some countries where the private sector is smallest (the Greek public sector, for example, accounts for approximately 40 percent of its GDP) the resultant minor tax base has made deficit financing the sole method available to finance these spending programs. Second, these spending programs will need to be paid back some day. When they are repaid, we can expect below potential growth, as resources will be redirected to the spending programs of today. It is questionable in some cases whether today's debts will ever be paid back. Ireland's bailout of €85 billion has come at an interest rate of 5.8 percent. Irish economic growth will almost assuredly be lower than this for the foreseeable future. As the ability of the country to repay these loans can be thought of as a ratio with GDP growth in the denominator, and the applicable interest rate as the numerator, we see that Ireland will have increasing difficulties finding the revenue to repay this loan as the recession progresses (Gros, 2010). Finally, government spending is rarely viewed as bringing high growth opportunities. At what price has the current increase in government expenditure come at? If we think of a generation of government projects returning lower yields than the comparable private sector investments were capable of, this loss of long-term growth potential could be devastating.

Indeed, although 'austerity' has been a new rallying cry within the EU, the Commission itself has taken a different approach. While urging national governments to control their deficits, the European Commission seeks a 5.9 percent increase in its own budget for 2011 (Castle, 2010). In total, the budget is about €3.5 billion more than the member states say they can afford. EU officials took a 'heroic' pay cut of 0.4 percent recently, and Spanish public workers took an across the board 5 percent wage reduction. Getting member state finances in order has taken precedence over that of the larger EU – a case of do as I say, not as I do.

Indeed, the levels of indebtedness are a little paradoxical to the uninitiated and may come as a shock to those who understand the founding principles of the EU and EMU. The signing of the Treaty of Maastricht in 1992 was supposed to usher in a period of stability for Europe, constrained by a rule of law designed to impose strict limits on the governments making up the new European Union. In particular one rule –that a member state government may only run a deficit of 3 percent of GDP in any one year except for rare and exceptional circumstances – was reckoned to be the tool necessary to rid Europe of its public spending excesses of the past. As Malte Tobias Kähler illustrates, the change from a rule-based regime to discretion over the course of the recession has brought a new crisis to the EU. Lacking clearly defined operating rules, uncertainty has increased as to what the future holds. The European Central Bank (ECB), founded upon the constrained rule-based operating policies of the German Bundesbank, has shed any semblance to rule-based management that could be thought of. At any rate, if the ECB is currently following a set of predefined rules we are hard pressed to identify what exactly they may be.

Rules are not established for the 'normal' times when events seem to unravel exactly as planned. Rules are thought out in advance and enacted for those exact moments when the tempest hits, and if there is no clear view of the way out of the storm, trust must be placed in a guiding compass to lead the way. Europe's rule-based compass was not designed for when the boom was in full force; rather it was to guide it to dry ground when market conditions significantly worsened. Now is just such a time.

Indeed, entrance to the European Union was initiated by many neighboring countries under the pretense of increased stability. Especially in Eastern Europe, years of post-communist political charades attracted voters to a more accountable and secure Western European existence.

Economics, like all the social sciences, lacks the ability to compare directly two specific groups when placed in similar situations. The fall of the Berlin Wall and the reunification of Eastern and Western Germany provide as close an approximation to a controlled test as we can normally hope to attain in the dismal science. Jiří Schwarz and Josef Šíma make use of another similar economic transition – the breakup of Czechoslovakia into its two component states of the Czech Republic and Slovakia – to assess how each fared during the last decade. While these two countries commenced from essentially identical starting points – similar geographies, standards of living, traditions and citizens – they diverged as Slovakia vied for entrance to the Eurozone and the Czech Republic opted for monetary independence.

As Schwarz and Šíma convincingly argue, entrance to the Eurozone provided a commitment mechanism that led to many meaningful and positive market reforms in Slovakia. The Slovak economy consequently pulled ahead of its western Czech neighbor. With the onset of the recession and Slovakia's simultaneous adoption of the Euro (finalized in 2009) a considerable cost was borne by the small nation's business community. While the longer-term benefits of increased investment may some day be realized, the short-term costs could not have come at a worse time. As the process of striving to meet the convergence criteria brought positive institutional change to Slovakia, it is difficult to say whether many additional gains will be made now that Eurozone entrance is secured. By opting not to join, the Czech Republic lacked the commitment mechanism to reform its political (and monetary) frameworks. Slow reform is better than none and it may well be that refraining from becoming entangled in an ever-expanding bureaucratic European monetary alliance will reap longer-term benefits on the Czech nation and its citizens.

Understanding where Europe stands today requires some knowledge of how it came to be here. The unification of Europe under its political and monetary unions promised important reforms, but an important step was missed. Already top-heavy bureaucratic countries joined an increasingly bureaucratic centralized union, whether centralized in Brussels or Frankfurt. While some evident advantages and liberties seemed to be gained (one could now travel from Barcelona to Paris without a passport), many unseen losses are unaccounted for.

In a timely piece, Brian Ó Caithnia looks into the EU's largest spending program, the Common Agricultural Policy (CAP). That the policy is one of the least understood EU policies is testament to the web of complications that underlie its organization. Indeed, the CAP has been the pride of European integrationalism since its inception in the late 1950s, yet it has grown to be a behemoth. It is a show of the strength of political will to ignore all evidence that it has overgrown its original purpose, uses a disproportionate share of the EU budget and has wasted untold billions of Euros in political rent-seeking and failed agricultural policies. Indeed, while the EU tries to secure its 2011 budget, earmarks for agriculture abound: €300 million for dairy farmers, €10 million for a school fruit plan, €8 million for beekeeping and €8 million just for promoting awareness of the bloc's agricultural policy (Castle, 2010).

Countries joining the European Union under the pretense of a forward-looking progressive future are soon greeted with a backward-looking monstrosity – a policy designed to keep farmers on their land, instead of allowing for productivity increases to permit (if they choose) these producers to strive for an alternative life. While some farmers have been better off, the vast majority have seen their livelihoods robbed from them. As Canny sums it up: 'Intellectually, the CAP is in tatters. It has failed on *all* of its intended objectives.'

The CAP is just one of many failed European policies over the last half-century. Europe, for better or worse, has a rich and long history – political, economic and cultural. Understanding where it came from is essential to understanding where its future lies. Europe's continuing recession exposes some of the deeper-rooted issues at stake. A drive for increased integration has failed to ask the critical question: at what cost? Europe could have achieved integration easily in a heartbeat. Opening the labor markets and reducing regulatory hurdles could have been enacted at any point (even unilaterally if need be). Instead a political apparatus was implemented that soon became the *raison d'être* for the new Europe. Exit from the political or monetary union is now so unthinkable that politicians are willing to save it at any cost.

While the essays contained in this volume were written in 2010, some recent events have proven their messages to be prescient. The deep-rooted issues of the common currency area have intensified, leading to a bailout of Portugal. Fiscal imbalances have not improved, and politicians have yet to learn that debt-fueled crises cannot be solved by running perpetual deficits. In my own country of Spain, valiant efforts to get the public deficit below 6 percent of Spanish GDP for 2011 have met resistance. It was not so long ago that the Maastricht Treaty calling for deficits of no more than 3 percent of GDP were strictly adhered to. While much has been learned over the past several years, there is still room for improvement.

Almost 20 years ago my own book, *Socialism, Economic Calculation and Entrepreneurship*, looked at a similar crisis (Huerta de Soto, 2010b). The failure of socialist doctrines, concretely manifested in the fall of the Berlin Wall, left an ideological gap. The years that followed witnessed a revival of liberalism in Europe – east and west. A similar crisis is before us now, this time operating in reverse. The current European recession is being offered as an excuse for a wider, more expansive centralized Europe. Failure to recognize the true causes of the recession – failed institutions that have plagued Europe for years, and will continue to do so if permitted to continue – will prolong the current malaise, and hold Europe back from its new future. Let us hope that the current volume does much to bring this new Europe to us.

NOTES

1. This is not to imply that Europe's recession is not severe, or that it will not worsen in the future. Already the future levels of longer-term European economic growth are suspect. Jörg Guido Hülsmann's chapter assesses some of the prospects for Europe's exit from recession. A depletion in the capital stock of European industry has left the continent with largely depreciated and increasingly obsolete means of production. This has not

been evident due to an anomaly in the calculation of the much-vaunted GDP that largely overlooks reinvestment in depreciated capital. While this anomaly has allowed for relatively buoyant GDP figures throughout the present recession, when recovery nears and the time for increased production comes, European entrepreneurs will be entrapped by capital equipment woefully unready for the recovery at hand. Mark Skousen (1990) and myself (Huerta de Soto, 2009, pp. 305–12) have both given alternatives to account for this capital investment. Replacing the current gross national product statistics, which exclude many of the intermediary productive works where much economic activity takes place, with a 'gross national output' figure to account for these activities could almost double our conception of the economic activity of an economy, according to Skousen.

2. We must note that Spain is a unique example of an excess supply of housing that was driven by a large influx of migrant workers – primarily Latin American, Romanian and Moroccan – into Spain. The fact that Spain constructed such an enormous excess of housing units in such a short period is indicative, however, of the extent to which cheap money flowed into the country in need of a use.

REFERENCES

Bagus, P. and D. Howden (2009a), 'The Federal Reserve System and Eurosystem's balance sheet policies during the financial crisis: a comparative analysis', *Romanian Economic and Business Review*, **4** (3), 165–85.

Bagus, P. and D. Howden (2009b), 'Qualitative easing in support of a tumbling financial system: a look at the Eurosystem's recent balance sheet policies', *Economic Affairs*, **29** (4), 60–65.

Castle, S. (2010), 'While Europe scrimps, European Union spends', *New York Times*, www.nytimes.com/2010/10/08/business/global/08austerity.html?_r=2, 7 October.

Cowen, T. (1997), *Risk and Business Cycles: New and Old Austrian Perspectives*, London: Routledge.

Gros, D. (2010), 'All together now? Arguments for a big-bang solution to Eurozone problems', VoxEU, www.voxeu.org/index.php?q=node/5892, 5 December.

Hayek, F.A. von (1931), *Prices and Production*, London: Routledge.

Howden, D. (2010), 'Knowledge shifts and the business cycle: when boom turns to bust', *Review of Austrian Economics*, **23** (2), 165–82.

Huerta de Soto, J. (2009), *Money, Bank Credit and Economic Cycles* (2nd edn), trans. Melinda A. Stroup, Auburn, AL: Ludwig von Mises Institute.

Huerta de Soto, J. (2010a), 'Economic recessions, banking reform, and the future of capitalism', Hayek Memorial Lecture, delivered at the London School of Economics and Political Science, http://mises.org/daily/4817, 28 October.

Huerta de Soto, J. (2010b), *Socialism, Economic Calculation and Entrepreneurship*, Cheltenham, UK and Northampton, MA, USA: Edward Elgar.

Huerta de Soto, J. (2010c), *The Theory of Dynamic Efficiency*, London and New York: Routledge.

Hülsmann, J.G. (1998), 'Toward a general theory of error cycles', *Quarterly Journal of Austrian Economics*, **1** (4), 1–23.

Mises, L. von (1951), *Socialism: An Economic and Sociological Analysis*, trans. J. Kahane, New Haven, CT: Yale University Press.

Mises, L. von ([1949]1998), *Human Action*, Auburn, AL: Ludwig von Mises Institute.

Skousen, M. (1990), *The Structure of Production*, New York: New York University Press.

Wagner, R.E. (1999), 'Austrian cycle theory: saving the wheat while discarding the chaff', *Review of Austrian Economics*, **12** (1), 105–11.

Yeager, L.B. (1997), *The Fluttering Veil: Essays on Monetary Disequilibrium*, Indianapolis, IN: Liberty Fund.

1. Institutional illusion and financial entrepreneurship in the European debt scheme

Gabriel A. Giménez-Roche

While the ongoing public debt crisis reveals the very bad condition of the public finances of the European PIGS nations (Portugal, Ireland, Greece and Spain), the misbehavior of certain private financial institutions – such as Deutsche Bank and Goldman Sachs (Chambers and Ridley, 2010) – has come under increasing scrutiny by public officials. These accusations are of the same nature as those made in the past against the financial players who did not respect the flawed rules of the financial game played by governments, central banks and the banking system in general. In spite of any misbehavior by a financial institution, it should be remembered that financial markets are essentially markets where capital funds are transferred, usually via bank intermediation, from net-saving individuals to net-borrowing individuals. Capital losses should thus be limited to the funds of the individuals engaging in only this kind of exchanges. The same is valid for futures and derivatives markets. In futures markets, although there is a financial operation involved, it only consists of a sales and acquisition operation without any actual creation of wealth sprouting from it. Although one party to a financial contract can be a loser while the other is a winner, the economy as a whole should not be either gaining or losing.

Yet financial markets move more funds in volume than the world's total funds, a most disturbing fact if one remembers that financial markets are primordially derived from the goods markets.[1] If the volume of financial transactions surpasses that of the goods markets, there can only be one answer: there are too many funds unbacked by real wealth. A comprehension of how this is possible represents the missing link in understanding why financial markets are so unstable, as is often pointed out by government officials and the general press (Kiff et al., 2009). Nevertheless, understanding this missing link demonstrates that no financial instability could ever be possible without institutional instability coming from the official authorities actually responsible for the production of money and credit. An institutionally unstable monetary system has as its foundation the fractional reserve system of banking that nourishes all financial markets from the short-term monetary markets to the long-term capital markets. The aim of this chapter is to show that the public debt scheme of the Eurozone countries and their unified fractional reserve banking system is the cause of financial instability and the very fiscal difficulties confronted by these same countries. This chapter will present a socially situated praxeological analysis of financial entrepreneurial behavior under fractional reserve banking in order to explain how the European fractional reserve system generates institutional illusions that falsify entrepreneurial decision-making (Hülsmann, 1998). First, the entrepreneurial mechanism of socially situated action will be presented. The distinguishing approach of socially situated praxeological analysis of entrepreneurship is the crossover between methodological individualism (Menger, 1994; Mises, 1996) and 'structurating-action' sociological analysis (Giddens, 1984; Merton, 1968; Parsons, 1949). It explains individual action through a means–end approach while contextualizing this action in the socio-institutional structure in which it takes place. Following this presentation, the analysis will be enriched by explaining how European governments and the European Central Bank (ECB) mold the socio-institutional structure of the financial entrepreneur, setting in motion the process of institutional illusion that leads to malinvestments and unsustainable speculation.

ENTREPRENEURSHIP AND THE FINANCIAL MARKETS

Socially Situated Individual Entrepreneurial Action

At the purely individual level, individual action is always entrepreneurial because it implies the use of the agent's means toward an uncertain end (Mises, 1996). Therefore, in order to be able to distinguish between entrepreneurs and non-entrepreneurs, it is not enough to simply define the functional individual's entrepreneurial action (Menger, 1994); rather it must be situated in its socio-institutional environment. Once individual action is socially situated it becomes evident that some actions are institutionally *integrated* as means *into* the actions of other individuals that are not institutionally integrated into the actions of others (though these actions are always institutionally connected). Actions are thus institutionally integrated as means into others' actions through contracts of provision of goods and services (Coleman, 1990; Giddens, 1984). The socially connected but institutionally non-integrated actions are what will be treated as entrepreneurial actions in this chapter.

Entrepreneurial action is further distinguished from non-entrepreneurial action by its praxeological tri-dimensionality. First, it is diachronically profit-seeking; full entrepreneurs seek differential gains through time. They use their stock of means of action – their capital funds – in the present for future revenue, which they hope will more than cover their present use of capital. Non-entrepreneurs do not engage in diachronic profit-seeking due to the contractual nature of their gains. Indeed, the contractual promise of payment a priori eliminates the diachronic nature of their profit-seeking. The gain of the institutionally integrated agent is contractually synchronous with the rendering of his or her service. Thus, the non-entrepreneur obtains gain within one exchange transaction, while the entrepreneur needs at least two exchange transactions separated in time (Huerta de Soto, 2009) – hence his gain is a diachronic differential between exchanges.

The second praxeological dimension of entrepreneurial action is uncertainty-bearing. Although entrepreneurs do not institutionally integrate their action into that of others, their actions still take place in a social environment beyond their control as they cannot control the motivations behind the actions of others as well as their consequences (Parsons, 1949; Giddens, 1984). Yet, entrepreneurs can at least try to eliminate one source of uncertainty; the one coming from agents with whom they associate in order to obtain means necessary for their own undertakings. In order to do this they must use their capital to integrate these agents. If the contract institutionally integrates the non-entrepreneurs into the action of the entrepreneur, it is the entrepreneurial capital funding of their remuneration that integrates their uncertainty to that of the entrepreneur. In fact, the entrepreneur's uncertainty is not reduced or increased by this integration; it is simply confirmed by it. In transferring capital in the present for an uncertain remuneration in the future, the entrepreneur makes one thing certain: if he fails, he will lose his capital. The institutional integration of non-entrepreneurs via contracts ensures that the entrepreneur is the uncertainty-bearer, while non-entrepreneurs bear no uncertainty of losing the capital of an enterprise which is not theirs (Mises, 1980a).

Finally, the third dimension distinguishing entrepreneurial from non-entrepreneurial action is the ultimate power of decision-making. Just like the other two dimensions, this is also derived from the fact that the entrepreneur is the one controlling the capital that funds the enterprise. The ultimate power of decision-making is the dimension that definitively distinguishes the entrepreneur from the non-entrepreneur in the enterprise. It is the dimension that personifies the ownership of capital within

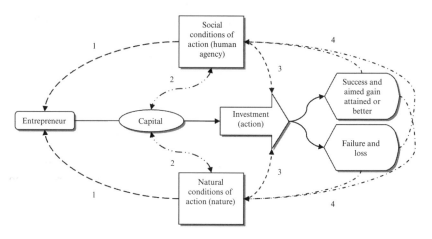

Figure 1.1   Structure of socially situated action

the entrepreneur. It should be noted that the ultimate power of decision-making is not the power of management, as this can be a hired service from a non-entrepreneur just like any other within the enterprise. The ultimate power of decision-making is the power of judgment over the very existence of the enterprise (Knight, 2006; Lewis, 1937). As long as the institution of private property over one's enterprise is in place, no one can decide on the continuation or termination of the enterprise but the owner of the capital.[2]

The three dimensions of entrepreneurial action are manifested interdependently within the structure of action, as shown in Figure 1.1. Figure 1.1 shows how the entrepreneur and his capital are linked, as the capital is the stock of means enabling his action. The fact that the agent acts implies that he is aiming at the success of his action, his end of gain – hence profit-seeking. Action, however, is undertaken when the decision is made to initiate the use of capital. This decision is based on the perception and acknowledgment of the conditions of action (dashed lines 1), that is, the aspects of the entrepreneur's socio-physical environment that are beyond his control. These conditions include natural phenomena – the knowledge of which is embodied in natural sciences – and social phenomena – the knowledge of which is embodied in social sciences, cultural and legislative institutions (Giddens, 1984). All available and objective knowledge of these phenomena allow for the calculation of class probability, which enables the agent to incorporate any foreseeable change in his action (also depicted by dashed lines 1).[3] The entrepreneur can also channel some social conditions of action into his capital by means of contracts of the provision of goods and services. He surrenders part of his capital fund to remunerate other agents who then surrender their goods and services to the capital stock of the entrepreneur (dashed lines 2).

Unfortunately for entrepreneurs, they cannot fully and/or correctly perceive or acknowledge all conditions of action. Such imperfect and/or incomplete knowledge of the conditions of action introduce the possibility of error, which embodies the temporal uncertainty of the action (O'Driscoll and Rizzo, 1996). Entrepreneurs can only account for the conditions in a subjective way that is not based on anything objective; they can only calculate case probabilities (or even nothing at all, thus indicating full ignorance), which are subject to error and subsequent losses.[4] Those aspects of the conditions of action that are ignored by entrepreneurs, then, are the ones that affect their actions in a beneficial or detrimental way (dashed line 3), thus making their success or failure something utterly uncertain.

Moreover, entrepreneurial action and its consequences have an impact on the very conditions of action; an impact that may influence reactions to one's actions thus changing or creating new conditions of action that must be held to account by the entrepreneur in the future (Merton, 1968). This feedback process demonstrates the socially reflexive character of action (Sandri, 2009). Entrepreneurial agents' actions are influenced by the conditions in which the agents are immersed, and at the same time influence those same conditions. In regard to the social conditions of action this means a feedback process relative to other agents, including other entrepreneurs.

Financial Entrepreneurship

In financial markets, entrepreneurs are providers of liquidity and of financial assets of all sorts (Machlup, 1940). Their capital can be composed either of money or of financial assets that they use to earn diachronic differentials either by buying and selling financial assets or by producing financial services such as credit or intermediation. The different types of financial entrepreneurship are depicted in Figure 1.2.

The primordial entrepreneur in financial markets is, in most cases, the credit entrepreneur (E_C), or capitalist. As can be seen in Figure 1.2, the credit entrepreneur sells credit capital in the present for principal plus interest payments in the future. Among the clients, the credit entrepreneur can find corporations (Co_2 in Figure 1.2) in need of working capital, as well as other entrepreneurs (such as E_I, to be analysed later). Thus, we see that credit entrepreneurs are essential to the maintenance of many production processes in the economy as they are among the main providers of capital to non-financial entrepreneurs. Indeed, the credit entrepreneur is one of the sources of basic financial assets (e.g. bonds and shares)

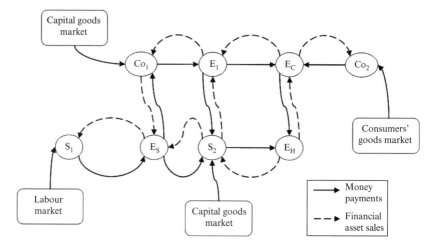

Figure 1.2   Social network and financial entrepreneurship types

among corporations and other similar enterprises, with the difference that
he specializes in obtaining diachronic profits in the financial markets,
while others obtain theirs in the consumers' or producers' goods markets.
Money-lending of all sorts, like credit banking and securities-based
mutual funds, are typical credit entrepreneur activities.

Entrepreneurs specializing in financial speculation (E_S) act by using
their capital to buy financial assets issued by other agents in the financial
markets in order to sell them later in those same markets. In this way,
speculators demonstrate their social role as both liquidity providers for
individuals desirous of liquidating their asset positions and as asset providers for those individuals desirous of assuming a position on an asset
(Machlup, 1940). In Figure 1.2, the entrepreneur-speculator is seen as
buying assets from either a corporation (Co_1) or a group of savers (S_2)
in order to resell those assets to another group of other savers (S_1). If it
were not for entrepreneur-speculators, many investors such as pension
and investment mutual funds would find that entering or leaving a
market would be greatly hindered. Entrepreneurial speculation in financial markets is a prime activity of investment banks and individual investors such as venture capitalists.

Among the most complex financial entrepreneurs is the financial
intermediary (E_I). The entrepreneur uses his or her capital to obtain
credit from providers such as savers or credit entrepreneurs, under the
promise of interest payment, and then relends that borrowed capital to
capital-deficient agents such as corporations (Co_1) for greater interest.

The financial intermediary thus earns its diachronic differential out of the spread between interest rates. Financial intermediation is the domain of commercial and savings banks, which are also among the biggest entrepreneurial entities in the financial markets, along with investment banks.

Finally, there are hedge entrepreneurs (E_H), those individuals specializing in using their capital funds in order to back their sales of futures and derivatives contracts that provide a hedge service to other agents in financial markets as well as the underwriting contracts of any financial asset sale and issuance. Their diachronic profit is to be found in the volume of payments they receive for those contracts. This is probably the most heterogeneous group of entrepreneurs, where one can find anything from commercial and investment banks to individual investors providing such services to other agents, usually by trying to protect their credit positions relative to other agents. This demonstrates the importance of hedge entrepreneurs in evaluating and absorbing risk from other entrepreneurs trying to cover any potential loss from credit or intermediary financial operations – hence the link between E_H and E_C, for instance, in Figure 1.2.

It should be mentioned that the financial entrepreneurial types analysed here are not necessarily manifested by different and separate kinds of entrepreneurial entities. In fact, one individual can be both a credit entrepreneur and a financial intermediary – commercial banks serve as intermediaries but also use their equity capital to issue credit. It will be seen in subsequent sections that this plurality of entrepreneurial forms within the same entrepreneurial entity is particularly important in understanding how institutional illusions in financial markets can easily spread within them and to other markets.

INSTITUTIONAL ILLUSIONS AND EUROPEAN FINANCE

The ECB and Fractional Reserve Banking

The ECB is the main institutional organization that sprouted from the Maastricht Treaty of 1992, which established the creation of the European Monetary Union (EMU) with the Euro as its currency. The idea of the Euro and the EMU arose from the failure of the European Monetary System (EMS) and the Exchange Rate Mechanism (ERM) in keeping stability between member countries' currencies and interest rates.[5]

The fundamentals of the ECB are similar to those of the German Bundesbank, whose fundamentals were modeled on those of the US Federal Reserve System (Fed) (Dominguez, 2006; Howarth and Loedel,

2003). It is a central bank with the monopoly of currency issuance in the Eurozone, charged with the monetary policy for all the Eurozone's member countries. The main similarity with the Bundesbank is that the ECB's primary goal is price stability, while full employment and low long-term interest rates are secondary goals subordinate to it – a hierarchy of policy goals different to those of the Fed, which considers all three as primary (Dominguez, 2006). The ECB's monetary policy is mainly carried through 'refinancing operations' – the ECB's sales and acquisitions of financial assets in the hands of the commercial banks – in the money market in order to manipulate interest rates via injection (acquisitions of assets) or withdrawals of ECB liquidity (sales of assets) – that is, ECB Euro notes.

In order for the ECB operations to take place, however, a fractional reserve system is necessary, otherwise commercial banks could have no interest in such operations. Why would a bank prefer a central bank over another kind of partner? In a 100 percent reserve system there would be no reason for such a preference, besides price (i.e. interest) competition, but in a fractional reserve system things are different. Commercial banks earn profits by collecting usage fees from their clients and by collecting an interest 'spread.' Interest 'spread' exists only in credit transactions where time deposits are involved; however, it is a well-known fact that in a fractional reserve system, banks create credit out of demand deposits (Mises, 1980a; Mishkin, 2004; Rothbard, 1983). The interest collected on such credit falls entirely to the bank. Moreover, if the bank succeeds in liquidating the fiduciary credit in question, it becomes obvious that the bank can easily increase its equity capital simply by creating credit as demand deposits to its debtor-clients (Mises, 1980b). Thus, in a fractional reserve system, the bank has a new and massive source of profit beyond fees and spread.

This is not without dangers, as there is no guarantee that the demand deposits from which the fiduciary credit originates will not be liquidated before that credit is repaid to the bank. In this manner, if information about the bank's balance were fairly available, the potential illiquidity of the bank could deter banks from engaging in fractional reserve (Mises, 1980b).[6] This is no longer true if the central bank institution – particularly if its primary goal is price stability – is available. Since fiduciary credit creation has an inflationist impact on the money supply and hence on price levels, central bank intervention through refinancing operations becomes a necessity (Huerta de Soto, 2006, p. 716). This is especially true if the central bank has among its attributions the role of lender of last resort.[7] Because of this institutional guarantee, deposit banks will have a lower perception of the uncertainty of potential illiquidity than they might otherwise have (Davies and Green, 2010; Mishkin, 2004). Moreover, the liquidity made available by a central bank's refinancing operations is cheaper than that available in the rest of the money market, which further incites deposit banks to assume more potentially illiquid positions (Bagus and Howden, 2010; Gerlach, 2010; Mishkin, 2004). In the end, given the institutional incentives and guarantees given by central banks to deposit banks, it is no wonder that monetary policy consists mostly of regulating the rate of growth of fiduciary media rather than outright creating or eliminating fiduciary media (Bagus and Howden, 2009a; 2009b). At no time since the introduction of the Euro did the ECB actually curtail expansion of M3, which is the monetary aggregate that includes most fiduciary media.

It should be pointed out that fiduciary credit enters the system as if it were new capital, even though no additional savings are actually being undertaken by the general public (Mises, 1980b; Rothbard, 1983). The relationship between savings and M3 presents a problem to the system, however. The monetary aggregate M3 reunites all financial contracts that are derived from real savings: roughly time deposits and those financial papers that are not backed by such deposits – fiduciary media. Nevertheless, the financial markets are supposed to be simply transfer markets for existing capital, that is real savings. If real savings are not following the expansion of fiduciary media, it means that the financial markets are transferring nonexistent capital through these newly issued fiduciary media. Since the end clients of financial markets are producers of non-financial goods and services, an illusion is created that more capital is available than the savings preferences of the public can possibly allow for (Huerta de Soto, 2006; Mises, 1980b). Moreover, this illusion is strengthened by the fact that the fractional reserve system is the very raison d'être for the central bank, as it 'controls' price stability by playing with the liquidity needs of deposit banks: liquidity needs that can only appear in a legal way under a fractional reserve system backed by a central bank.

Although in the short run the fractional reserve system apparently represents an opportunity for banks to make extra profits and for enterprises to obtain cheap and extra credit where they could not otherwise, in the long run it proves problematic. Even if one assumes that all enterprises are able to obtain productivity gains without the holders of demand deposits withdrawing their deposits – which would force banks to cut off fiduciary media creation – there would still be a lack of money as all fiduciary media contracts are reckoned in monetary terms. If productivity gains were obtained by all entrepreneurs who contracted fiduciary credit, they would not be able to get enough money revenue to pay their credit if the monetary base supply did not increase.[8] The problem is that fiduciary credit contracts are established in monetary terms, thus, even if the output capacity of entrepreneurs increased, they would simply get the same amount of money that was available before contracting the credit, but they would need to pay more money than is effectively available. Add to this the fact that productivity gains imply a downward pressure on prices, and it becomes obvious that unless productivity gains result in greater volumes of real money revenues flowing in, the entrepreneur will not be able to get enough money to pay the fiduciary contracts. This is the deflation problem so feared by central bankers (Bernanke and Reinhart, 2004), feared to threaten price stability.[9] As the threat of deflation lingers, liquidity needs to build up because the potential illiquidity of deposit banks now comes from their debtor-clients and not from their creditor-clients. It comes as no surprise that central banks lower interest rates and inject liquidity when the threat of deflation is in the air.

Fiscal and Banking Illusions

A central bank justifies its existence by implementing and supporting a fractional reserve system, but the question to be asked is: *Cui bono?* Deposit banks benefit from the opportunity to increase their equity capital exponentially through credit expansion unbacked by savings – at the cost of incremental potential illiquidity – while enterprises benefit from the possibility of disposing of a greater amount of credit than would otherwise be possible, also at the cost of illiquidity. But what is the interest of the main institution behind the central bank, that is, the state?

Assuming that the state is run by political entrepreneurs,[10] the main concern of these individuals is to maintain themselves and their associates in power for whatever reason they may have – idealistic or corrupt. These political entrepreneurs must invest in political means (i.e. government means) in order to remain in power either by providing services to voters, whether the system is a democracy or a dictatorship. Investment in political means, however, is equivalent to government expenditure and this expenditure has to be financed a priori by taxation. The problem is that the growth of the European governments' expenditures have long outrun their tax revenues, as shown in Figure 1.3.

Therefore, it can be estimated that taxation has become less and less reliable as a European revenue source. Since state expenditures are usually directed at subsidizing consumption or unprofitable productive activities – profitable activities would not need state intervention on their behalf in the first place – it is no wonder that the problem with taxation is its capital-consuming nature (Rothbard, 2004). Therefore, rising tax rates in order to meet increasing government expenditures would prove an immediate problem to the state, as it would eventually result in less revenue being

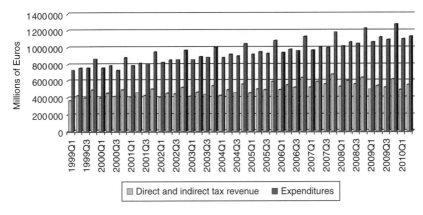

Figure 1.3   Expansion of European government expenditures relative to tax revenues

available in the long run. This is further aggravated by the fact that the tax burden in the Eurozone is already heavy, which makes any further increase in taxation dangerously unpopular (Hallerberg et al., 2009). Thus, debt becomes an attractive alternative to taxation – particularly because of its low popularity costs in the short-run (Salerno, 2010, pp. 245–59).

Nevertheless, public debt in a 100 percent reserve system is quite limited by the fact that only time deposits – that is real savings, not fiduciary – can give existence to credit. Moreover, increasing public debt in a 100 percent reserve system would mean that governments would have to compete more aggressively for funds against private agents and, given the limited availability of credit, this would mean interest rates rising quite fast. Fractional reserve banking, however, allows governments not only to increase the availability of credit but also to cheapen it. Since fractional reserve banking increases the supply of credit in the credit market, the downward pressure on interest rates is much stronger than it could be in a 100 percent reserve system. Yet, this is not enough to secure an easy access of funds to the state. Given governments' consumptive use of credit, creditors could still prefer to loan to private agents instead because their engagement in productive wealth-creating activities would indicate an estimated greater capacity of debt-reimbursement than governments' activities. The 'risk-freeness' of state bonds – based on the state's supposed capacity to print the money necessary to pay its debts or to tax the population for the money instead – would not really matter as it simply means that state bonds are free of the risk of default, but not of purchasing power loss.

Therefore, the master stroke of a state-sponsored monetary system would be not only to increase and cheapen the supply of credit but *to make it necessary for banks to make credit continuously available to the state.* This need will be created by the central bank institution supporting the fractional reserve banking of deposit banks. The ECB's refinancing and discount operations are not collateral-free liquidity lending operations. In order for a bank to be eligible for such operations, it must hold mainly Eurozone government securities in its assets; securities that are asked as collateral for refinancing and discount operations by the ECB.[11] In conclusion, if a deposit bank wants to prepare for any eventual liquidation of its demand deposit liabilities, it must allocate a part of its fiduciary credit creation to government debt. The more the bank wants to cover any eventual liquidity loss, the more it will have to lend credit to governments, further contributing to the latter's increasing debt (Candelon and Palm, 2010). Since Eurozone government securities are accepted under much more advantageous terms than other issuers' securities, a priori, the ECB-sponsored fractional reserve system works as an apparently endless source of credit for European governments.[12]

The whole situation is thus very propitious for the formation of *fiscal illusions*, the illusion that citizens – taxpayers or not – have of their state benefits relative to what they actually pay, in terms of direct or indirect taxes and in terms of purchasing power losses due to state capital consumption (Mourão, 2010; Puviani, 1903).[13] Thanks to the central bank-backed fractional reserve system, political entrepreneurs will dispose of a greater source of funds without needing to tax citizens immediately or to provoke *crowding out* effects in credit markets. Due to deposit banks' continuous need for central bank liquidity, and consequent need to hold government securities, amassing public debts will not be a problem for political entrepreneurs. Citizens will apparently receive more benefits from governments without paying the actual costs; costs will be socialized while their specific benefits are privatized. This fiscal illusion is evident when one examines the social security debt-to-GDP ratio of European countries in Figure 1.4. Indeed, an effective payment of social security debt would represent an outright taxation of more than 50 percent of the GDP for most Eurozone countries.

One could argue that deposit banks could choose to cover liquidity losses by simply holding greater reserves instead of creating credit and allocating a part of it to governments. This ignores the opportunity cost of deposit banks in terms of the profits they could get out of the interest paid on fiduciary credit and, more importantly, of the huge equity capital build-up that they could obtain by means of fiduciary credit (Mises, 1980b; Rothbard, 1983). But again, one could counter that the building up of government debt cannot really be sustainable as it will grow to heights that cannot be backed by either taxation or money supply inflation. This

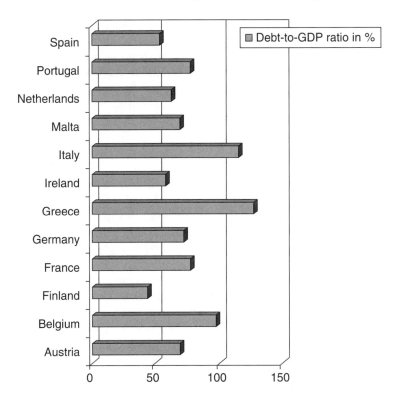

Figure 1.4   Social security debt-to-GDP ratio in the Eurozone

is true, but fiduciary credit expansion without cover from holding government securities is also a problem for deposit banks.

This does not mean that deposit banks will blindly engage in accumulating government securities. The accumulation of financial entrepreneurial functions and the financial innovations derived thereof allow deposit banks to provide credit for governments without necessarily putting their balance sheets at much risk. In fact, this is the main role of the derivatives markets today, where securitization and hedging take place daily, allowing deposit banks to write off risky credit from their assets while also hedging against the default of retained debt (Altunbas et al., 2009; Gertchev, 2009).

The debt scheme of Eurozone governments today, then, is a complex system in which the ECB acts as liquidity provider for the fractional reserve banking system in order to ease the provision of cheap credit to governments. The whole system is a circle where the national central banks (NCBs) of the Eurosystem act as investment bank underwriters of Eurozone government securities, which are then largely bought by deposit

banks in need of eligible assets for the refinancing and discount operations of the ECB. As governments build up debt and as deposit banks
build up liquidity needs, more government securities will be issued and
more of these will be acquired for further use in refinancing operations.
Securitization and derivative hedging will allow further expansion of fiduciary credit and greater risk positions being assumed by banks.

ILLUSIONS AND FINANCIAL ENTREPRENEURSHIP

The fractional reserve banking debt scheme of Eurozone countries will set
up institutional illusions in the financial markets that will distort entrepreneurial planning in those markets. First, since fiduciary credit is created
in deposit banks fed with ECB liquidities, it can be said that an alteration
is made to their financial intermediary entrepreneur function. With the
legal authorization and backing to create fiduciary media, financial intermediary entrepreneurs such as deposit banks become credit entrepreneurs
without any real capital backing their activities. This fiduciary media
creation involves negligible costs and allows fiduciary entrepreneurs to
practice a downward pressure on interest rates, which traditional credit
entrepreneurs and non-deposit intermediary institutions cannot compete
with. As long as deposit banks remain institutionally backed by the ECB
via refinance operations, it will be difficult and costly for traditional credit
entrepreneurs and non-deposit intermediary institutions to use precipitated clearing of any fiduciary media issued to liquidate fiduciary banks to
bankruptcy. Fiduciary media creation enables deposit banks to enjoy scale
economies both in terms of price and quantity, thus allowing them to fetch
bigger and more clients than traditional credit entrepreneurs can. Credit
entrepreneurs will then specialize in pulverized consumer credit, particularly to those consumers with difficulties in getting credit from other
institutions such as deposit banks.[14] Meanwhile, non-deposit intermediary
institutions will shift to channeling their clients' funds toward other kind
of investments rather than credit, in mutual funds and other collective
investment schemes in organized and non-organized markets, for example.
Although in both instances more risk might be involved, the pulverization
of investment tries to mitigate this risk through diversification.

The problem, however, is that the non-financial clients of credit entrepreneurs and of non-deposit intermediary entrepreneurs might also be
funded through fiduciary media. Moreover, the non-financial clients of
fiduciary deposit banks might be issuing too many securities that will
circulate in the market and can thus become part of the portfolios of non-
deposit intermediary institutions. Risk mitigation through diversification

might prove insufficient as these institutions begin to have their specialized business infected with riskier unbacked securities.

Financial speculators are doubly affected by fiduciary media creation. On the one hand, they might access greater funds made available to them by fiduciary deposit banks – in fact, fiduciary deposit banks might also indulge in financial speculation with their own fiduciary funds either directly or indirectly where the law forbids it.[15] On the other hand, fiduciary media creation means a greater circulation of both 'money' and of financial assets. If financial speculators function as liquidity and asset reserves that eliminate price disequilibria between markets and intertemporally (Kirzner, 1985; Machlup, 1940), this will be seriously affected by the creation of fiduciary media. Fiduciary media implies money-supply inflation and consequently an upward pressure on prices. This upward pressure will prevent price differences from disappearing if speculative action lags behind fiduciary media creation. Since financial speculators find their profits in price differences, they will keep investing their capital in exploiting such differences continuously, without any increase in real wealth lying behind the price difference, thus nourishing a speculative bubble.

Finally, hedge entrepreneurs will also see their business affected by the creation of fiduciary media. As all other financial entrepreneurs, as well as non-financial entrepreneurs, are indulging in greater risks due to fiduciary media creation, more hedge will be demanded by all these parties. Fiduciary deposit banks will revisit hedge entrepreneurs in order to hedge their growing fiduciary credit assets. This entails a vicious circle of moral hazard where fiduciary deposit banks increase their fiduciary credit offer to over-indebted clients, such as governments, in spite of this knowledge because they can hedge their positions in the derivatives market. This hedge can be direct, when the fiduciary deposit bank buys, for example, swap contracts or credit default swaps (CDS) from hedge entrepreneurs, or indirect, when the fiduciary deposit bank uses securitization of their credit assets in order to write off these risky fiduciary credit positions from their balance sheets (Stulz, 2004). Securitization thus allows fiduciary deposit banks to: 1) write off strongly risk-weighted assets from their balance sheets; 2) liquidate risky assets and increase the banks' reserves; and 3) increase fiduciary media creation due to the increase of reserves (Gertchev, 2009).

Similarly, traditional credit entrepreneurs and non-deposit intermediary entrepreneurs might also make use of hedge and securitization, as their risk positions increase due to fiduciary media creation. Given that both entrepreneurs will specialize in riskier investments, the hedge and the securitization sought by these entrepreneurs will lead to greater volatility being traded in derivatives markets.

The greater availability and diversity of derivative assets in the market will prove an additional venue for speculator entrepreneurs to invest, but also new opportunities for bubbles to appear. The problem is that fiduciary media create illusions not only for those buying hedge and selling securitized derivatives but also to those selling hedge and buying the securitized derivatives. Hedge entrepreneurs might agree to hedge more assets and positions than usual because they might have a greater access to funds such as fiduciary lines of credit provided by banks.[16]

The question that arises then is: Is it all sustainable? The operations of all financial entrepreneurs are altered but boosted by fiduciary media creation. More funds are available and more opportunities appear to be available. Yet, most of these funds and opportunities are based on fiduciary media and not on the actual availability of real wealth, that is, goods. The problem of fiduciary media expansion is that it makes it seem possible for individuals both to consume and to invest at the same time, but such a phenomenon is impossible. Greater consumption – that is, greater quantity of goods available to be *used* and not simply more money available for *spending* – follows greater production. Greater production, however, cannot take place without greater investment, and greater investment demands greater quantities of real capital – that is, more goods at the disposition of producers. Consumption and investment can grow, but not immediately together. Savings for investment go first and then allow for greater consumption. In the end, there is more consumption *and* investment, but only after a time of frugality.

Fiduciary media expansion does not increase the availability of real capital, but only of payment promises on future real capital. Since consumption is not necessarily falling in order for real capital to be formed through savings, production cannot go far just with fiduciary media. Liquidation of fiduciary media for acquisition of real goods will reveal that there are not enough real resources in the fiduciary issuers' safes. The use of financial markets, particularly of securitization and hedge, to extend the circulation of fiduciary media proves to be a possibility. This is particularly true if fiduciary media can be used as collateral, as in credit-based obligations (CBOs).

Extension of circulation is not tantamount to savings, and sooner or later fiduciary media will be liquidated; when this happens the whole fiduciary boom crumbles. Financial speculators will find themselves with too many assets that lost their value. Hedge entrepreneurs cannot hedge all the losses of their contracts and default on payment. Credit entrepreneurs cannot recover the capital lent, while non-deposit intermediary entrepreneurs cannot repay their investors. Finally, deposit intermediary entrepreneurs have too many obligations for few valuable assets. The illusion thus gives way to a reality lowly-endowed with capital.

CONCLUSION

Financial markets are not the cause of crises, past or future. They are institutional processes in which individuals exchange useful services of capital transfers and insurance on investments that cannot usually be found in other markets (e.g. the insurance market). Just like any other market, exchange operations imply transfers of goods and services, that is, transfers of produced goods and services. Paraphrasing Lavoisier: in the market economy, nothing is created nor destroyed, just *transferred*. If there is a problem of creation or destruction, it is to be found either in the production process or in the preferences of consumers. In other words, market value creation or destruction depends on the utility attributed by consumers to the production decided by producers.

Now, financial markets are markets derived from goods markets. The fact is that financial markets transfer capital from net-saving individuals to net-borrowing individuals in order to sustain production or consumption processes. These transfers are defined by contracts known as shares, securities, futures, forward contracts, and so on. If something happens to the production or consumption processes underlying these contracts, they lose or earn exchangeability in the market and hence value. Derivatives markets, being derived from traditional financial markets, are no different from them. The value of swap, options, CBO, CDS, MBS contracts and so forth are all derived from the value of the underlying shares, securities, futures and other contracts. The only way for a problem to arise is if a problem arises with the real capital structure of the economy.

In this chapter, it has been shown that the distortion of capital structure comes from the illusion produced by fractional reserve banking backed by a central bank that more capital is available either for production or consumption, or both, than is actual available. This illusion comes from the production of fiduciary media by deposit banks; a fiduciary media production that is institutionally backed by central bank, and more specifically to the context of this book, the ECB. The legitimacy of the ECB institutional guarantee comes from none other than the Eurozone member states who thus put in motion a vicious circle of debt and fiduciary money inflation. Deposit banks create fiduciary media based on their ECB liquidity reserves. These reserves are provided by the ECB in exchange for eligible securities, preferably Eurozone government debt. In this manner, the more debt is contracted by the Eurozone governments, the greater the amounts of ECB liquidities that can be acquired by deposit banks, and the more the quantity of fiduciary media that can be created.

If government over-indebtedness and excessive speculation are a problem, it surely does not come from the 'market' but from the non-market entity institutionally distorting the capital perceptions of market participants.

NOTES

1. The term 'goods' refers here to both physical goods and services in general.
2. This is an argument that is technically confirmed by the very fact that any enterprise constituted as a firm has to register its equity capital as a liability, as it is an obligation that the firm has to the original individuals financing it: the owners of the enterprise's founding capital.
3. Class probability accounts for events, the frequency of which can allow them to be grouped into classes presenting similar characteristics (Mises, 1996). Class probability thus includes both mathematically objective frequency probability and Bayesian probability based on knowledge of frequency probabilities.
4. Case probability is a pure subjective estimation of probability (Mises, 1996). Even if it can have a mathematical form, the probability distribution is attributed by entrepreneurial instinct and not on the basis of any frequency. Case probability includes Bayesian probability, but only that kind based on entirely subjective knowledge.
5. This failure was due to the incapacity of the member countries to keep their fiscal accounts in order, particularly on the occasion of the German reunification, which was financed by considerable public deficits on the part of West Germany. These deficits led to an inflationary pressure – proving that the Bundesbank had more to do with the inflationary pressure than previously thought – that was met with a rise in German interest rates that the remaining countries could not follow without further deteriorating their own public debt (Howarth and Loedel, 2003). In the end, the EMS fell apart when Italy, Spain and the United Kingdom had to leave it in order to depreciate their currencies, a step followed by France months later (Dominguez, 2006; Mulhearn and Vane, 2008).
6. It is no surprise, then, that in the times before central banks, banks were engaged in issuing fractional reserves in a deceitful way (Huerta de Soto, 2006). Bagus and Howden (2010) have recently explored some of the difficulties involved in a fractional reserve banking system whose fundamental raison d'être is issuing loans against demand deposits – deposits which are viewed and treated as being continually available at par by the depositing agents.
7. Although the Maastricht Treaty did not establish any explicit 'lender of last resort' function to the ECB (Dominguez, 2006; Mulhearn and Vane, 2008), article 105.6 of the treaty could be interpreted as a 'lender of last resort' clause (Howarth and Loedel, 2003). For the moment, the Eurozone has not yet reached a critical situation in which it has had to test this interpretation (Cottarelli et al., 2010; Sgherri and Zoli, 2009).
8. This is the more unlikely the greater one assumes those productivity gains to be. Even if the new fiduciary credit-based investments are eminently capital intensive, the new capital-goods must be produced first, indicating that the productivity gains must come primarily from the workforce. Productivity gains in labor before new productivity-boosting capital goods are available must forcibly come from increased labor effort relative to nominal wages (Hayek, 1975).
9. No wonder, then, that the goal of central banks is to control price *stability* and not price *inflation*. The goal of price stability implies intervention in the eventuality of either price inflation or price deflation (Davies and Green, 2010; Mishkin, 2004). Not only is this true of mainstream economists but it is also recurrent among some Austrian economists (Bagus, 2003).
10. Political entrepreneurs aim at ends linked to the state machine, such as state positions involving some degree of power of intervention (Baumol, 1990; Holcombe, 2002).

Non-political entrepreneurs may also integrate the state, but their aims will not involve political positions as an end, only as a means for their non-political ends.

11. Implications of the artificial demand for Eurozone member state debt via the ECB's collateral requirements for its refinancing operations are discussed by Philipp Bagus in Chapter 7 in the present volume.

12. Although articles 17 and 18 of the Protocol on the Statute of the European System of Central Banks and of the European Central Bank are quite open to which financial assets can be accepted as collateral in refinancing operations (Howarth and Loedel, 2003, p. 196), '[I]n apparent response to the lack of enforcement of the Stability and Growth Pact, in November 2005 the ECB stated that it would only accept member government securities with a rating of A− or above as collateral in its refinancing operations' (Dominguez, 2006, p. 76). The ECB's restrictive policy regarding collateral and the apparently juridical impossibility of countries bail-out by the ECB is leading debate on the creation of an 'European Monetary Fund' in order to avoid rescue by a non-European entity such as the International Monetary Fund (Candelon and Palm, 2010, p. 97).

13. In many ways this illusion is similar to the one outlined in Howden (2010). In the latter case, entrepreneurs more distant from the credit inflation's origin (i.e. small business owners, individuals, etc.) are harmed to a larger degree than those entrepreneurs closest to the inflation's origin (i.e. primary dealers, large banks, etc) as they have access to less knowledge of the extent and subsequent sustainability of the credit-creation process. When the collapse finally ensues, these entrepreneurs incur the full wrath of the inflationary boom, unaware of its magnitude because of the illusion hiding its origin.

14. For recent analyses of the consumer credit markets, see Bertola et al. (2006). For a detailed analysis of consumer credit in Europe, see Vandone (2009).

15. Real world examples of such use of fiduciary media creation are the financial fraud perpetrated by Barings Bank's former derivatives trader Nick Leeson and the financial loss supposedly provoked by Société Générale's former trader Jérôme Kerviel.

16. This is something typical of naked financial operations and markets such as the Service de Règlement Différé (SRD) in France, which authorize participants to take naked sale or buy positions based on a minimal capital provision during a month and having only to liquidate them at the end of it. Of course, what is actually covering such operations is the clearing house of the SRD market.

REFERENCES

Altunbas, Y., L. Gambacorta and D. Marqués-Ibañez (2009), 'Securitisation and the bank lending channel', *European Economic Review*, **53**, 996–1009.

Bagus, P. (2003), 'Deflation: when Austrians become interventionists', *Quarterly Journal of Austrian Economics*, **6** (4), 19–35.

Bagus, P. and D. Howden (2009a), 'Qualitative easing in support of a tumbling financial system: a look at the Eurosystem's recent balance sheet policies', *Economic Affairs*, **29** (4), 60–65.

Bagus, P. and D. Howden (2009b), 'The Federal Reserve System and Eurosystem's balance sheet policies during the financial crisis: a comparative analysis', *Romanian Economic and Business Review*, **4** (3), 165–85.

Bagus, P. and D. Howden (2010), 'The term structure of savings, the yield curve, and maturity mismatching', *Quarterly Journal of Austrian Economics*, **13** (3), 64–85.

Baumol, W.J. (1990), 'Entrepreneurship: productive, unproductive, and destructive', *Journal of Political Economy*, **98** (5), 893–921.

Bernanke, B.S. and V.R. Reinhart (2004), 'Conducting monetary policy at very low short-term interest rates', *American Economic Review*, **94** (2), 85–90.

Bertola, G., R. Disney and C. Grant (eds) (2006), *The Economics of Consumer Credit*, Cambridge, MA: MIT Press.

Candelon, B. and F.C. Palm (2010), 'Banking and debt crises in Europe: the dangerous liaisons?', *De Economist*, **158** (1), 81–99.

Chambers, A. and K. Ridley (2010), 'Greece not alone in exploiting EU accounting flaws', www.reuters.com/article/idUSTRE61L3EB20100222.

Coleman, J.S. (1990), *Foundations of Social Theory*, Cambridge, MA: Harvard University Press.

Cottarelli, C., L. Forni, J. Gottschalk and P. Mauro (2010), 'Default in today's advanced economies: unnecessary, undesirable, and unlikely', IMF Staff Position Note.

Davies, H. and D. Green (2010), *Banking on the Future: The Fall and Rise of Central Banking*, Princeton, NJ: Princeton University Press.

Dominguez, K.M. (2006), 'The European Central Bank, the Euro, and global financial markets', *Journal of Economic Perspectives*, **20** (4), 67–88.

Gerlach, P. (2010), 'The dependence of the financial system on central bank and government support', *BIS Quarterly Review* (March), 51–7.

Gertchev, N. (2009), 'Securitization and fractional reserve banking', in J.G. Hülsmann and S. Kinsella (eds), *Property, Freedom, and Society: Essays in Honor of Hans-Hermann Hoppe*, Auburn, AL: Ludwig von Mises Institute, pp. 283–300.

Giddens, A. (1984), *The Constitution of Society*, Cambridge: Polity Press.

Hallerberg, M., R.R. Strauch and J. von Hagen (2009), *Fiscal Governance in Europe*, Cambridge: Cambridge University Press.

Hayek, F.A. (1975), *The Pure Theory of Capital*, Chicago, IL: University of Chicago Press.

Holcombe, R.G. (2002), 'Political entrepreneurship and the democratic allocation of economic resources', *Review of Austrian Economics*, **15** (2), 143–59.

Howarth, D. and P. Loedel (2003), *The European Central Bank: The New European Leviathan?* New York, NY: Palgrave Macmillan.

Howden, D. (2010), 'Knowledge shifts and the business cycle: when boom turns to bust', *Review of Austrian Economics*, **23**, 165–82.

Huerta de Soto, J. (2006), *Money, Bank Credit, and Economic Cycles* (2nd edn), Auburn, AL: Ludwig von Mises Institute.

Huerta de Soto, J. (2009), *The Theory of Dynamic Efficiency*, London: Routledge.

Hülsmann, J.G. (1998), 'Toward a general theory of error cycles', *Quarterly Journal of Austrian Economics*, **1** (4), 1–23.

Kiff, J., J. Elliott, E. Kazarian, J. Scarlata and C. Spackman (2009), 'Credit derivatives: systemic risks and policy options', IMF working paper 254, International Monetary Fund.

Kirzner, I.M. (1985), *Discovery and the Capitalist Process*, Chicago, IL: University of Chicago Press.

Knight, F.H. (2006), *Risk, Uncertainty, and Profit*, Mineola, NY: Dover Publications.

Lewis, B.W. (1937), 'The corporate entrepreneur', *Quarterly Journal of Economics*, **51** (3), 535–44.

Machlup, F. (1940), *The Stock Market, Credit, and Capital Formation*, New York, NY: Macmillan.

Menger, C. (1994), *Principles of Economics*, Grove City, PA: Libertarian Press.

Merton, R.K. (1968), *Social Theory and Social Structure*, New York, NY: Free Press.

Mises, L. von (1996), *Human Action: A Treatise on Economics* (4th edn), Irvington-on-Hudson, NY: Foundation for Economic Education.

Mises, L. von (1980a), 'Profit and loss', in L. von Mises, *Planning for Freedom* (4th edn), Grove City, PA: Libertarian Press, pp. 103–44.

Mises, L. von (1980b), *The Theory of Money and Credit*, Indianapolis, IN: Liberty Classics.

Mishkin, F. S. (2004), *The Economics of Money, Banking, and Financial Markets* (7th edn), Boston: Pearson.

Mourão, P.R. (2010), 'Debate: the dangers of fiscal illusion', *Public Money & Management*, **30** (5), 267–8.

Mulhearn, C. and H.R. Vane (2008), *The Euro: Its Origins, Developments and Prospects*, Cheltenham, UK and Northampton, MA, USA: Edward Elgar.

O'Driscoll, G.P. and M.J. Rizzo (1996), *The Economics of Time and Ignorance*, New York, NY: Routledge.

Parsons, T. (1949), *The Structure of Social Action: A Study in Social Theory with Reference to a Group of Recent European Writers*, New York, NY: Free Press.

Puviani, A. (1903), *Teoria della illusione finanziaria*, Palermo: Sandron.

Rothbard, M.N. (1983), *The Mystery of Banking*, New York, NY: Richardson & Snyder.

Rothbard, M.N. (2004), *Man, Economy, and State with Power and Market*, Auburn, AL: Ludwig von Mises Institute.

Salerno, J.T. (2010), *Money, Sound and Unsound*, Auburn, AL: Ludwig von Mises Institute.

Sandri, S. (2009), *Reflexivity in Economics: An Experimental Examination on the Self-Referentiality of Economic Theories*, Heidelberg: Physica-Verlag.

Sgherri, S. and E. Zoli (2009), 'Euro area sovereign risk during the crisis', IMF working paper 222, International Monetary Fund.

Stulz, R.M. (2004), 'Should we fear derivatives?' *Journal of Economic Perspectives*, **18** (3), 173–92.

Vandone, D. (2009), *Consumer Credit in Europe: Risks and Opportunities of a Dynamic Industry*, Heidelberg: Physica-Verlag.

2. A stock-taking of the impact of the crisis[1]

Jörg Guido Hülsmann

The present crisis of the global economy started with the publication of massive defaults of US subprime mortgage loans in July 2007. During the following 12 months, these initial defaults set in motion a wave of consolidation and contraction in the global financial industries. This wave has been followed by another wave of bankruptcies that swept over financial markets worldwide. The burgeoning financial tsunami has been slowed down, but not stopped, through massive interventions by the world's major central banks, which greatly expanded the money supply and eased credit conditions. In the summer and fall of 2008, it reached a climax when two of the five largest US investment banks went bankrupt, and the three remaining banks abandoned their status to become commercial banks in order to benefit from public bailout.

The defaults within the investment-bank sector were at the point of spilling over to a large US insurance company and to several public and semi-public banks. Within a few weeks or even days it would in all likelihood have entailed a complete meltdown of the financial markets. Few if any banks would have survived; their failures would have set in motion a deflationary spiral. The debt-ridden global financial industries would have been wiped out. Any sort of credit – public or private – would have become unavailable. The meltdown would have swept over the rest of the global economy: With bank credit unavailable or greatly reduced, most companies could not have financed their spending on wages, supplies, and investment. Unemployment could have soared to 30 percent and more. The evaporation of the value of financial titles would have drastically impaired household spending in general and consumption expenditure in particular. Retirement plans would have been in shambles.

It did not come to this point because the major governments and central banks intervened massively to bail out the threatened institutions.

A bankrupt company can be bailed out by and large in one of two ways. Either one has to raise new capital to cover the losses, or one has to create artificial markets for the company's products. Both techniques were applied on a massive scale, starting in the fall of 2008. Central banks have been subsidizing the banks through artificially low interest rates and by exchanging hundreds of billions of dollars of their relatively sound assets against the defaulting assets of the commercial banks, at nominal values. Governments have launched massive spending programs designed to: 1) invest public funds into commercial banks, thus partly nationalizing them; 2) provide credit guarantees for companies and households; and also 3) stabilize stimulate aggregate spending within the economy. These policies were extended through 2009 and were still continuing in 2011. Most notably, monetary policy is in 2011 still being conducted at an acute crisis level (with interest rates close to zero, standard repo maturities of one year, and great leniency in regards to collateral).

Despite these massive interventions, the global recession has not yet been overcome, and according to most estimates it is not expected to be overcome in the immediate future. In several important respects, the world economy today is structurally in worse shape than before the crisis broke out. Most notably, the very measures that have so far been taken to confront the crisis have raised new problems, and aggravated some of the problems that led to the crisis.

IMPACT ON LABOR MARKETS

In the European Union (EU), the unemployment rate reached almost 10 percent out of a labor force of 236 million persons in August 2010, which corresponds to some 23 million unemployed persons. These figures need to be put into perspective in three regards. First, EU unemployment is some 3 percent (or 7 million persons) up from the level of the first quarter of 2008, when it had reached a boom-induced low point; but only 1 percent up from the pre-boom level of the years 2002–05. Second, these figures do not convey the greater precariousness of employment conditions caused by the marginally greater weight of part-time work, of temporary labor contracts, and of increased youth unemployment. Third, these figures represent only an EU-wide average. The concrete local situations differ widely. In Spain and the Baltic countries, unemployment hovers near 20 percent.

IMPACT ON REAL-ESTATE MARKETS

Real-estate markets boomed from 2002 to 2006, especially in the Anglo-Saxon countries.[2] They were the focal point of the unhealthy developments of the boom years. Naturally, therefore, they were first in line to be hit by the subsequent bust. In 2006, that is, at the height of the real-estate boom, the aggregate value of real estate owned by US households and non-profit organizations was almost $25 billion, with outstanding mortgages of a total volume of $9.8 billion. At the end of the second quarter of 2010, the aggregate value had shrunk to $18.8 billion, while the outstanding mortgage debt stood at $10.2 billion.[3] In other words, households and non-profit organizations suffered a loss corresponding to some 43 percent of current US GDP. Again, this fact needs to be put into perspective, emphasizing in particular that these are only average figures. In many individual cases the value of the real estate owned has dropped below the value of the mortgage (negative equity); the consequence is mortgage delinquencies and foreclosures – in other words, another round of financial defaults which threatens mortgage banks and thus all financial industries by implication. In 2011 the real-estate markets in the US and the EU remain particularly fragile because the extremely low level of interest rates that has resulted from massive monetary interventions is unlikely to persist, especially for long-term interest rates.

IMPACT ON CAPITAL MARKETS

All over the world, stock markets collapsed in 2008, with market capitalization declining by about 50 percent in average (see Table 2.1). As a consequence, pension funds, mutual funds, and other financial companies that were heavily invested in stocks suffered a corresponding meltdown of their capital. A rally followed in 2009, but at the end of that year the total market capitalization still remained some 26 percent below the peak attained in 2007. This dramatic setback has entailed a massive redistribution of wealth, from the owners of capital stock to those who were invested in other asset classes (fixed income, cash, etc.). The meltdown of the stock markets also greatly impaired the potential for companies to raise new capital on the stock markets (initial public offerings – IPOs – have plummeted and remained low).

Private fixed-income securities in many cases lived through a similar setback, and several companies (such as General Motors) defaulted on their bonds. However, government bonds were a notable exception, especially the bonds of major governments. They actually experienced a mini boom during the crisis, primarily because investors considered them to be safe havens. As a consequence, interest rates on such bonds plummeted in the fall of 2008 and remained low all through 2009, which has facilitated greater public debt and therefore greater public expenditure.

Table 2.1   Stock market capitalization (billions of US dollars)

Year	Americas	Asia-Pacific	Europe, Africa, and the Middle East	Total
2006	22 653	12 908	16 189	51 750
2007	24 320	19 792	18 615	62 727
2008	13 896	9 959	9 444	33 299
2009	18 934	13 135	14 223	46 292

Source: World Federation of Exchanges; author's calculations.

The great losers of the stock-market meltdown have been households. Firms and other market institutions to a very large extent have been spared thanks to government support.

IMPACT ON HOUSEHOLDS

For most families in most countries, labor is the main source of income, and the bulk of savings are usually invested in the family residence. Additional savings are invested on the capital markets or held on savings accounts with banks. The meltdown of real-estate prices combined with the meltdown of stock markets has destroyed much of this wealth. In many cases, most notably in the US, the market value of the family residence has become lower than the remaining debt to be paid.

From an aggregate point of view, the net worth (total assets minus total liabilities) of households and non-profit organizations, even in the countries that so far have been most affected by the crisis, is still largely positive. However, the picture is different if we turn from the aggregate to the many individual cases of families who lost both their capital and the income from labor. For them, the disastrous events have caused much frustration and often despair. Three circumstances have so far prevented even greater suffering among those who were affected: 1) the fact that the crisis had a rather moderate impact on employment; 2) in the case of the US, the relative ease of personal bankruptcy; and 3) government subsidies.

Families have adjusted to the crisis by cutting expenditure, getting out of debt, and building up savings. Much more than any other sector of the economy, families had to solve, and did solve – and often chose in advance to solve – their financial problems the hard but virtuous way, usually with great financial and personal sacrifice. At present they still have to cope with forced sales of their property (financial titles, houses, and vehicles), with the struggle to find new employment, accepting new jobs at conditions much inferior to those that they previously enjoyed, often moving to new locations, leaving relatives and friends, starting new lives. Those who are willing to make such efforts are often hampered by the loss of their residential property value, which in normal times would ease the movement from one labor market to another. Not all families survive shocks of such magnitude, especially not in a culture that is geared towards material success and where uninterrupted material improvement is often taken for granted. Fragile families disintegrate under the humiliation of failure, through despair and its fruits: self-neglect and neglect of others, social isolation, violence, alcoholism, suicide, and so on.

The reduction of household spending particularly concerned expenditure on education, charitable giving, and financial contributions to associations. As a consequence, church revenues, private foreign aid, and associative life have experienced setbacks.

IMPACT ON BUSINESS

In market economies, business spending is usually the citizens' main source of revenue. It is also the main source of government revenue, to the extent that government spending is financed by taxes and loans to the government, which in turn are obtained from revenue earned in firms. The total volume of business spending is determined by savings (and also by money production), and the concrete investment projects that are realized are determined by relative household spending on the various consumer goods. The crisis has unsettled both the volume of savings and relative consumer spending. As a consequence it has disrupted both the volume and the direction of investment.

Because of the combined meltdown of real-estate and stock markets, households spent less, spent their money differently, and had less money available for saving and investment. As a result of the banking crisis, bank credit in general, and bank money creation in particular, dried up. Because of the stock-market crisis, it was almost impossible to raise new capital. This in turn has shaken trust in the business community and impaired the availability of commercial credit, thus reinforcing the curtailment of bank credit. As a consequence, many firms and investment projects that had been started in the boom years before the crisis were no longer viable, because of either a lack of finance and/or shifting consumer preferences.[4] In other words, the structure of production was no longer adjusted to the new crisis-induced circumstances. The financial crisis had entailed and reinforced a structural crisis; as a consequence, many firms went bankrupt,

Table 2.2   Recent evolution of private investment in the EU and the US

Year	European Union (15) (billions of Euros)			United States (billions of US dollars)		
	GDP	Gross private fixed capital formation	Net private fixed capital formation	GDP	Gross private domestic investment	Net private domestic investment
2005	10 405	1 841	571	12 638	2 172	881
2006	10 950	1 987	650	13 399	2 327	936
2007	11 525	2 137	731	14 078	2 295	819
2008	11 504	2 093	665	14 441	2 097	560
2009	10 911	1 753	325	14 256	1 589	53
2010	11 212	1 787	N/A	14 592	1 826	N/A

Sources: Eurostat; DG Economic and Financial Affairs; Bureau of Economic Analysis.

many production projects had to be discontinued, and employment in those firms and projects decreased. Structural unemployment resulted.

Not all unviable firms and business projects were in fact discontinued. A great number of them – most notably in the banking, construction, and automobile sectors – benefited from the increased public spending designed to combat the crisis. Unviable firms and projects by definition destroy more resources than they create. Their preservation therefore implies a sapping of the capital base of the economy. In the medium and long run, this will entail a reduction of aggregate production (not necessarily in absolute terms, but relative to the level of aggregate production that would otherwise have been possible) and thus an impoverishing of the world population.

Another factor has encouraged the same nefarious tendency. In order to overcome a structural crisis, it is not sufficient to discontinue unviable business projects that have been started in the past; it is also necessary to give new directions to investment, directions which it is hoped are more in tune with present and future conditions. At present, this has not yet been achieved: in virtually all countries private investment expenditure has plummeted during the crisis and remains low. There is a widespread reluctance on the part of businesses to invest, especially in long-term projects (Table 2.2).

In 2009, private gross fixed capital formation in the EU[5] had declined by 18 percent from its 2007 peak level and in 2010 was expected to be 16.4 percent below that level. As a percentage of GDP, it declined from 18.5 percent in 2007 to 16.1 percent in 2009 and to 15.9 percent in 2010.

Estimated private net fixed capital formation declined by 55.5 percent from 2007 to 2009 and in 2010 represented only 3.0 percent of GDP, down from 6.3 percent in 2007.

In the US, the deterioration was even more dramatic. In 2009 gross private domestic investment declined by a huge 31.7 percent from its 2006 peak level and in 2010 was expected to be 21.5 percent below that peak. As a percentage of GDP, it declined from 17.4 percent in 2006 to 11.1 percent in 2009 and 12.5 percent in 2010. Turning to the estimate of net private domestic investment, in 2009 it had fallen by 94.3 percent from its 2006 peak and, as a percentage of GDP, plummeted from 8.5 percent to 0.5 percent.

This state of affairs is a heavy burden on the future welfare of the citizens in Europe and the US. However, the extent of the damage has so far barely become visible in conventional national accounting statistics, which turn around the GDP concept. Indeed, because of increased government spending, GDP figures have declined only in the single year of 2009, by 5.2 percent in the EU and a mere 1.7 percent in the US. It would be wrong to infer from these figures that government spending has stabilized the overall level of production, at least in the short run and possibly also in the long run. GDP figures portray the monetary value of that part of annual domestic production which has been sold to final users. They include additions to the capital structure (which include most notably 'gross fixed capital formation' and 'gross domestic private investment' respectively), but do not take into account that part of annual domestic production that comes in the form of labor services and intermediate products and which is sold to intermediate users. This omission is deliberate, the purpose being to avoid a double-counting of the monetary value of factor services and intermediary goods, which is held to be included in the monetary value of final goods. However, the fact is that the residents of a country in any given year do produce more than just the goods destined for final users.[6] In order to estimate the aggregate production of economic goods in general one has to include business spending on intermediary goods and employed labor.

Table 2.3 applies these considerations to analyse the impact of the crisis on the US. Total intermediate output (TIO) – the total spending on intermediate goods – can be inferred from BEA input–output tables. The sum of TIO and gross private domestic investment (GPDI) represents the total of business-to-business expenditure (TBB). When we add to this sum the compensation of employees (CE), we obtain total business spending (TBS). Note that both TBB and TBS are multiples of the GPDI figure, and that TBS is also a multiple of GDP. In other words, the great bulk of US domestic production (and also of all other developed countries) serves firms and other intermediate users, not final users. Next, notice that from

Table 2.3   Aggregate commodity production and aggregate business spending in the US

| | Total commodity output (TCO=GDP+TIO) (US$) | GDP | | | Total intermediate output (TIO) (US$) | Total business-to-business spending (US$) (TBB=GPDI+TIO) | Compensation of employees (CE) (US$) | Total business spending (US$) (TBS=GPDI+TIO+CE) | TBB/TCO (%) | TBS/TCO (%) | TBS/GDP (%) |
		Total (US$)	of which: gross private domestic investment (GPDI) (US$)	GPDI/GDP (%)							
2005	23 074	12 638	2172	17.2	10 435	12 607	7072	19 679	54.6	85.3	155.7
2006	24 481	13 399	2327	17.4	11 082	13 409	7484	20 893	54.8	85.3	155.9
2007	25 796	14 062	2295	16.3	11 735	14 030	7863	21 893	54.4	84.9	155.7
2008	26 566	14 369	2096	14.6	12 197	14 293	8068	22 361	53.8	84.2	155.6
2009	24 804	14 119	1589	11.3	10 685	12 274	7820	20 094	49.5	81.0	142.3
2010	N/A	14 592	1826	12.5	N/A	—	N/A	—	—	—	—

Source: Bureau of Economic Analysis; author's calculations.

2008 to 2009, total business spending declined by $2.267 billion (from $22.361 billion to $20.094 billion), which corresponds to 15.8 percent of GDP. In other words, despite the momentous surge in government spending, there has been a substantial decline of aggregate spending which is not reflected in the 2009 GDP figure.

Even more important, Table 2.3 reinforces the conclusions we have drawn from the recent evolution of private domestic investment (Table 2.2). The decline of both gross and net private domestic investment within a by and large constant GDP means that present consumption has been increased at the expense of future consumption. However, net private domestic investment is still estimated to be positive. It is therefore tempting to believe that future growth has merely been slowed down or at most come to a halt. By contrast, Table 2.3 shows that aggregate production for intermediate users has declined substantially. Hence, the future production for final users must equally be expected to diminish, rather than merely stagnate.

By 2011 this trend is still barely visible. Real GDP figures have declined only slightly, reflecting the reduced capital formation springing from the reduction of private domestic investment. Indeed, when business expenditure plummets (with the short-term consequence of capital consumption), it does not have an immediately negative impact on real GDP because in the short run the economy continues to churn out the consumer goods that were close to completion. Nominal GDP might actually increase, to the extent that some of the funds that would otherwise have been invested are now being used for consumption expenditure.

The current reluctance of businesses to commit to long-term investment projects is, to a large extent, the unintended consequence of the attempts of governments and central banks to manage the crisis. Indeed, these attempts have made the business environment deteriorate, most notably by aggrandizing the uncertainty concerning the future evolution of the economy in four respects:

1. The momentous surge of government expenditure has been financed through a corresponding increase of public debt (national, regional, and municipal). In most countries, public debt was already high before the crisis. Deficit spending in an attempt to manage the crisis has brought it to new record levels.[7] This threatens to unsettle government finance, and in several cases has already done so, bringing most notably the Greek and Irish governments to the brink of default. Government default can be prevented in three ways: a) by cutting public expenditure; b) by loans from other governments at lower interest rates than those offered on the market; and c) by loans from

the printing press of the central bank (monetization of the public debt). Solution b) can work only if some major governments have not yet accumulated a large public debt. At present, only the Chinese government is in this felicitous situation; in all other cases, the debt problem is merely shifted from one government to another. Only solutions a) and c) are therefore ultimate remedies against government default,[8] but both solutions entail major macroeconomic disruptions – deflationary spirals in the case of a), and strong inflation or even hyperinflation in the case of c).

Hence, one way or another, the excessive public debt of the major governments today has the potential to create macroeconomic disturbances of a magnitude far in excess of even our current problems. It is true that such a disaster is not yet imminent, but if current deficit spending goes on unchecked, and if historical experience provides any guide, we might be only five or six years away from it.[9] Meanwhile, this dire prospect slows down and often stops the execution of long-term business plans, as prudent investors who take their mandate seriously refuse to gamble with their own family savings or the life-time savings of their clients in such an uncertain environment.

2. The sheer magnitude of the changes of additional public expenditure is likely to create great fortunes where they fall. For example, in the US, the budget of the federal government was been increased in 2009 through 2011, each year by an amount corresponding to some 10 percent of GDP. These fortunes will be gained only by those who are well positioned to deliver the goods that are then in public demand; it is not always clear which goods will be concerned and when.

3. This expenditure is for the moment essentially short term, while it is not clear if and to what extent these public-spending programs will be extended.

4. Various legislative processes, initiated by the heads of major states, have been announced to bring about sweeping changes to business regulation and sometimes even to the whole structure of the economy. In some cases a relatively concrete objective of these changes is announced ('green economy'), while their dimension remains unclear and the measures (public spending, business regulation, etc.) remain vague. In other cases, even the objective is elusive ('ending capitalism', 'empowering the state') and as a consequence the political measures cannot yet be ascertained.

Each of these four factors creates policy-induced or regime uncertainty that impair long-term investment.[10] Taken together, they go a long way to account for the current stifling of business investment, which, if it persists, threatens to undermine in the medium and long run the material welfare of the world population.

IMPACT ON BANKING

Even more than the stock markets, the banking sector has been the epicenter of the current crisis. Much less than the stock markets, banks have been penalized for their own excesses, which had, after all, contributed quite substantially to magnitude of the crisis. In the EU the number of bank failures has been much smaller than in the US, essentially because the European governments were much more determined to prevent bank failures by providing open and hidden subsidies (in Europe corporate finance is essentially bank based, rather than market based as it is in the US). This concerned in particular public and semi-public banks. In Germany, the Länder-owned Landesbanken had invested heavily in mortgage-backed securities (MBS) which they had bought, as it turned out, at excessively high prices. Only public bailouts prevented their bankruptcy.

Just as the private commercial banks and investment banks, public and semi-public banks were engaged in business practices that have been making the financial system as a whole more fragile and have decisively contributed to the magnitude of the current crisis. Three such business practices can be singled out:

1. Banks have operated with extremely low cash balances, which made them vulnerable to bank runs. They were thus dependent on permanent assistance from the central banks to prevent such runs. They have done this to invest the money that would otherwise have been 'idle' in their cash balance, thus profiting from the return on this investment.
2. Banks have operated with extremely low equity ratios in an attempt to leverage a higher than average return on equity capital. This technique of leveraging, and the implied under-capitalization, is pervasive on the financial markets and is their most serious structural problem. It accounts for much of the magnitude of the current crisis. Banks typically operate with equity ratios much lower than 10 percent, and in the case of large government-sponsored enterprises (GSEs) such as Fanny Mae and Freddie Mac, their equity ratio was in the order of a mere 1 percent. Consider the following example: suppose an investment entirely in the form of equity capital of €50 million yields a net profit of €5 million. This is equivalent to a return on equity (ROE) of 10 percent. If the investment is no longer entirely financed by equity, but in a more or less large part by debt, then the net profit diminishes

(because the investor has to pay interest on the debt), but it increases relative to the equity capital that is still invested. Thus, if €45 million out of the €50 million investment are financed through credit at 5 percent, then the net profit is €2.75 million (€5 million less €45 million at 5 percent). But this net profit of €2.75 million is now the remuneration of only €5 million of equity capital. In other words, it represents an ROE of 55 percent. This technique can conceivably be applied ad infinitum, as long as the total return on investment is higher than the cost of credit. Thus, suppose the above investment is financed by €1 million equity capital and €49 million of debt, then the net profit is €2.55 million (€5 million less €49 million at 5 percent), now representing an ROE of 255 percent.

3. Banks have systematically invested too much money in relatively high-return (but also, therefore, high-risk) assets. Or, what amounts to the same thing, they have systematically underestimated the risks associated with these assets.

As we have stated, these practices have long been pervasive. It is obvious that they engender a higher profit and a higher return for the investor, at the cost of greater vulnerability. Interest-rate hikes, unexpected revenue losses, unexpected technical problems, and so on can easily upset the calculations of the ardent risk-taker. The risk-takers may quickly face insolvency, especially if they have reduced their equity basis to an almost symbolic minimum. If only one or a few banks are such excessive risk-takers, only they become vulnerable, and their behavior represents no threat for the banking system and the financial system as a whole. But if more or less all banks choose to apply these financial techniques on a massive scale, then they all become vulnerable. And because the assets of one financial firm are more than often the liability of another, the failure of one of them – if sufficiently large – is likely to trigger a snowball of further failures. Such firms, which are big enough to trigger snowballing failures, are 'systemically relevant' in current economic jargon.

These problems, and in particular the pervasive problem of undercapitalized financial agents, have been known to public banking supervisors for many years. It is true that nobody was able to predict the exact timing and the extent of the current crisis, but many economists – some of them associated with government financial institutions such as the Bank for International Settlements and the Federal Reserve System – ever since the acceleration of the global real estate boom in 2002 had warned in scholarly articles, in the daily press, and in public speeches that it was only a question of time until these structural problems would usher in a new crisis.

They have at times been heard, but governments have not listened to them. In short, there was no lack of intelligence, but there was a lack of political will to tackle the issues.

One of the factors that paralyzed the determination of governments to solve these problems in time was their self-interest in preserving inflationary (that is, leveraged) finance, and in promoting rather than curtailing the banking industry's credit-creation powers. Now, it needs to be stressed right away that this is not a recent phenomenon, but a constant feature of mankind's financial and monetary history. Until the 17th century, governments sought and obtained inflationary finance through the debasement of the coinage. They then discovered that the same end could be reached much more cheaply, safely and efficiently by banks producing redeemable paper notes and demand deposits on a fractional-reserve basis. They therefore started to create such banks on their own account, and encouraged similar initiatives from businessmen and financial promoters.

The central problem of bank-based inflationary finance is the virtual illiquidity of the banks. It is impossible for them to redeem all of their notes and deposits at once, even though they give a promise of immediate redemption to each bearer of their notes and to each owner of a deposit. If the banker correctly speculates on the volume asked for redemption, the virtual illiquidity remains just that – virtual. However, it turns into manifest illiquidity if the banker is a poor speculator. Such illiquidity very quickly turns into insolvency if, as is often the case, the banker is forced to sell assets to replenish the cash balance. The insolvency of one banker more than often snowballs into the insolvency of others, as everybody scrambles for cash and is forced to sell. In short, with the new banking industry there appeared the phenomenon of the banking crisis.

While the banking industry was young, its crises were small and did not have much impact on the rest of the economy. But when it grew into importance at the end of the 18th and through the middle of the 19th century, its crises became a nuisance for public finance. Thus governments sought to prevent bank runs and financial crises by the institution of central banks, starting with the Bank of England in 1844.[11]

These new institutions centralized the country's reserves of base money, which at the time was usually a currency of silver or gold. Thus they could bail out the other banks in times of liquidity crises. However, this institutional solution was short-lived because it did not attack the problem of inflationary finance at the root; rather, it aggravated the basic illiquidity problem, which was soon 'reproduced on a larger scale,' as the Marxists used to say. Central banks were supposed to preserve, not to curtail, the ability of commercial banks to inflate the money supply, and thus to inflate the supply of bank credit. They themselves were operating on a fractional-reserve basis, even though they were not quite as leveraged as the other banks. Not surprisingly, commercial banks did not reduce their issues but on the contrary increased them. They did not increase their equity capital so that they would have a greater buffer in bad times, but increased their leverage because they knew the central bank was behind them. This behavior was rational from their individual point of view, given the incentives that had been created through the centralization of reserves. The new institutional environment had made them less responsible for their actions; they no longer had to shoulder the full negative consequences of their choices, yet they still enjoyed all the benefits (current economic jargon calls this 'moral hazard'). They acted accordingly, and the system as a whole became much more leveraged and fragile. In short, the centralization of banking ultimately reinforced the problems of fractional-reserve banking by making the industry as a whole more fragile. As a consequence, financial crises became even larger, threatening the entire banking system as well as government finance, and increasingly had international ramifications.

Again, governments stepped in to rescue the banking system. Yet again, they did so at least in part out of self-interest, without going to the root of the matter. The new solution consisted of giving legal tender status to the money substitutes issued by central banks, and granting the central banks the right to suspend their payments. This implied that central bank issues were no longer redeemable into some underlying natural base money such as gold. Rather, these issues now were the base money of the country. This is the origin of the present system of immaterial fiat monies, which underlies the architecture of global finance (Hülsmann, 2008, esp. part 3).

To understand the economic consequences of immaterial fiat money, one has to realize that in such a monetary system there are no more technical or commercial limits to the production of base money. Under a silver standard, or a gold standard, the production of base money is constrained by the costs of mining and minting. No such constraints exist in our present fiat money system. Central banks can produce money in unlimited amounts and with virtually no time restriction. This implies most notably that a central bank cannot go bankrupt as long as its debts are denominated in its own currency. Similarly, no public or private organization can go bankrupt as long as it enjoys the unmitigated solidarity of the central bank that produces the money that it has to pay back.

This institutional solution promotes moral hazard on an even greater scale than the system it replaced. The very presence of central banks producing immaterial paper money, which moreover have the official mission to stabilize the banking sector and the financial markets, encourages precisely those nefarious practices that we have singled out above. Thus, commercial banks run down their cash balances because they can obtain cash in unlimited amounts and at a moment's notice at the trading desks of the central banks. Commercial banks run down their equity ratios as far as legally allowed, because there is no more need for them to take any precautions against adverse market tendencies. Indeed, the monetary values of their assets are stabilized through the central banks, and they themselves are 'systemically relevant' and can therefore expect to be bailed out in the worst of all cases. Finally, for the same reason, commercial banks make riskier investments. These risks do not fully fall on them; a significant part of the risks is 'socialized' through public bailout money.

These practices cannot be fully prevented through the control mechanisms that are successfully applied in other areas. Both credit rating and bank audits are hapless in markets that are fundamentally biased by the presence of a pervasive moral hazard. Rating agencies and auditors rely on past and current market prices to assess the possible benefits and risks of a firm's operations. But those very prices are being asked and paid by agents that are not fully responsible for their actions. The prices 'lie,' so to say.

Similarly, financial regulation is ultimately powerless in the presence of institutionalized moral hazard, as long as it leaves the banks any freedom of choice to innovate and develop new products and markets. The minimum capital ratios imposed on the banking system starting in the 1990s (under the Basel I agreements) have merely shifted the locus of excessive behavior. Banks have developed a whole panoply of new financial techniques, most notably securitization, to get around those rules legally. Often this has been done with the connivance of public and semi-public partners. For example, under the Basel rules, private-sector claims have to be secured by a minimum equity ratio of 8 percent. But if a GSE holds these claims and uses them as backing for some new asset-backed securities (ABS) that it sells on the market, then a commercial bank that buys one these ABS has to secure this purchase by a mere 1.6 percent of equity, even though the underlying asset (and thus the underlying risk) has not changed in the least.

In the past, financial and banking regulation has been 'captured' by the very firms – usually major firms – which were supposed to be regulated. These firms used the regulation process to fight competitors whom they could not successfully confront on the market. Financial and banking regulation has also been full of exceptions and exemptions designed to allow inflationary finance in the service of the state. For example, again under the Basel rules, any credit granted to a national government requires no equity basis.

The institutional fragility of the global financial sector and of banking in particular is therefore quite essentially the result of rational individual adjustments to an ill-conceived institutional environment. Banks have not mindlessly followed a greedy appetite for greater profits and market shares, not caring for the downside this could have in store for them. They have not just mimicked other banks or other investors who applied hazardous strategies. Quite the reverse: they have coolly and rationally pondered the pros and cons of these practices. And the turn of the events of the past two years demonstrates that the bankers have been right, at least as far as their own business is concerned. Unsound practices in finance and banking have, as a rule, *not* been penalized through bankruptcy. To the contrary, as a rule, they have been rewarded by bailouts in the form of expansionary monetary policy, credit guarantees, and direct subsidies (partial or full nationalizations). These bailouts have been justified with the 'systemic relevance' of those banks and financial firms. Their executives are therefore encouraged to count on similar bailouts in the future.

This amounts to nothing less than a destruction of the incentive system without which a market economy cannot operate. When profits are private, while losses are socialized, the beneficiaries are encouraged to behave in ways that are no longer conducive to the common good. To sum up, longstanding political interventions into the monetary system were primarily designed to preserve inflationary finance in the service of the state (and of others). These interventions have entailed: an increase of the overall volume of the banking sector relative to the rest of the economy; a concentration within the banking industry that set in when regulations were set up that slowed down the creation of new banks; and a greater overall fragility of the banking industry, as manifest in under-capitalization.

The current crisis does not provide a clear-cut demonstration that free and unfettered markets – financial markets in particular – cannot work and rather need vigorous political control to be conducive to the common good. The evidence for this often-made assertion is weak, if not outright lacking. A much stronger case can be made for the exact opposite claim: namely that the current crisis delivers yet another demonstration that political interventionism just does not work, and that only the genuinely free (and responsible) actions of entrepreneurs and other market participants can make financial markets operate to the benefit of the common good. Without even entering into any detailed argument, the basic and widely known institutional facts lend prima facie credence to this claim. As a starter, in historical perspective, financial markets and financial agents (especially banks) are, to a large extent, political creatures. The history of organized financial markets is very much the history of governments trying to make sure there are enough buyers of government bonds.[12] The history of banking is very much the history of money creation in the service of the state (Gouge, 1968 [1833]; Hammond, 1957; Rothbard, 2002). In our own day, banks are often state-owned, and in all other cases they are licensed by public administrations according to rules fixed by legislation (Barth et al., 2006). On the financial markets, governments feature a massive presence, not only as regulators, but also as financial agents, and especially as large consumers of financial services. The major governments of the world taken together absorb a good third of the world's savings. Financial markets are not free from political intervention, not by any stretch of the imagination or common use of grammar.

THE CONSEQUENCES OF ANTI-CRISIS GOVERNMENT INTERVENTIONS

Apart from the top echelon of banking, government – especially the governments of major countries, in economic terms – has been the only sector to benefit from the current crisis. Governments all over the world have assumed the mission to manage the crisis and thus to bring the world economy back on track. The essential means have been greater public spending and further regulations of the financial markets and other sectors of the economy. The bulk of these activities have taken place on a national level, but regional and communal governments have often mimicked the same approach. The result has been an across-the-board momentous surge of public spending. The order of magnitude has very often been in the double digits of percentage of GDP. Virtually all of this additional spending has been financed by an increase in public debt.

At the risk of laboring the obvious, it should be noted that the momentous growth of government activity (including central banking) at the onset of a crisis is not an inescapable law of nature. Rather, it is a characteristic fruit of the culture of statism that has come into dominance in the 20th century and is today deeply entrenched in the political class and its organizations, as well as in public administrations, in education, in higher education, in religious organizations, and in the media (with the exception of the Internet). Statism can be defined as an exaggerated belief in the power of political interventions to create or to restore a beneficial social order.[13] In its mildest form, it holds that such interventions, if used wisely and as a complement to the order-creating activities of civil society, may benefit social order. In a stronger form, it holds that political interventions are always a necessary element in creating social order, though they may be counter-productive if used without circumspection. In its most extreme form, it does not recognize any limitations to the power of the state in realizing its objectives (the fiction of government omnipotence). Statism is grounded on various factual claims. It is therefore open to be challenged by scientific inquiry and is, indeed, being challenged constantly.

Government management of the present crisis rests on three related claims: 1) that interventionism has not itself been a major cause of our present calamities; 2) that further interventionism is a suitable means – possibly the only means – to bring the world economy back on track; and 3) that interventionism has worked on similar occasions in the past, most notably in combating the Great Depression of the 1930s. All three claims are at the centre of current debate.[14] In any case, increased government activity (including central banking) in the name of economic problem solving means an increased role of government in the economic and social spheres. Individuals, families, firms, associations, and communal governments are learning to rely, both in addressing present concerns and in their planning of future activities, on the very same political institutions: national governments and their supra-national institutions. In short, civil society and civil institutions become less self-reliant, while political power is being enhanced and centralized.

This tendency to turn governments and their institutions, including central banks, into 'problem solvers of last resort,' far from putting society on a more solid footing, makes the social fabric as a whole more fragile. On the one hand, the manifold prudential measures for economic self-protection taken by individuals and civil institutions in the light of their different subjective assessments of present and future risks are homogenized. On the other hand, the overall volume of economic self-protection is reduced because of the economies of scale implied in centralized all-risk economic insurance offered by the state. In short, the buffers and cushions of the social fabric, providing protection to each against the errors and abuses of others, dwindle in orientation, number, and overall volume. The expansion and concentration of political action implies that any errors in government (and, *a fortiori*, abuses of government power) have a greater and immediate impact on all members and institutions of civil society. The reinforcement of political institutions entails increased overall institutional fragility. In the words of current economic jargon, it creates and respectively increases systemic risks.

The evolution of western banking, which we have briefly reviewed above, stands as a warning illustration of this dangerous tendency. From a political point of view, increased government activity (including central banking) bodes ill for the preservation of free societies, even if the current expansion and centralization of government power is meant to be temporary. Indeed, throughout the 20th century and into the present day, temporary increases of government power to confront a military or economic crisis have never been fully scaled back after the crisis has been overcome.[15] All in all, there has been a tendency for government to grow at the expense of civil society, with only a few occasional and minor setbacks.

CONCLUSION

Our overview of the main features of the current crisis of the global economy, up to the present point (December 2010), can be summarized in eleven points.

1. The magnitude of the current crisis of the global economy results especially from the fragility of virtually the entire financial sector, which is too weak to reform itself and too weak to accommodate sudden and major adjustments in business.
2. The fragility of the financial sector has been known for many years. Governments have neglected to address this problem, inter alia, because of their own material self-interest.
3. The major manifestation of the crisis so far has been the dramatic meltdown of stock markets on a worldwide scale in the year 2008, and the implied massive redistribution of wealth, essentially to the detriment of households.
4. The crisis did not entail an institutional meltdown because of immediate and massive action of public authorities (central banks and national governments). In particular, the momentous expansion of government and central bank spending has prevented a great number of bankruptcies in the financial industries and in other sectors of the economy.
5. Because of 4), unemployment has been kept at a relatively low level, as compared to major crises in the past, even though there are significant regional disparities.
6. Because of 4), many unviable firms and business projects have been kept in existence that sap the capital basis of the economy and thus undermine the future productivity of labor.
7. Because of 4), the incentive system of the market has been further eroded, especially in the 'systemically relevant' banks and financial firms. The resulting waste of capital undermines the future productivity of labor.
8. Because of 4), public debt has reached critical levels in several countries. If unchecked, it threatens to entail major macroeconomic disruptions.
9. Because of 4), the network of social institutions is becoming more fragile, and systemic risks are building up.

10. Because of 4), political freedom is being undermined.
11. Because of 4), and also because of current legal activism motivated by the desire to 'use the crisis' to impose social change, the business environment has deteriorated and private investment slowed down.

All in all, therefore, the crisis of the global economy is far from over. Due to immediate and vigorous bailout interventions on the part of the major central banks and governments, much human suffering has so far been prevented. However, this achievement has been essentially short term in nature, and it has been bought at a great price.

Fundamental structural problems of the world economy (both in business and in finance) have not been solved, and have often been reinforced through their bailouts. Virtually all banks and financial firms are still seriously under-capitalized, a great number of industrial firms survive only thanks to overt and hidden subsidies, and private investment in general is sluggish. The massive interventions of central banks and governments have also created and aggravated other problems, such as the institutional fragility of civil society (systemic risks), the erosion of political liberty, the undermining of public finance (potential of major macroeconomic disruptions in the near future), and the further erosion of entrepreneurial responsibility, one of the pillars of a genuine market economy.

NOTES

1. This chapter is a revised and shortened version of my 'General overview of the magnitude of the crisis' (2011).
2. Anthony Evan's chapter in the present volume assesses the boom-time growth of Ireland, one specific Anglo-example.
3. See Federal Reserve, 'Flow of funds accounts of the United States (second quarter 2010)', Table B.100.
4. It is questionable whether all of them were viable before, because consumption and saving-investment under boom conditions is, by definition, unbalanced.
5. To facilitate comparisons with the US, we use data for EU-15 (the first 15 member countries, before enlargement of the Union on 1 May 2004), which represent more than 92 percent of the total GDP of the current Union of 27 member states.
6. For a systematic critique of this shortcoming in conventional national accounting, see Reisman (1996, pp. 674–82). See also the more general discussion in Rothbard (1993, pp. 313–50).
7. At the end of 2009, public debt in the EU (27 countries) stood at 73.6 percent of GDP, and at 78.7 percent in the Eurozone (16 countries).
8. Only solution a) is a genuine ultimate remedy against government default, because solution c) amounts to covert default.
9. On the theory and history of hyperinflations see Bernholz (2003).
10. On the theoretical and historical significance of the concept of regime uncertainty, see Higgs (1997).
11. Huerta de Soto (2006, p. 713) and Bagus and Howden (2011) describe this process by

which the fractional reserve banking system demands and eventually creates a central bank to coordinate credit expansion and act as a lender of last resort during the ensuing bust.

12. On the early history see Ehrenberg (1896).
13. Political interventions must not be confused with a mixed economy. In the latter, the government is one of several owners and it controls only its own property. By contrast, an interventionist government commands other property owners to use their resources in a different way than these owners themselves would have used them. See Mises (1977 [1929], ch. 1).
14. See for example Ferlito (2010); Higgs (2006); Huerta de Soto (2006); Paul (2009); Powell (2003); Rothbard (2005); Salin (2010); Shlaes (2007); Taylor (2009); Woods (2009); and the papers published in *Critical Review* (2009) **21** (2–3).
15. This is known as the 'ratchet effect' of government expansion. See Higgs (1977).

REFERENCES

Altmiks, P. (ed.) (2010), *Im Schatten der Finanzkrise. Muss das staatliche Zentralbankwesen abgeschafft werden?* Munich: Olzog.

Bagus, P. and D. Howden (2011), 'Fractional reserve free banking: some quibbles', *Quarterly Journal of Austrian Economics*, **13** (4), 22–55.

Barth, J., G. Caprio and R. Levine (2006), *Rethinking Bank Regulation: Till Angels Govern*, Cambridge: Cambridge University Press.

Bernholz, P. (2003), *Monetary Regimes and Inflation*, Cheltenham, UK and Northampton, MA, USA: Edward Elgar.

Ehrenberg, R. (1896), *Das Zeitalter der Fugger. Geldkapital und Creditverkehr im 16 Jahrhundert*, Jena: Fischer.

Gouge, W. (1968 [1833]), *A Short History of Paper Money and Banking in the United States*, New York: Kelley.

Ferlito, C. (2010), *Dentro la crisi*, Chieti: Solfanelli.

Hammond, B. (1957), *Banks and Politics in America from the Revolution to the Civil War*, Princeton, NJ: Princeton University Press.

Higgs, R. (1977), *Crisis and Leviathan*, New York: Academic Press.

Higgs, R. (1997), 'Regime uncertainty: why the Great Depression lasted so long and why prosperity resumed after the war', *Independent Review*, **1** (4), 561–90.

Higgs, R. (2006), *Depression, War, and Cold War. Challenging the Myths of Conflict and Prosperity*, New York: Oxford University Press.

Huerta de Soto, J. (2006), *Money, Bank Credit, and Economic Cycles* (2nd edn), Auburn, AL: Ludwig von Mises Institute.

Hülsmann, J.G. (2008), *The Ethics of Money Production*, Auburn, AL: Ludwig von Mises Institute.

Hülsmann, J.G. (2011), 'General overview of the magnitude of the crisis', in J.T. Raga and M.A. Glendon (eds), *Crisis in a Global Economy: Replanning the Journey*, Vatican: Pontifical Academy of the Social Sciences, pp. 95–117.

Mises, L. von (1977 [1929]), *Critique of Interventionism*, trans. H.F. Sennholz, Irvington-on-Hudson, NY: Foundation for Economic Education.

Murphy, R. (2009), *The Politically Incorrect Guide to the Great Depression*, Chicago, IL: Regnery.

Paul, R. (2009), *End the Fed*, New York: Grand Central Publishers.

Powell, J. (2003), *FDR's Folly: How Roosevelt and His New Deal Prolonged the Great Depression*, New York: Crown Forum.

Raga, J.T. and M.S. Sorondo (eds) (forthcoming), *Crisis in a Global Economy: Replanning the Journey*, Vatican: Pontifical Academy of the Social Sciences.

Reisman, G. (1996), *Capitalism*, Ottawa, IL: Jameson.

Rothbard, M.N. (2002), *A History of Money and Banking in the United States: The Colonial Era to World War II*, Auburn, AL: Ludwig von Mises Institute.

Rothbard, M.N. (2005), *America's Great Depression* (5th edn), Auburn, AL: Ludwig von Mises Institute.

Salin, P. (2010), *Revenir au capitalisme, pour éviter les crises*, Paris: Odile Jacob.

Shlaes, A. (2007), *The Forgotten Man: A New History of the New Deal*, New York: Harper Perennial.

Taylor, J.D. (2009), *Getting Off Track. How Government Actions and Interventions Caused, Prolonged and Worsened the Financial Crisis*, Stanford, CA: Hoover Institution Press.

Woods, T.E. (2009), *Meltdown*, Chicago: Regnery.

3. The Irish economic 'miracle': Celtic tiger or Bengal kitten?

Anthony J. Evans

The Irish economic story is one well told – Barry (1999), Burnham (2003), De la Fuente and Vives (1997), Gray (1997), MacSharry and White (2000), Powell (2003) and Sweeney (1998) all offer admiring accounts of a remarkable transformation from one of Europe's poorest economies to one of its most prosperous. Between 1990 and 2007 real GNP quadrupled, and GNI per capita (at PPP) overtook that of the UK. And yet the rags-to-riches story has an Act III: in 2009 Irish GNP fell by 10.7 percent,[1] and compared to the 2007 peak had plunged by a huge 17 percent within two years, constituting 'the deepest and swiftest contraction suffered by a Western economy since the Great Depression' (Kelly, 2010). Just as economists were trumpeting the employment gains of the Irish 'miracle,' we have witnessed a total fall in employment of 266 000 from 2007 to 2009, with an unemployment rate that has doubled from 6.3 percent in 2008 to 13.25 percent in 2010.[2] Figure 3.1 shows the massive increase in Irish GNI since 1990, overtaking the UK in 2006 but then falling back below it since 2008.[3]

The 'Celtic tiger' analogy is a curious one. It originates from a 1994 report by Morgan Stanley, and alludes to the infamous East Asian 'tiger' economies of the same period. The Austrian theory of the trade cycle rests on a conflict between expected future incomes and the stock of real resources required for production. According to the conventional story, artificially low interest rates (typically caused by excess credit creation from the banking sector) generate an illusion of wealth as businesses and consumers are enticed into excess borrowing.[4] In the case of the recent housing bubble consumers were borrowing against the expected future value of their homes, and businesses were borrowing against the expected future profits of their investment plans. When house prices fell, and growth prospects slowed down, the mistakes were revealed.

Notice that many of the mechanisms that create such a crisis are present in simple narratives. When the British chancellor Gordon Brown declared

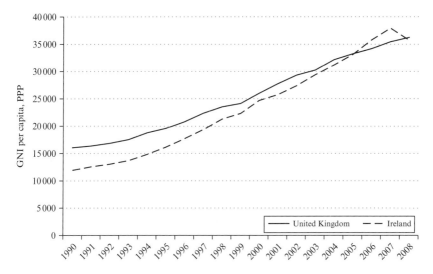

Figure 3.1   British and Irish GNI per capita

that he had brought an end to boom and bust, it encouraged people to overestimate the future growth prospects of the economy. Notice how the widespread belief in a 'tiger' economy has the potential to lead to similar errors – if the general public act as though incomes will perpetually increase they may well engage in unsustainable levels of current consumption and investment. To be sure there are large degrees of truth in the characterization of the Irish economy as a 'tiger'; however, this chapter presents an alternative view.

Consider the 'Bengal' breed of cat, which derives from the cross-breeding of Asian leopards and the domestic feline. Although superficially similar to the Bengal tiger (sharing striped markings and a light undercarriage), they have a gentle temperament and only grow to a size similar to a normal domestic cat. Drawing on this analogy, this chapter augments the 'Celtic tiger' thesis by suggesting that when an economy is still developing it can be easy to get carried away with growth projections. If a pet owner confuses a Bengal kitten for a tiger they will misallocate resources by investing in products (such as a large pen) that are inconsistent with their future needs. Similarly if people act as though the economy is a 'tiger' – and that house prices and business profits will rise indefinitely – when in actual fact it is a 'Bengal', this will generate a bubble, malinvestments will occur, and a bust will follow.[5]

CAUSES OF GROWTH

Before attributing too much to domestic (or indeed deliberate) policy changes, it is important to consider the extent to which broader, exogenous shocks play a role in the development of an economy such as Ireland. O'Grada warns, 'small open economies, no matter how successful, get buffeted by exogenous shocks' (2002, p. 12), and it is important not to underestimate the favorable conditions such as increased globalization and EU integration in the 1990s, or indeed the impact of the global financial crisis of 2008. To some extent the Irish economy is simply a reflection of broader, external factors. That said, domestic policy can have an impact, although it needn't necessarily be economic policy or even intended. Bloom and Canning point out that the legalization of contraception in 1980 and subsequent fall in birth rate 'has given Ireland a "bulge" cohort of working-age people' (2003, p. 230) that they posit played an important role in the latter economic boom. While economists can focus on relatively trivial details, broad forces such as demography can create these predetermined elements of change.

The conventional view is that these 'accidental' factors are outweighed by deliberate domestic policy design. For example, 'Ireland illustrates how large the pay-offs from better policies can be in a few critical sectors in the presence of favorable external factors' (Burnham, 2003, p. 537). Ireland was well placed to take advantage of the fortuitous rise in the international high-tech sector (51 percent of jobs created in the 1990s were in 'internationally traded and financial services, where telecommunication is a critical factor' (ibid., p. 554)).

Powell (2003) highlights the importance of economic freedom, and indeed Ireland's economic reforms have been reflected in their rankings across a variety of measures. According to the Fraser Institute's Economic Freedom of the World index, Ireland scored 5.8 in 1975 rising to 6.8 in 1990 and jumped to 8.2 in 1995 (but it plateaued in the subsequent decade). This index is compiled based on five broad areas of 'freedom': the size of government; the legal protection of private property rights; access to sound money; free trade; and business regulation (see Gwartney et al., 2010). Note that in Ireland's case the key drivers are 'sound money' and 'freedom to trade internationally,' ranking 14th and 6th globally respectively (in 2008). In terms of 'size of government,' however, they were ranked 116th in the world, demonstrating that while benefiting from being an open economy, the public sector remains significant. The Heritage Foundation's Index of Economic Freedom shows a slightly later spike in Ireland's ranking, from 1995 to 2000.

There is no doubt that Ireland is a pioneer of efforts to stimulate entrepreneurship: the Industrial Development Agency (IDA) was founded in the 1950s and has served as a subsequent model for targeted spending at encouraging investment through tax breaks and direct subsidies. Shannon was an early example of a state-created 'free trade zone,' as domestic policy clearly targeted economic growth. With zero percent corporate tax on the profits of manufactured exports, later rising to 10 percent, it is no surprise that companies queued up to relocate (Dorgan, 2006; Murphy, 2000, p. 13). Burnham (2003) lists four major examples of supply-side reforms – low corporate profit tax rates; reducing personal tax rates; education; and telecommunication infrastructure – while Dorgan adds that 'the advantage for business of the low tax rate is enhanced by a wide network of double-taxation agreements, favorable treatment of foreign dividends, and supportive administrative rules' (2006, p. 11). Barry (2003) provides examples of specific ways, such as transfer pricing, in which US-based companies could benefit from their Irish operations. Note that these changes occurred well in advance of the 'tiger' years: 'By 1975, more than 450 foreign-owned industrial projects, covering a wide range of manu-facturing sectors, accounted for two-thirds of Ireland's total industrial output' (Dorgan, 2006, p. 6).

In 1997, 30 percent of the economy and 40 percent of exports were derived from foreign-owned companies (Powell, 2003, p. 44), while foreign investment accounted for 17 percent of GDP in 2003, (Dorgan, 2006, p. 1), and 'at the heart of these policies was a belief in economic openness to global markets, low tax rates, and investment in education' (ibid., pp. 1–2). This was not just any foreign investment; the Irish 'boom' coincided with a surge in the US economy and an influx of high-growth US mul-tinational corporations (MNCs) seeking access to the European market (Dorgan, 2006, p. 8). By 1994 US companies had invested $3,000 per Irish head in the Irish economy (*Economist*, 1997) and by 2006 US companies were responsible for 'two-thirds of all investment projects and 80 percent of capital invested' (Dorgan, 2006, p. 11). It is not a gross exaggeration to consider Ireland to be an offshore US tax haven, as Murphy accentuates: 'it is more accurate to look at it as a predominantly U.S. high-tech multi-national tiger nurtured in a special Irish tax reserve which is part of the united states of Europe' (2000, p. 14). Barry (2003) compares the average effective corporate tax rate facing US MNCs in 1997, showing a rate of 9.1 percent in Ireland, compared to 24.9 percent in the UK, 29 percent in France, and 24.6 percent in Spain. Indeed this is a lower rate than in Australia, Hong Kong, or China.

Indeed for this reason it is important to make a distinction between GDP calculations (measures of economic output produced in Ireland) and GNP (that which is produced by Irish residents) – Barry, Hannan and Strobl (1999, p. 14) estimated that 13 percent of Irish GDP are profits being repatriated by MNCs and more recent estimates put these 'profit transfers' as closer to 20 percent (Johnson, 2010). Focusing on GDP (as economists tend to do) can thus overstate the health of the domestic economy. Indeed, from 1994 to 1997, while GDP growth averaged 8.4 percent, GNP growth was considerably lower at 7.5 percent (Murphy, 2000, p. 6). Barry, Hannan and Strobl (1999, p. 15) estimate that in the 1990s GNP was only 81 percent of GDP.

One of the main debates regarding Ireland's growth is the role that transfer payments from the EU had. By some measures they were such a boost to the economy that when stripped out of the figures the 'miracle' becomes more normal. With regard to EU spending, 'these expenditures may have raised GNP in the late 1990s by 3 to 4 percentage points above what it would otherwise have been' (Barry, Bradley and Hannan,1999, p. 115).[6] However, important theoretical and empirical objections relate to the role of such transfer payments.

TRANSFER EXPANSION

Consider the following quote:

> The difficulties of economic calculation and public choice problems present theoretical reasons why transfers to the Irish government cannot be a major cause of growth . . . There is no sound theoretical case for viewing EU structural funds as the cause of Ireland's economic growth. Government officials have no way to know what investment projects will generate the most growth and, even if they did, they have little incentive to undertake them. (Powell, 2003, pp. 442–3)

This chapter does not challenge the skepticism about attributing growth to transfer payments,[7] but note that there are two ways to interpret all of this. The first is to say that since transfer payments do not cause economic growth the EU funds must have had little impact (and therefore other factors such as economic institutions are the primary cause). The second interpretation is to say that since transfer payments do not cause economic growth, the economic 'growth' must have partly been an illusion. It seems to be taken as given that Ireland achieved rapid economic prosperity, and therefore the only way to respond to the channels of transfer payments is to downplay their importance (or deny their scale). An alternative explanation is to view these payments as evidence that part of this growth might have been an unsustainable boom. Indeed, the Austrian theory of the trade cycle provides exactly the explanation for how economists confuse the two

– an over reliance on faulty macroeconomic aggregate variables. GDP is not a valid measure of economic activity and CPI is not a valid measure of inflation (Skousen, 1990). By taking this data at face value economists miss the Austrian insights into how 'you can't eat growth rates' and that inflation can exist within a period of stable prices. When economists trumpet, 'from 1990 to 2005, employment soared from 1.1 million to 1.9 million' (Dorgan, 2006, p. 1) the subtle question is 'what kind of jobs?' As previously mentioned, those who are keen to ascribe Ireland's economic performance to pro-market reforms fail to consider whether that growth is genuine or not: the possibility that some of the growth drivers are bubble activity simply does not appear. With the benefit of hindsight (which I do not intend to underplay) it is clear that some of the rises in GDP (especially in the last decade) were based on a bubble.[8]

Boyfield (2009) argues that in 1990 EU structural and cohesion funding constituted 3 percent of Irish GDP, which is less than in Greece (4 percent) or Portugal (3.8 percent). Since these countries did not exhibit the strong growth rates of Ireland, 'these figures indicate that the justification for EU regional development funding is not as convincing as its proponents claim' (ibid., p. 5). Powell (2003) also presents other countries that received EU structural funding as counterpoints for the theory that transfer payments cause growth. However, this oversimplifies the concept of falsification. Examples of low-growth countries that also received transfer payments does not prove that transfer payments cannot lead to growth in certain conditions, and it is a straw man to put forward the idea that transfer payments alone cause growth.

It is important to pass judgment on whether Ireland's receipts were indeed substantial. Ireland's net EU receipts rose from 4 percent of GDP in the late 1980s to 5.1 percent in 1990, 6.2 percent in 1991, before returning to 3–4 percent until 1998, after which it fell further.[9] According to Powell, 'Net receipts from the EU averaged 3.03 percent of GDP during the period of rapid growth from 1995 through 2000, but during the low growth period, from 1973 through 1986, they averaged 3.99 percent of GDP' (2003, p. 444). The obvious rejoinder is that there's a lag between such investment and growth. Even if 'transfers were relatively most important in the 1980s and the early 1990s, but their importance has declined sharply since then' (Burnham, 2003, p. 544), this does not undermine the notion that such transfers led to growth – indeed it suggests that the 'miracle' occurred just after this spending reached its peak. Powell says, 'the government made further policy changes in the 1990–95 period, which helped to bring about the higher rate of growth' (2003, p. 436), but seems to discount the transfer payments that occurred in the same period of time.

Also, while Powell is correct in saying that, 'in absolute terms, net receipts were at about the same level in 2001 as they were in 1985' (Powell, 2003, p. 444), he neglects to mention that they had doubled in the meantime, rising from €1.16m in 1985 to €2.35m in 1991 and reaching a peak at €2.54m in 1997 (just as the boom took off).[10] Braunerhjelm et al. (2000, fig. 5.1, p. 67) provide support for the conventional wisdom that on a per capita basis Ireland has been the most favored recipient of EU funding.

There are a number of possible sources for a boom, some of which can be ruled out in the case of Ireland. First, it was not fueled by debt. The level of national debt has been consistently below €40bn from 2000 to 2007, only spiking as a recent response to the financial crisis (rising to €50.4bn in 2008, and €75.2bn in 2009).[11] As a proportion of GDP it has steadily fallen from over 90 percent in 1994 to 25 percent in 2007 (before rising back to 44 percent in 2008 and 65.6 percent in 2009).[12] Second, it was not fueled by central bank money creation, nor the monetization of debt. Since Ireland is in the Eurozone it does not have control of the domestic money supply. Having said this, 'Ireland's decision to adopt the Euro (which required the country to reduce interest rates) contributed to a substantial increase in prices, especially in property prices' (Burnham, 2003, p. 551).[13]

There are two further sources of monetary injection that do seem more relevant – transfer payments and cheap credit. The Austrian theory of the trade cycle is typically viewed as a credit-induced boom, and indeed the vast majority of empirical work has focused on these cases. However, Garrison (2001, p.75) outlines a theory of a transfer expansion (in contrast to a credit expansion). He posits that: (i) output would exhibit a consumption bias; (ii) this would draw investment from early to later stages of production; (iii) the economy would move beyond its sustainable growth rates; (iv) the subsequent recalculation would be less severe than compared to a credit boom since late-stage investment is more easily liquidated than early-stage, thus 'we would expect a transfer expansion to be less disruptive than a credit expansion' (Garrison, 2001, p. 71).

It is not being claimed that Ireland is an ideal example of a transfer-induced boom, but we might expect to find signs of this. For example, from 2004 to 2008 consumption expenditure rose by 33 percent, while gross domestic fixed capital formation rose by 9 percent.[14] It is important not to oversimplify these aggregate measures, because gross domestic fixed capital formation tends to be more volatile than consumption expenditure (Skousen, 1990). Indeed, while consumption rose by 8.9 percent in 2004–05 and fell by 11.1 percent in 2008–09, investment rose by 19.4 percent and fell by 44 percent in the same periods.[15] And while consumer spending fell by 7 percent in 2009 in real terms, investment in construction and capital equipment fell by 31 percent.[16]

Some have argued that it is appropriate to view Ireland as experiencing two separate booms – the first based on the 'tiger' growth due to increased competitiveness and export growth, and the second in construction (Kelly, 2010). There can be little doubt that, despite claims of low inflation, Ireland has experienced an epic housing boom and that this has been financed by bank leverage.[17] House building accounted for 5 percent of national income in the 1990s but rose to 15 percent at the 2007 peak (with other forms of construction accounting for a further 6 percent) (Kelly, 2010). Indeed this shows up in standard measures of house prices, with first-time mortgages rising from three times average earnings in 1995 to eight times in late 2006 (with even higher multiples for new homes and city homes) (Kelly, 2010).[18] It may be a highly simplified story of the US economy – that easy money led to the dot.com boom and mild recession, but expansionary policy by the Federal Reserve manifested itself in a new bubble in housing – but it provides a close mirror to events in Ireland.

Indeed, Ireland's banking system has been fueling this bubble activity – Irish bank lending in 2008 was 200 percent of national income, significantly higher than in other EU countries (Kelly, 2010, fig. 1). Recent work exposes the extent to which the Irish economy was built on unsustainable leverage (McWilliams, 2009; O'Toole, 2009; Ross, 2009), and while it is a common narrative that these banking failures followed the irrational exuberance that the myth of the Celtic tiger created, to some extent they must also have been a cause.[19] We therefore see indications that a transfer expansion contributed to the 'tiger growth' of the early boom years, only to be replaced with a credit expansion boom in line with the UK and US housing bubbles. The case of the Anglo Irish Bank (AIB) exemplifies this narrative – by September 2008 it was owed €5.8bn by Irish homebuilders and €2.2bn by builders in the UK, reflecting the vast majority of their total loan book (Garvey, 2009, estimates it as being almost its entirety). By comparison the Bank of Ireland had about 70 percent of its lending in property, and AIB had 60 percent (ibid.). When Anglo Irish was nationalized in December 2008 it demonstrated the inherent instability that had developed in the financial system.

Paul Krugman (2010) has cast doubt on the extent to which Ireland's property market played an important role: 'Ireland had none of the American right's favorite villains: there was no Community Reinvestment Act, no Fannie Mae or Freddie Mac.' However, he does point out the similar 'irrational exuberance' (or 'illusion of wealth' referred to earlier) and that 'there was a huge inflow of cheap money . . . it came mainly from the rest of the euro zone, where Germany became a gigantic capital exporter' (ibid.). It is important here to look into Irish housing policy in more detail, because as Constantin Gurdgiev points out:

The squeeze on the property market was complete – the supply was artificially restricted, demand was artificially inflated and the Government was actively 'talking the market up'. The banks were encouraged to lend and the regulators were directly selected to be complacent, inactive and on some occasions – outright unsuited to run the complex world of finance. (Gurdgiev, 2010)

In short, attempts to simplify the causes of the 1995–2007 growth have backfired spectacularly, and the challenge now is not only to factor in the easy money and transfer payments that led to a 2004–08 housing boom, but also to establish how much of that 'tiger' growth was merely a bubble.

CONCLUSION

Ireland has, historically, been a nation open to trade. With its combination of a well-educated workforce and low wages, plus its unique position as an English-speaking country in the Eurozone, it is not hard to see why foreign investors would find it appealing. Indeed, the dramatic tax breaks that actively encouraged FDI clearly led to remarkable economic growth and prosperity. However, it is tempting to attribute too much to domestic policy, and it is too simplistic to conclude that the advances in economic freedom simply dominate other events. In reality Ireland experienced a complex combination of: genuine economic freedom; a credit bubble fueled by an influx of cheap capital; and massive transfer payments from the EU.

It is beyond the scope of this chapter to attempt to disentangle all three factors, as doing so would require a comparative analysis involving other cases (or at least detailed counterfactual analysis). It is also beyond the scope of this chapter (and possibly beyond the capabilities of the economics profession) to tease out which effects dominate, so that we can make reasonable predictions about the scale of capital misallocations and the duration of any adjustment processes. What this chapter does show, however, is a rare historical example (albeit not an idealized type) of an Austrian-style 'transfer payment' boom, and a reminder of the caution that economists must display when passing judgment on such recent case studies. The lessons of the 'Irish tiger' are yet to be learned. It may still turn out to be a Bengal kitten. There will still be an Act IV.

ACKNOWLEDGMENT

The author wishes to thank Constantin Gurdgiev, C.J.L. Lauder, Benjamin Powell, Robert Thorpe, and especially David Howden for helpful comments on early drafts. The usual disclaimer applies.

NOTES

1. In 2009 GDP fell by 7.6 percent, but for reasons discussed later GNP represents a more appropriate measure. See Central Statistics Office, 'National Income and Expenditure: Annual Results for 2009', 30 June 2010. Using an alternative data source, GNI at constant market prices was €33 931 per head of population in 2004. This rose to €35 205 in 2005, €36 525 in 2006, and reached €37 220 in 2007, before falling to €35 274 in 2008, and a preliminary forecast of €31 278 in 2009. Note that this constitutes a 16 percent fall within two years. (See Table A of Central Statistics Office, 'National Income and Expenditure: Annual Results for 2009', 30 June 2010.)
2. From the Economic and Social Research Institute (ESRI), 'Quarterly Economic Commentary', summer 2010.
3. The figure shows GNI per capita, at PPP, in international dollars. From World Bank Databank, http://data.worldbank.org/indicator/NY.GNP.PCAP.PP.CD, 25 September 2010.
4. Indeed this is supported by an experience of wealth as people nearest the source of credit creation see their real incomes rise faster than general prices.
5. Other authors have played on the 'tiger' metaphor (again, mostly operating with the benefit of hindsight). O'Sullivan (2009) shows how the heavy reliance on the property sector has created problems in the Irish banking system, shifting 'from Celtic tiger to Celtic mouse.' Murphy (1994) investigates whether the Irish economy is 'Celtic tiger or tortoise.'
6. If we take this to be referring to GNP growth rates (otherwise it does not makes sense to refer to percentage points) this implies that the underlying growth rate of the economy was a more modest 3.5–4.5 percent. However, it may be the case that it is referring to the absolute level of GNP, in which case tiger growth remains. Indeed Dorgan (2006) cites Barry et al. (2001) to claim that 'studies have shown that these contributions added about 0.5 percent per year to the growth rate, while the growth has averaged over 6.5 percent per year since 1987' (Dorgan, 2006, p. 8).
7. Even if transfer payments do lead to growth, this does not mean that they pass a simple cost–benefit test and should be favored. It should be obvious that if you collect money from dispersed taxpayers across Europe (or indeed 'Germany') and concentrate the spending on a few small locations (e.g. 'Ireland'), you will expect to see a positive impact in the net beneficiaries. The broken-window fallacy does, after all, provide the most telling critique of transfer payments. Free-market economists run the risk of overstating their position when they argue that the 'multiplier' of a transfer payment – in the area in which it is concentrated – is negative. Having said this, there is a strong argument that transfer payments have a tendency to promote rent seeking and thus retard growth (Powell, 2003, p. 443).
8. I am being deliberately careful with my words here. In most histories of the 'Celtic tiger' it appears as though none of the growth is due to bubble activity. It would be similarly foolish to claim that all of it is. I doubt whether we possess the tools to judge whether 'most' or 'a little' are accurate depictions. Thus I think 'some' is an appropriate term since it is the most vague. When Powell says, 'a general tendency of many policies to increase economic freedom has caused Ireland's economy to grow rapidly' (2003, p. 431), I do not doubt it. However I also feel that a great deal of that 'growth' was an illusion and that this was due to a transfer expansion and a credit expansion.
9. See Department of Finance, 'Budgetary and Economic Statistics', September 2009, table 10, and also 'Ireland's 40-year bonanza of foreign aid from the European Union will amount to €41 billion by the time we become a net contributor in 2013', 22 February 2008, www.finfacts.ie/irishfinancenews/article_1012675.shtml, 30 July 2010.
10. See Department of Finance, 'Budgetary and Economic Statistics', September 2009, table 10.
11. From National Treasury Agency, www.ntma.ie/NationalDebt/LevelOfDebt.php, 29 July 2010.

12. From National Treasury Agency, www.ntma.ie/NationalDebt/debtGDP.php, 29 July 2010.
13. Irish interest rates were harmonized with German ones in 1997/8, and many commentators argued that they were artificially low (Honohan and Leddin, 2006).
14. See Central Statistics Office, 'National Income and Expenditure: Annual Results for 2009', 30 June 2010, table 5.
15. See Central Statistics Office, 'National Income and Expenditure: Annual Results for 2009', 30 June 2010, table 5.1.
16. See "Central Statistics Office, 'National Income and Expenditure: Annual Results for 2009', 30 June 2010.
17. In addition to the boom in housing a permanent expansion of the public sector can be observed, and indeed this is probably a more important factor in the ongoing public finance catastrophe.
18. It is important to stress that a housing boom is not an inevitable consequence of easy money – it depends on unique institutional circumstances. Generous tax relief on housing is one example of specific policy decisions that combined to channel much of the artificial credit into the housing industry.
19. Consider the unfortunate timing of Dorgan's bragging that 'leading banks, insurers and fund managers were persuaded of the advantages of Dublin for financial services' (2006, p. 12).

REFERENCES

Barry, F. (ed.) (1999), *Understanding Ireland's Economic Growth*, New York and London: St Martin's Press and Macmillan.
Barry, F. (2003), 'Tax policy, FDI and the Irish economic boom of the 1990s', *Economic Analysis and Policy*, **33** (2), 221–36.
Barry, F., J. Bradley and A. Hannan (1999), 'The European dimension: the single market and structural funds', in F. Barry (ed.), *Understanding Ireland's Economic Growth*, New York and London: St Martin's Press and Macmillan, pp. 99–118.
Barry, F., J. Bradley and A. Hannan (2001), 'The single market, the structural funds and Ireland's recent economic growth', *Journal of Common Market Studies*, **39** (3), 537–52.
Barry, F., A. Hannan and E. Strobl (1999), 'The real convergence of the Irish economy and the sectoral distribution of employment growth', in F. Barry (ed.), *Understanding Ireland's Economic Growth*, New York and London: St Martin's Press and Macmillan, pp. 13–24.
Bloom, D.E. and D. Canning (2003), 'Contraception and the Celtic tiger', *Economic and Social Review*, **34** (3), 229–47.
Boyfield, K. (2009), 'Good money after bad: an analysis of EU regional aid', Adam Smith Institute briefing paper.
Braunerhjelm, P., R. Faini, V. Norman, F. Ruane and P. Seabright (2000), *Integration and the Regions of Europe: How the Right Policies Can Prevent Polarization*, London: Centre for Economic Policy and Research.
Burnham, James B. (2003), 'Why Ireland boomed', *Independent Review*, **7** (4), 537–56.
De La Fuente, A. and X. Vives (1997), 'The sources of Irish growth', in Alan W. Gray (ed.), *International Perspectives on the Irish Economy*, Public Policy Series, Dublin: Indecon Economic Consultants, pp. 112–34.

Dorgan, S. (2006), 'How Ireland became the Celtic tiger', *Heritage Foundation Backgrounder* 1945, 23 June.

Economist, The (1997), 'Europe's Tiger Economy', *The Economist*, 15 May.

Garrison, R.W. (2001), *Time and Money: The Macroeconomics of Capital Structure*, London: Routledge.

Garvey, G. (2009), 'One-trick commercial loan lender came unstuck', Independent. ie, www.independent.ie/business/irish/onetrick-commercial-loan-lender-came-unstuck-1603989.html, 16 January.

Gray, A. (ed.) (1997), *International Perspectives on the Irish Economy*, Dublin: Indecon.

Gurdgiev, C. (2010), 'Replying to Prof Krugman', True Economics blog, http://trueeconomics.blogspot.com/2010/03/economics-11032010-replying-to-prof.html, 11 March.

Gwartney, J., J. Hall and R. Lawson (2010), *Economic Freedom of the World 2010 Annual Report*, Vancouver: Fraser Institute.

Honohan, P. and A.J. Leddin (2006), 'Ireland in the EMU: more shocks, less insulation?' *Economic and Social Review*, **37** (2), 263–94.

Johnson, S. (2010), 'The very bad luck of the Irish', Baseline Scenario, http://baselinescenario.com/2010/05/20/the-very-bad-luck-of-the-irish/.

Kelly, M. (2010), 'Whatever happened to Ireland?' VoxEU.org, www.voxeu.org/index.php?q=node/5040, 17 May.

Krugman, P. (2010), 'Irish mirror', *New York Times*, 7 March.

MacSharry, R. and P. White (2000), *The Making of the Celtic Tiger: The Inside Story of Ireland's Boom Economy*, Dublin: Mercier Press.

McWilliams, D. (2009), *Follow the Money*, Dublin: Gill & Macmillan.

O'Grada, C. (2002), 'Is the Celtic tiger a paper tiger?' Centre for Economic Research working paper, University College Dublin, January.

O'Sullivan, O. (2009), 'From Celtic tiger to Celtic mouse', *Bank Systems and Technology*, **46** (3), 30–35.

O'Toole, F. (2009), *Ship of Fools: How Stupidity and Corruption Sank the Celtic Tiger*, London: Faber & Faber.

Murphy, A.E. (1994), *The Irish Economy: Celtic Tiger or Tortoise?* Dublin: MMI.

Murphy, A.E. (2000), 'The "Celtic tiger": an analysis of Ireland's economic growth performance', EUI working paper RSC 2000/16.

Powell, B. (2003), 'Economic freedom and growth: the case of the Celtic tiger', *Cato Journal*, **22** (3), 431–48.

Ross, S. (2009), *The Bankers: How the Banks Brought Ireland to its Knees*, London: Penguin.

Skousen, M. (1990), *The Structure of Production*, New York: New York University Press.

Sweeney, P. (1998), *The Celtic Tiger: Ireland's Economic Miracle Explained*, Dublin: Oak Tree Press.

4. Europe's unemployment crisis: some hidden relief?

David Howden

The European continent has long been plagued with what Americans may consider high rates of unemployment. This high natural level of unemployment has for some time been attributed to several elements of European-type social assistance schemes. More generous unemployment insurance benefits remove an important incentive for European workers to find new jobs compared to their American counterparts. The average Frenchman receives 58 percent of his former wages, and the average Belgian 51 percent, when they find themselves freshly unemployed. By comparison the average Americans will enjoy an average of only 25–29 percent of their former salary upon job separation (Conerly, 2004). Despite Congress lengthening the duration of American unemployment benefits during the current recession, European workers have in contrast regularly seen these benefits extending for two to three years after unemployment, with some countries extending them indefinitely. Stephen Nickell finds that the greatest effect on European unemployment comes from 'generous unemployment benefits that are allowed to run on indefinitely, combined with little or no pressure on the unemployed to obtain work' (1997, p. 72). Indeed, individual unemployment durations are substantially longer, and the flows of workers finding and being separated from jobs substantially lower than in the US (Blanchard, 2004a; Blanchard and Portugal, 2001).

Exogenous to the labor market, Edward Prescott (2004) argues that the higher European natural rate of unemployment is due to differences in tax systems relative to the US. Europeans face both higher tax rates than Americans, and these tax rates have risen more quickly over the past several decades than in America.

A separate hypothesis stresses the role of higher European unionization. Alesina et al. (2005) find that European union-lobbied holidays explain 80 percent of the difference in the number of weeks worked a year vis-à-vis Americans, and 30 percent of the difference in the supply of labor between the two regions. These results are largely compatible with Prescott (2004) as taxes and unionization rates are positively correlated – the effects

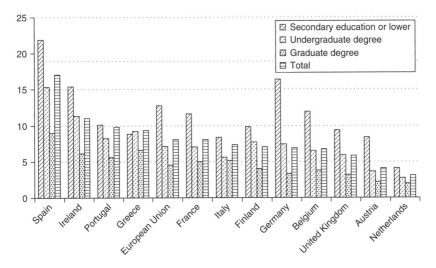

Source: Eurostat (2010).

Figure 4.1 European unemployment rates as per education level

of higher taxes and those of widespread unionization are difficult to disentangle.

Finally, higher European unemployment may be largely preference based. Blanchard (2004b) reckons that the 'main difference is that Europe has used some of the increase in productivity to increase leisure rather than income – while the U.S. has done the opposite.' As Mankiw (2010) points out, as a European working in the US, Blanchard may have a 'special insight' into this phenomenon.

While unemployment benefits partly explain the tendency toward longer periods of unemployment in Europe, entry to the labor force is likewise negatively affected. Relatively high minimum wages, especially when normalized for country-specific levels of worker productivity, block many unskilled workers from directly participating in the labor force. With the recent broadening of the European Union's (EU) freedom of movement zone, relatively unskilled Eastern European laborers particularly find their dreams of a better Western life upset when they cannot offer the productivity necessary to earn Western minimum wages.

The current recession marks a significant deterioration in Europe's unemployment situation. Spain, the country with the worst unemployment imbalance, has approximately 20 percent of its total workforce officially out of the job (see Figure 4.1). The interesting peculiarities of Europe's labor imbalances are only apparent when we delve into the specifics of each member state. The Netherlands, for example, has less than 5 percent of its workforce currently looking for a job – fewer than most European countries can lay claim to during the best of times. In all countries there is a bias toward uneducated labor being unemployed. This in itself is unremarkable: as a general rule human capital, and hence productivity, increase with education. What is remarkable is the volume of educated masses in some countries. Over 9 percent of Spaniards with either a master's or a doctoral degree are searching for work – almost as many as the average for the whole US population.[1]

While this troublesome situation seems to point to its primary problems being centralized in the southern European economies of Portugal, Italy, Greece and Spain, and Ireland (the PIIGS), as with most phenomena in economics, things might not be exactly as they seem. These southern countries all share one commonality – the existence of a thriving underground, or shadow, economy. While functioning separately of the official, and officially recorded economy, shadow employment provides a substantial portion of these countries' unemployed masses at least some type of income.

This burgeoning underground economy may be one cause for relief as we assess these crisis-stricken economies, but there are caveats to be aware of. We may well assume that most of the individuals working in the shadow economy are drawing on some type of social assistance benefit program.[2] At the same time a dwindling tax-paying portion of the official economy is contributing to these programs, worsening an already tenuous fiscal imbalance. Unfortunately, European governments treat these fiscal imbalances as symptoms of their troubles, and not as results of the deeper underlying issues. Failing to understand that fiscal imbalances have been brought forward by these unemployment imbalances is now leading to detrimental policy prescriptions. Further interventions in their economies – by increasing taxes or regulations – will only serve to drive more productive capacity into the shadow economy. This shift will in turn worsen the already bleak fiscal situation. The vicious cycle sets in.

THE SHADOW ECONOMY: NO LONGER A GANGSTER'S PARADISE

Although commonly viewed as the domain of drug dealers and gangsters, the modern underground, or shadow, economy is nothing of the sort. While illegal activity does comprise a not insignificant part of the underground economy, some other less negative activities are increasingly dominating it. Sennholz (2003 [1984], p. 5) lists the four main categories that we can group the underground economy into.[3]

1. The portion of the economy that yields income without reporting it to the tax authorities. 'Under the table' transactions, common for small goods and services, dominate this group. In an effort to evade taxation, entrepreneurs and consumers can agree on a price that neglects the applicable taxes. Note that welfare gains are realized through such bargaining – consumers and producers can mutually agree on a selling price more advantageous to both of them than if a tax was paid, and this mutually agreeable price will coincide with an increased level of economic activity due to the evaded tax – the commonly cited welfare losses of taxation are largely avoided. The welfare gains from such underground activity show that not all forms of the shadow economy are detrimental to those involved (Fleming et al., 2000).
2. Economic production that violates one or more laws or mandates. These mandates include compulsory licensing, inspections, labor laws or export and import controls. Violators in this group may not be evading the payment of taxes, although they will all be producing goods and services illegally. Hiding production output, techniques or inputs (including, in some instances, employees) from government inspectors places this group firmly in the underground economy.
3. The productive activity of those who are transfer beneficiaries or otherwise draw public assistance may be seen as being confined to the underground. Recipients of social security, for example, are commonly barred from partaking in other pecuniary-enhancing activities. Their freedom to work is consequently restricted. Any attempt to increase their monetary wellbeing will be restricted to the underground economy. This group will define themselves as non-taxpayers to avoid detection by the fiscal authorities.
4. The productive capacity of illegal aliens lacking a proper residence status. This group may or may not pay income taxes or make social security contributions, but remains subjected to the underground for fear of deportation.

These four categories allude to the fact that not all underground activity is undertaken to avoid paying taxes. In fact, only one of the four categories has a direct and targeted goal of evading taxes. This is not to say that the other three categories do report their taxable income to the fiscal authority; only that their main motive for operating underground is not to evade such taxes.[4]

Rothbard (2009 [1962], ch. 12) provides a typology of interventions that proves helpful in discerning the distinct causes why an individual chooses to work in the shadow economy. First, autistic interventions are those that order an individual not to make use of something they possess.

Legislation dictating the maximum hours of permitted labor to be worked in a week falls into this category. Binary interventions are those where two parties are forced to associate in a given way with each other. The payment of labor taxes, for example, causes both parties – employees and employers – to contract at a price different to what would otherwise be agreed on between them. Finally, triangular interventions are those that prohibit exchanges between two other sets of individuals. Licensing requirements, price controls or state monopolies provide examples of this type of intervention.

Of these three types of interventions we see that the third type – triangular – is by far the most damaging to the economy. Their scope is much broader as they automatically affect more than one party each time they are followed. As a result these interventions will also be the ones more likely to be evaded via production and employment in the shadow economy. While tax rates – a form of binary intervention – most definitely affect a contracting party in a negative way, they are more or less easy for the entrepreneur to plan round. Especially if they are relatively stable over time, entrepreneurs can factor in taxes as an added cost of doing business and proceed as they otherwise would. In contrast, triangular interventions – due to their scope and uncertain nature – serve to complicate operations in the formal economy. Although all types of intervention will, *ceteris paribus*, increase the incentives for an individual to work in the shadow economy, triangular interventions in particular will more forcibly entice this shift.

One way to operate in the underground economy and to avoid detection from the proper authorities is to transact via nonmonetary means. Given money's role as an intermediate good that allows for an increased scope for trade, it is doubtful whether these nonmonetary transactions can be substantial. Nonmonetary transactions appear as bartered services. You may help your neighbor with one task in return for an in-kind payment; babysitters may be paid by movie vouchers or other gift cards. Growing illegal drugs for one's own consumption or stealing a car to trade for some other good represent items of this economy.

More often the underground economy is marked by its prevalence of monetary transactions. With no paper trail left to trace the illegal activity, cash is by far the preferred means of payment. However, not all underground market activity need be illegal – at least not completely. Household services performed by one's spouse are not tallied in the official economy. An illegal alien or social security recipient, although themselves being unable to work legally, may be employed in the production of a good that is completely legal.

Following Lippert and Walker (1997, p. 13) we categorize these underground activities as per the nature of their legality and whether they

Table 4.1   Categories of underground economic activity

	Legal	Illegal
Market-based production	Production and sale of legal goods not reported to the proper regulatory or fiscal authority	Production and sale of illegal goods (drugs, prostitution, some pornography, etc.)
Nonmarket-based production	Household tasks not subject to regulatory or fiscal authorities	Production of illegal goods for private consumption (i.e. personal drug use)

Source: Lippert and Walker (1997, p. 13).

are market-based activity or not (Table 4.1). In this categorical scheme, we find that the scope of 'illegal' economic activity is, in all likelihood, dwarfed in size by that of its legal counterparts. Especially within the Western European economies, production of drugs and pornography is a relatively small fraction of these economies' greater output. Prostitution is legal or accepted as a grey area in most Western European economies, thus being excluded from the underground. This leaves us with the size of the underground economy largely determined by those economic activities that are of a legal or quasi-legal nature: the production and sale of goods that are themselves legal, yet are undertaken in such a way that they avoid regulations concerning labor or production processes.

The shadow economy is the realm of legal business activities that are performed outside the reach of the watchful eye of the regulatory authorities. It does not include illegal activities – such as crime, smuggling or money laundering – which by law do not need to be registered with the government (Schneider, 2010). For our purposes, we follow Schneider et al. (2010, p. 4) in defining the shadow economy as that market-based production of goods and services that is deliberately hidden from the public authorities for four reasons: 1) to avoid the payment of taxes; 2) to avoid payment of social security contributions; 3) to avoid meeting certain labor market requirements (i.e. the minimum wage); and 4) to avoid compliance with certain administrative procedures.

BEM-VINDO/BENVENUTI/ΚΑΛΩΣΟΡΙΣΜΑ/ BIENVENIDA TO THE UNDERGROUND

Estimating the size of the shadow economy is fraught with peril. By definition it aims to exist in an undetected state creating apparent estimation problems. One method involves a straightforward question-naire. Interviewees can be asked to give honest responses to questions such as 'Did you yourself carry out any undeclared activities in the last 12 months?' (Buehn and Schneider 2009, p. 3). One problem with this direct approach is the questionable accuracy of responses. Both employers and employees of the underground economy are in their position due to a desire to be undetected.

Schneider et al. (2010) use a combination of the currency demand approach with the multiple indicators multiple causes (MIMIC) method to estimate the size of the shadow economies of 162 countries around the world.[5] Assuming that most transactions occurring in the under-ground economy are cash based, increases in the shadow economy should increase the demand for currency. Unobserved variables and their relationships to observed variables are analysed under this approach via the MIMIC method. In particular, Schneider et al. (2010) proxy the size of the shadow economy through four indicator variables: 1) the growth rate of GDP/capita; 2) the labor force participation rate; 3) the growth rate of the labor force; and 4) the growth rate of currency in circulation. Any 'excess' increase in currency that cannot be explained by these other conventional factors can be attributed to work undertaken in the shadow economy.

Based on these parameters, Schneider et al. (2010) estimate the sizes of the shadow economies (Table 4.2).

Several points become clear. First, the shadow economy is significantly larger in the southern economies than in their northern counterparts. The average size of the shadow economies of the OECD countries is 14 percent of GDP, and that of northern European countries is slightly lower. The southern PIGS of Europe have an average shadow economy equivalent to 21.7 percent of their total GDP; well above the OECD average. This divergence between north and south can be largely explained by the dif-ferent types and scopes of interventions that each area implements. The distinction in the type of intervention helps to explain why it is that the southern European countries, while offering relatively lower tax rates, foster larger shadow economies than their northern neighbors (Bovi, 2002, p. 18). While it is true that average northern European and Scandinavian tax rates are much higher than in the south, their economies are hampered by much lower levels of triangular interventions. Bureaucratic red tape and regulations are well-known features of southern European economies. Entrepreneurs often find it easier to exist in the underground economy rather than try to fulfill these regulatory requirements in the official economy.

Second, the trends seem to show that the size of Europe's shadow

Table 4.2 *Shadow economies of Europe (percentage of GDP)*

	Average 1999/2000	Average 2001/02	2003	2004	2005	2006	2007	2008	2009	2010
Portugal	22.7	22.5	22.2	21.7	21.2	20.1	19.2	18.7	19.5	19.7
Italy	27.1	27.0	26.1	25.2	24.4	23.3	22.3	21.4	22.0	22.2
Greece	28.7	28.5	28.2	28.1	27.6	26.2	25.1	24.3	25.0	25.2
Spain	22.7	22.5	22.2	21.9	21.3	20.2	19.3	18.7	19.5	19.8
Average PIGS	25.3	25.1	24.7	24.2	23.6	22.5	21.5	20.8	21.5	21.7
Austria	9.8	10.6	10.8	11.0	10.3	9.7	9.4	8.1	8.5	8.7
Belgium	14.3	14.1	13.7	13.2	12.6	11.4	11.7	10.6	10.9	11.1
Finland	18.1	18.0	17.6	17.2	16.6	15.3	14.5	13.8	14.2	14.3
France	15.2	15.0	14.7	14.3	13.8	12.4	11.8	11.0	11.6	11.7
Germany	16.0	16.3	17.1	16.1	15.4	15.0	14.7	14.2	14.6	14.7
Ireland	15.9	15.7	15.4	15.2	14.8	13.4	12.7	12.2	13.1	13.2
Netherlands	13.1	13.0	12.7	12.5	12.0	10.9	10.1	9.6	10.2	10.3
United Kingdom	12.7	12.5	12.2	12.3	12.0	11.1	10.6	10.1	10.9	11.1
OECD average	16.8	16.7	16.5	16.1	15.6	14.5	13.9	13.3	13.8	14

Source: Schneider et al. (2010).

economies has been stable over the past decade. In fact this stabilization is part of a larger 15-year trend which has seen shadow economies in most of the developed world shrink in size.

Finally, the current recession has disrupted this downward trend as the shadow economies are now showing mild growth (Rettman, 2009; Schneider, 2010). In fact, not one of the sample economies has seen a reduction in the size of its shadow economy since 2008. Spain has undergone a larger growth in its shadow economy in 2009–10 than any other Western European economy, at 1.3 percent of its GDP.

While countries with relatively low tax rates, few laws and regulations and a well-established rule of law minimizing corruption tend to favor smaller shadow economies, several changes during the recession have drastically altered these three aspects with the European Union.

Taxes and social security contributions add to the cost of labor in the official economy and are drivers of growth in the shadow economy. The larger the spread between the total cost of labor and the after-tax earnings from work, the greater the incentive for both employees and employers to avoid these costs by operating underground. In some instances these differences are quite large. In Spain, for example, employers must pay an amount approximately equal to their employees' wages in tax, insurance and social security contributions. This problem is also exacerbated by what taxpayers expect to get from their taxes. In the case of social security contributions there is a slowly growing realization that employees will not be able to draw on their retirement funds as they had expected. Several countries have already changed the retirement age at which workers may receive their 'promised' social security. As public perception shifts to view current taxes as having a reduced future value, an increased incentive to avoid paying them today results.

Regulations such as licensing requirements, labor regulations, trade barriers and restrictions on foreign labor may substantially raise the cost of labor in the official economy. Employers that shift a significant portion of these costs onto employees through decreased wages give employees a reason to seek relatively higher-paying work in the shadow economy. Most European governments place stringent restrictions on the number of hours that a worker may work during the week. Workers seeking increased incomes are forced into the shadow economy to find employment. For example, in Table 4.3 we see that a Frenchman is legally barred from working more than 40 hours per week, regardless of his need for income or desire to work. Anecdotally we see that those countries with the fewest legally allowable work hours per week correspond well (with the exception of France) with those countries that have the largest shadow economies.

Table 4.3   Legal maximum weekly work hours

Country	Legal maximum weekly hours
France	39.68
Belgium	40.71
Spain	41.68
Italy	45.20
Germany	48.00
Netherlands	48.00
United Kingdom	48.00
European Union	48.00
Austria	50.00

Note: Legal maximum employable hours include overtime, and are averaged over the whole year, thus resulting in fractional weekly hours.

Source: Federation of European Employers.

Lastly, we find that smaller shadow economies exist in those countries where government institutions are strong and efficient. Governments exercising high degrees of discretion – an abandonment of the rule of law – result in booming underground economies (Johnson et al., 1998b). Incidentally, these are also regimes that typically allow corruption to flourish, with economic activity largely occurring out of the enforcing eye of the general public.[6]

HOW BAD ARE THINGS REALLY?

The situation of the official economy plays an important role in determining participation in the shadow economy (Bajada and Schneider, 2005; Feld and Schnieder, 2010; Schneider and Enste, 2000). During boom times, workers (especially unemployed workers) face growing opportunities to earn income in the official economy. As recession sets in and the official economy enters decline, workers move into the shadow economy to compensate for their loss of income (Schneider et al., 2010, p. 8).

The shadow economies of Europe are a vital source of income for many, and increasingly so as the recession progresses. Despite this source of income for the officially unemployed, Schneider and Enste (2002) conclude that 'it is difficult to evaluate whether the shadow economy ultimately affects the official economy in a positive or a negative way'. As most of the earned income in the shadow economy filters quickly into the

Table 4.4   Shadow economy employment (percentage of workforce)

Source	Employed in shadow economy (1997/8)	Employed in shadow economy (2007)	Official unemployment rate (2007)
	Schneider and Enste (2002)	Fialová (2010)	Eurostat (2010)
Portugal	n.d.	n.d.	8.5
Italy	30–48	23.6	6.2
Greece	n.d.	38.6	8.4
Spain	11.5–32.5	24.0	8.3
Austria	16.0	11.1	4.5
Belgium	n.d.	21.5	7.5
Finland	n.d.	10.9	6.9
France	6.0–12.0	n.d.	8.0
Germany	19.0–23.0	n.d.	8.7
Ireland	n.d.	23.3	4.6
Netherlands	n.d.	6.8	3.2
European Union	n.d.	n.d.	5.6

official economy (and is hence taxable), governments themselves have little incentive to reduce the shadow economy, lest they realize a decrease in tax revenue at exactly this moment when they need it most.[7]

While it is relatively easy to proxy the size of the informal economy as a percentage of formal activity, data on the number of workers informally employed is much more difficult to obtain. Many workers in the formal economy are employed in the informal as well. Shop owners and bartenders – individuals who in every other respect are legally and formally employed – may from time to time take cash payments to avoid regulatory or tax detection. Several studies do proxy these employment levels, which Table 4.4 compares with the unemployment rate for the official economy.

What is immediately clear is that not only are large proportions of Europeans working in the shadow economy, but also that this trend seems more pronounced in the southern countries than in the north. While this could be expected from the size of production that we previously estimated to occur in the southern undergrounds, several points immediately jump out.

First, in not a single instance is a country's informal labor force as productive as its formal one. Ireland provides the most extreme case in point. With 23.3 percent of its population laboring in the shadow economy in 2007, the informal economy is able to produce only half its share of relative GDP (12.7 percent) compared to its formal counterpart. Indeed, it is to be expected that the shadow economy would be less productive than the formal. Typically it is the most productive laborers who are able to demand employment in the formal economy – complete with its security, benefits and higher pay. The marginalized laborers who are relegated to the underground are typically those of lower skills, education levels or with fewer social connections.

Second, we may see that, provided that not every single laborer in the shadow economy also has a job in the formal economy, a significant amount of official unemployment is alleviated through shadow employment. In 2007 if it was only a fraction of the 24 percent of the Spanish workforce working in the shadow economy that did not hold concurrent jobs on the formal side, the official unemployment rate would be much lower than its then-recorded 8.3 percent. Today (December 2010), with Spanish unemployment hovering around the 20 percent mark, one wonders how many of these unemployed masses are actually working in the underground. Although it is difficult to say, we can safely assume that it is more than zero, thus making the seemingly horrific unemployment figures somewhat less severe.

There are two ways to look at the relationship between employment in the shadow and official economies (Giles and Tedds, 2002). First, an increase in official unemployment could imply a decrease in shadow employment as workers would prefer, *ceteris paribus*, to work in the official economy. This would imply a negative correlation between the underground and official economy unemployment rates. Conversely some officially employed people could spend some of their time working in the shadow economy, thus giving a positive correlation between the two. Yet, while the traditional view has held that there is only an ambiguous relationship between the two employment rates (Tanzi, 1999, p. 143), there is growing evidence that there is a positive relationship between official unemployment and the growth of the shadow economy (Boeri and Garibaldi, 2002; Carrillo and Pugno, 2004; Dell'Anno et al., 2007; Loayza and Rigolini, 2006). This counter-cyclical aspect of the shadow economy – that it grows as the formal economy contracts – bodes increasingly well for the sluggish European economies and their unemployed masses. Unfortunately, wages in the informal sector are largely procyclical (Bajada and Schneider, 2009; Busato and Chiarini, 2004; Tyrowicz and Cichocki, 2010). Newly unemployed workers are left finding solace in knowing that jobs are increasingly available in the shadow economy, even if those jobs will be increasingly lower paying as the recession progresses.

On a positive note, by sidestepping interventions that hamper economic growth, increased employment in the shadow economy will result in a more robust economy – official and unofficial – than would otherwise be the case. As Huerta de Soto (2010, ch. 2 and esp. pp. 26–7) makes clear, the driving force of society's advance is the competitive force of entrepreneurs striving to unearth ever greater amounts of knowledge to aid coordination. Interventions act as inhibitors to these information flows of preferences. As these interventions hinder coordination it follows that any action to bypass them – through the shadow economy, for instance – will aid in this coordination process.

The growth of the shadow economy in Europe may just be an entrepreneurial response to circumvent unnecessarily rigid labor markets and excess regulation, similar to the decline in fixed labor contracts in favor of temporary ones (Michon, 2006). Indeed, some evidence demonstrates the positive benefits of avoiding the rigid formal labor markets. Italy observed a large increase in its informal economy during the 1960s and 1970s. The increased flexibility in the shadow workforce allowed firms to expand and contract production more easily to meet market demands, resulting in positive benefits for the greater Italian industry (Benton, 1990, p. 18; Brusco, 1982). Spain experienced a similar result during its own period of increasing informalization of the workforce, also in the 1960 and 1970s (Benton, 1990, p. 28).

The shadow economy may provide an income source for large swaths of the European population, but this is a far from ideal situation. A lack of benefits, job security and lower wages make these working conditions less desirable than official employment. In light of a worsening economic situation, we may do well to remember a simple fact of economics: 'People respond to incentives, and money is very persuasive. If you are unemployed and unable to find work in the official economy, do you pass up a job in the unofficial economy even if it pays below minimum wage or does not fully comply with labor standards?' (Davidson, 2010).

WHERE TO NEXT?

The recession has reversed much of the employment progress made in Europe over the previous decade. The resurgence of unemployment, and especially long-term unemployment, has left the continent reeling with lost productivity from an unused yet available labor supply. At the same time it has negatively affected many countries' balance sheets as government spending on social benefits has surged amid severe tax revenue cutbacks.

To combat this perceived unemployment crisis the European Commission is enacting a series of policies. These policies are especially aimed at the youth and least educated – two groups that are most affected by the recession. The European 2020 Strategy set out by the European Commission aims to create a new European social vision for the 21st century. Key to this initiative are two programs: An Agenda for New Skills and Jobs, and Youth on the Move. These target education and training institutions as key components to producing higher labor productivity, and hence higher participation rates in the labor market.

An increase in productivity may help those who are locked out of the labor market due to binding minimum wage laws, but for the vast majority the unemployment crisis is not a question of wages, nor of productivity. Indeed, to view the unemployment situation in Europe today as a 'crisis' is to miss a key point. There is a buoyant employment market in the underground economy. To make the most of this revival – for both employers and employees – a shift to allow these shadow workers to return or enter afresh into the formal economy is necessary. Increased education opportunities will do relatively little to aid this integration.

In light of the fiscal crisis in Europe there has been a steady movement to reduce the size of the shadow economy in an attempt to increase tax revenues and social security payments. While the shadow economy exists today in some degree to evade tax and social security payments it is likely that going against individuals' preferences will result in greater welfare losses. Be that as it may, political will for the time being seems content to transfer production from the informal to the formal sector of the economy. In light of the evidence of the substantial and growing shadow economies of Europe, there are three primary methods to reduce their scope and size (Schneider et al., 2010). First, a reduction in the total tax burden will alleviate the economic incentive to avoid the payment of such taxes by operating underground. Second, a reduction in fiscal and business regulations will reduce the bureaucratic red tape causing many entrepreneurs to operate in the shadows. Last, increased financial transparency can aid in reducing the size of the shadow economy.

Empirical evidence bears out the strong positive correlation between taxation levels on the size of the shadow economy (Schneider, 2005). An increased intensity of regulations compromises the ability of individuals to engage in production in the official economy. Theory (Johnson et al., 1997) and evidence (Johnson et al., 1998a) find a significant influence from labor regulations (minimum wages, dismissal protections and restrictions on the free movement of foreign workers) on the size of the shadow economy. Friedman et al. (2000) find that every measure of regulation is significantly correlated with the size of the unofficial economy. More regulation, in other words, unambiguously creates a larger underground economy.

Increased European integrationalism has been heralded for decades as a necessary step to combat Europe's long-term unemployment issues

(Symes, 1995). After almost 20 years of European political union and 10 years of a monetary union it is time to reassess what the root cause of Europe's unemployment crisis is, and how best to solve this thorny issue. The heterogeneity of the individual labor markets – their regulations, insurance schemes, minimum wage laws and so on – all act to create different hurdles to overcome in this current recession.

Spain, for example, has a shadow economy largely driven by its high unemployment rate (Ahn and De la Rica, 1997; Alañon and Gómez-Antonio, 2005). Whereas direct taxation does not seem to be a significant cause of participation in the shadow economy, the evidence does suggest that social security contributions and indirect taxation levels are significant factors (Dell'Anno et al., 2007). In addition, high levels of economic regulation and state intervention are both shown to be significant factors in Spanish shadow market participation (Dell'Anno et al., 2007). In Spain it would seem that one course of action to reduce shadow economy output – and hence increase the ability of workers to integrate themselves into the official economy – is through social security reform, changes to labor market laws to increase flexibility and a drastic reduction in the over-regulation and excessive bureaucracy that plagues entrepreneurs (Dell'Anno et al., 2007).

In the Greek case, as taxes (especially indirect taxes) are significantly easier to evade than in other Western European economies, tax simplification, reduction and reform would do much to reduce shadow economy participation. A reduction in social security contributions, especially among low-wage workers, would also reduce the size of the underground economy (Leibfritz and O'Brien, 2005).

While many European countries lament that 2009–10 has brought setbacks to their efforts to rein in the shadow economy, many of the policy actions undertaken during the recession will exacerbate it. Recent hikes in taxes, and especially value-added taxes, increases in social security contributions and corporate profit tax rates will serve to heighten the incentives for both employees and employers to move to the underground (Kearney, 2010).

One thing remains clear: '[I]n order to reduce shadow employment, it is necessary to reduce unemployment' (Boeri and Garibaldi, 2002, p. 29). While the shadow economy is, in and of itself, providing an important outlet for unemployed Europeans – and especially southern Europeans – during this recession, a shift to the official economy would be beneficial. Indeed:

> There is no doubt that the underground economy is essentially an employment phenomenon. Where government causes disemployment the underground offers ample opportunities for employment. It offers jobs to the officially unemployable.

It does so although it is besieged and harassed by government officials and their spokesmen in the media. It functions admirably although it is handicapped by a legal system that not only denies protection to its contract parties, but also threatens to fine and imprison them. (Sennholz, [1984] 2003, p. 9)

Of the two broad avenues that European governments have to reduce shadow economy participation – tax reductions and simplified (or in many cases eliminated) regulation – only one will target the root cause of the underground's emergence. Those unable to secure more optimal employment in the formal economy feed the supply side of the shadow economy. Reducing the regulations hampering these otherwise unemployable workers would do much to allow them to integrate into the formal economy.

What is necessary is a political reassessment of the problems at hand. Indeed, as Schneider concludes: 'Unless policy makers are prepared to accept continued growth of the shadow economy, they will have to consider reducing the burden of taxes and social security contributions' (2000, p. 85). A thriving shadow economy should serve as a signal to European politicians that past policies have failed. Social security payments are being evaded, either because they are stiflingly high or because workers do not see the future benefit as a realizable outcome. Excessive regulations – on labor, production processes and finished goods – all serve to cause production to occur away from the watchful eye of the regulator and tax collector.

As Schneider and Enste (2002) concluded in their assessment of the world's shadow economies for the International Monetary Fund almost a decade ago, there are six facts that are useful to policymakers in combating this underground phenomenon:

1. Even major tax reductions will not substantially shrink the shadow economy, although they may be sufficient to stabilize its size.
2. Marginal tax rates are of a greater concern to workers than average rates. If taxes cannot be lowered or eliminated, substituting direct for indirect taxes will likely increase tax compliance.
3. An emphasis should be placed on liberalizing certain markets – most importantly, labor markets.
4. Regulation reducing or eliminating reforms should be accelerated. This will result in the reduced corruption and encourage firms to enter the official economy.
5. Governments should return to a rule of law. By providing certainty to entrepreneurs a clear incentive to not be hesitant to operate in the official economy is apparent.

6.   More frequent tax audits and heavier fines will reduce the size of the shadow economy.

What Schneider and Enste (2002) miss with this final 'fact' is that it ignores the core reason for entrepreneurs choosing to operate in the shadows in the first place. Excessive risks of fines and audits in the formal economy breed an atmosphere of fear, with repercussions that can be avoided in the underground economy. While it is undoubtedly true that more controls and heavier fines on unofficial firms, workers and products will reduce their existence, this will not necessarily translate into a shift of production to the official economy unless one of the previous five facts are properly accounted for.

Instead of viewing the shadow economy as a good or a bad thing, it should start to be seen for what it is. It is an important signal to policymakers that the old policies have failed, that the current course of events is going in the wrong direction and that any sustainable future must have meaningful change if full and open labor participation is to be a part of it. Reducing bureaucracy, regulations and taxes would be a step in the right direction.

NOTES

1.   It could be that Spanish labor problems developed more quickly than in other EU countries and the US, but have now stabilized.
2.   We assume here that the shadow economy employs workers legally eligible to draw on social assistance programs. With the broadening scope of the European Union over the past decade, an increasing number of formerly illegal workers in the shadow economies have become legal. One repercussion is that they are now allowed to draw from their new home country's social system.
3.   A substantial and growing literature is forming concerning the shadow or underground economy. Schneider and Enste (2000) and Feld and Schneider (2010) provide comprehensive surveys.
4.   It is a mistake to view labor market interventions only in terms of wage rates or tax levels – important non-wage interventions also prohibit or otherwise hamper the allocation of labor services. It is also erroneous to view labor market interventions as isolated events as their repercussions will eventually flow through and affect both the capital and money markets. See Mises ([1949] 1996, pp. 614–17)
5.   Though not without its faults, the MIMIC approach has its strengths and weaknesses assessed in Dell'Anno and Schneider (2009).
6.   As the recession progresses, both the EU and the European Monetary Union have made a steady shift away from being rules-based regimes (as they were originally intended and prided for) to more discretionary stances. Malte Tobias Kähler's chapter in the present volume assesses the changes that have ushered in discretionary political and monetary unions.
7.   Schneider and Enste (2002) estimate that about two-thirds of income earned in the shadow economy filters to the official economy almost immediately.

REFERENCES

Ahn, N. and S. De la Rica (1997), 'The underground economy in Spain: an alternative to unemployment?', *Applied Economics*, **29**, 733–43.

Alañon, A. and M. Gómez-Antonio (2005), 'Estimating the size of the shadow economy in Spain: a structural model with latent variables', *Applied Economics*, **37**, 1011–25.

Alesina, A., E. Glaeser and B. Sacerdote (2005), 'Work and leisure in the United States and Europe: why so different?', *NBER Macroeconomics Annual*, **20**, 1–64.

Bajada, C. and F. Schneider (2005), *Size, Causes, and Consequences of the Underground Economy: An International Perspective*, Aldershot: Ashgate.

Bajada, C. and F. Schneider (2009), 'Unemployment and the shadow economy in the OECD', *Revue Économique*, **60** (5), 1033–67.

Benton, L.A. (1990), *Invisible Factories: The Informal Economy and Industrial Development in Spain*, Albany, NY: State University of New York Press.

Blanchard, O.J. (2004a), 'Explaining European unemployment', *NBER Reporter: Research Summary*, summer.

Blanchard, O.J. (2004b), 'Is Europe falling behind?', *The Globalist*, www.theglobalist.com/StoryId.aspx?StoryId=3954, 8 June.

Blanchard, O.J. and P. Portugal (2001), 'What hides behind an unemployment rate? Comparing Portuguese and U.S. unemployment', *American Economic Review*, **91** (1), 187–207.

Boeri, T. and P. Garibaldi (2002), 'Shadow activity and unemployment in a depressed labour market', CEPR discussion paper 3433.

Bovi, M. (2002), *The Nature of the Underground Economy: Some Evidence from OECD Countries*, Rome: Instituto di Studi e Analisi Economica.

Brusco, S. (1982), 'The Emilian model: productive decentralisation and social integration', *Cambridge Journal of Economics*, **6**, 167–84.

Buehn, A. and F. Schneider (2009), 'Corruption and the shadow economy: a structural equation model approach', IZA discussion paper 4182.

Busato, F. and B. Chiarini (2004), 'Market and underground activities in a two-sector dynamic equilibrium model', *Economic Theory*, **23**, 831–61.

Carrillo, M.R. and M. Pugno (2004), 'The underground economy and underdevelopment', *Economic Systems*, **28**, 257–79.

Conerly, W.B. (2004), 'European unemployment: lessons for the United States', *National Centre for Policy Analysis, Brief Analysis* 475, www.ncpa.org/pub/ba475.

Davidson, C. (2010), 'World Bank Report finds underground economies more affected by economic conditions than policy measures', report by the Financial Integrity and Economic Development Task Force, www.financialtaskforce.org/2010/08/06/world-bank-report-finds-underground-economies-more-affected-by-economic-conditions-than-policy-measures/.

Dell'Anno, R. and F. Schneider (2009), 'A complex approach to estimating the shadow economy: the structural equation modelling', in M. Faggini and T. Lux (eds), *Coping with the Complexity of Economics*, Heidelberg: Springer, pp. 110–30.

Dell'Anno, R., M. Gómez-Antonio and A. Alañon-Pardo (2007), 'The shadow economy in three Mediterranean countries: France, Spain and Greece: an MIMIC approach', *Empirical Economics*, **51** (1), 51–84.

Feld, L.P. and F. Schneider (2010), 'Survey on the shadow economy and undeclared earnings in OECD countries', *German Economic Review*, **11** (2), 109–49.

Fialová, K. (2010), 'Labor institutions and their impact on shadow economies in Europe', IES working paper 29/2010.

Fleming, M.H., J. Roman and G. Farrell (2000), 'The shadow economy', *Journal of International Affairs*, **53** (2), 387–409.

Friedman, E., S. Johnson, D. Kaufmann and P. Zoido-Lobaton (2000), 'Dodging the grabbing hand: the determinants of unofficial activity in 69 countries', *Journal of Public Economics*, **76** (4), 459–93.

Giles, D.E.A. and L.M. Tedds (2002), *Taxes and the Canadian Underground Economy*, Toronto: Canadian Tax Foundation.

Huerta de Soto, J. (2010), *Socialism, Economic Calculation and Entrepreneurship*, trans. M. Stroup, Cheltenham, UK and Northampton, MA, USA: Edward Elgar.

Johnson, S., D. Kaufmann and A. Schleifer (1997), 'The unofficial economy in transition', Brookings papers on economics activity 2.

Johnson, S., D. Kaufmann and P. Zoido-Lobaton (1998a), 'Corruption, public finances and the unofficial economy', World Bank discussion paper.

Johnson, S., D. Kaufmann and P. Zoido-Lobaton (1998b), 'Regulatory discretion and the unofficial economy', *American Economic Review*, **88** (2), 387–92.

Kearney, A.T. (2010), 'The shadow economy in Europe, 2010: using electronic payment systems to combat the shadow economy', report prepared by Friedrich Schneider.

Leibfritz, W. and P. O'Brien (2005), 'The French tax system: main characteristics, recent developments and some considerations for reform', OECD Economics Department working paper 439.

Lippert, O. and M. Walker (1997), *The Underground Economy: Global Evidence of Its Size and Impact*, Vancouver: Fraser Institute.

Loayza, N.V. and J. Rigolini (2006), 'Informality trends and cycles', *World Bank Technical Report*.

Mankiw, N.G. (2010), 'The rise of European leisure', *Greg Mankiw's Blog*, http://gregmankiw.blogspot.com/2010/01/rise-of-european-leisure.html, 13 January.

Michon, F. (2006), 'Temporary agency work in Europe', in S.E. Gleason (ed.), *The Shadow Workforce: Perspectives on Contingent Work in the United States, Europe, and Japan*, Kalamazoo, MI: W.E. Upjohn Institute for Employment Research, pp. 269–304.

Mises, L. von ([1949] 1996), *Human Action: A Treatise on Economics*, Auburn, AL: Ludwig von Mises Institute.

Nickell, S. (1997), 'Unemployment and labor market rigidities: Europe versus North America', *Journal of Labor Perspectives*, **11** (3), 55–74.

Prescott, E. (2004), 'Why do Americans work so much more than Europeans?', *Federal Reserve Bank of Minneapolis Quarterly Review*, **28** (1), 2–13.

Rettman, A. (2009), 'Europe's black market on the rise', *Bloomberg Businessweek*, www.businessweek.com/globalbiz/content/apr2009/gb20090414_329193.htm, 13 April.

Rothbard, M.N. ([1962] 2009), *Man, Economy and State. Scholar's Edition*, Auburn, AL: Ludwig von Mises Institute.

Schneider, F. (2000), 'Dimensions of the shadow economy', *Independent Review*, **5** (1), 81–91.

Schneider, F. (2005), 'Shadow economies around the world: what do we really know?', *European Journal of Political Economy*, **21** (3), 598–642.

Schneider, F. (2010), 'The influence of the economic crisis on the underground economy in Germany and the other OECD-countries in 2010: a (further) increase', working paper.

Schneider, F. and D. Enste (2000), 'Shadow economies: size, causes, and consequences', *Journal of Economic Literature*, **38** (1), 77–114.

Schneider, F. and D. Enste (2002), 'Hiding in the shadows: growth of the underground economy', *International Monetary Fund Economic Issues* 30, http://www.imf.org/external/pubs/ft/issues/issues30/.

Schneider, F., A. Buehn and C.E. Montenegro (2010), 'Shadow economies all over the world: new estimates for 162 countries from 1999 to 2007', World Bank policy research working paper WPS5356.

Sennholz, H.F. ([1984] 2003), *The Underground Economy*, Auburn, AL: Ludwig von Mises Institute.

Symes, V. (1995), *Unemployment in Europe: Problems and Policies*, London and New York: Routledge.

Tanzi, V. (1999), 'Uses and abuses of estimates of the underground economy', *Economic Journal*, **109**, 338–47.

Tyrowicz, J. and S. Cichocki (2010), 'Employed unemployed? On shadow employment during transition', University of Warsaw working paper 5/2010 (28).

5. Europe's crisis of accounting

Maria Alvarado, Laura Muro and Kirk Lee Tennant

Since the European financial crisis began, the reaction has mainly been political. Following political pressure, financial institutions such as the European Central Bank (ECB) and the individual national central banks that comprise the Eurosystem instigated policies aimed at stemming the tide of unemployment through deficit spending. The ECB facilitated this greatly by an expansive monetary policy that accepted increasing amounts of Eurozone government debt under less stringent collateral requirements than before the crisis emerged (Bagus and Howden, 2009a; 2009b).

In addition to these early monetary and fiscal responses, European politicians were some of the earliest proponents of regulatory changes to the financial industry. Talk of compensation and bonus limits for bankers became common place (especially in the United Kingdom), while increasing regulatory constraints in collateral and financing operations were rushed through.[1] Politically speaking, the proposed accounting rule changes were to accomplish two purposes. First, accounting data were to be reported in a manner that better represented the underlying substance of the economic transactions. Second, and more importantly, the new rules were to enact regulatory changes that would affect both the micro-economic and macroeconomic behavior of the financial markets.

No matter what position one takes with regard to the proposed and adopted changes to accounting rules, a strong caveat must be attached to their effectiveness. The measurement of the effects of these changes is dependent on the ability of the proposed rule changes to affect microeconomic and macroeconomic behavior quickly. Measurement must be made in a timely manner so that both regulators and politicians (and, indirectly the general public) can assess the effectiveness of these policy changes.

The purposes of this chapter are threefold. First, it will review the European accounting rule makers' reaction to the financial crisis and the political pressure (specifically, from the G-20) that called for changes in accounting rules. Second, it will assess the economic and political aspects of the European financial crisis and ensuing recession on the formation of accounting rules. Finally, it will evaluate the likely effects that will result from these accounting rule changes.

ACCOUNTING FOR THE CRISIS

The global economic crisis, and specifically the European financial crisis, has brought with it the political desire to change the accounting rules and policies that govern financial companies. As the foundation of the modern economy is a well-developed financial system, global companies under the jurisdiction of a myriad of regulatory regimes and agencies have come under increasing scrutiny. The leaders of the G-20 countries pledged at its 15 November 2008 meeting in Washington DC to implement reform policies consistent with the following five criteria: a strengthening of transparency and accountability, enhanced regulation, promoted financial market integrity to boost investor confidence, an increase in international cooperation to ease cross-border transactions and a reform of international financial institutions (in particular the International Monetary Fund) to identify financial vulnerabilities better (G-20, 2008). These criteria were concretely set out in the Washington Action Plan to implement the reforms, and which would take effect by 31 March 2009. The plan included major reforms related to the Financial Stability Board (FSB), increased cooperation among international regulatory agencies, more prudential regulatory schemes (including the oversight of compensation packages), enhanced scrutiny of existing tax havens and other non-cooperative jurisdictions, accounting standard reform and an overview of the role of credit rating agencies, as well as their rating criteria.

In regard to financial reporting, the G-20 agreed that the international accounting standard setters – the International Accounting Standards Board (IASB) and Financial Accounting Standards Board (FASB) – should improve standards for the valuation of financial instruments based on their liquidity and investors' prospective holding horizons, while reaffirming the framework of fair value accounting.

At its Pittsburg Summit (24–25 September 2009) the G-20 called on the international accounting bodies to redouble their efforts to achieve a single set of high-quality global accounting standards in the context of their independent standard setting processes, and complete the ongoing convergence project by June 2011. The goal of these changes would be to secure the economic recovery and to move the economy into an era of 'strong, sustainable, and balanced economic growth.' The institutional framework of the IASB was to enhance further the involvement of various stakeholders.

Finally at the G-20 Toronto Summit (26–27 June 2010), the importance of achieving a single set of high-quality improved global accounting standards was reiterated. The G-20 urged the IASB and the FASB to increase their efforts to complete their convergence projects by the end of 2011.

The IASB responded to the recommendations of the G-20 and undertook the measures shown in Table 5.1 (IFRS, 2010). The FASB responded to the G-20 recommendations and chronologically developed the following measures (IASB, 2009):

1. In September 2008, in an attempt to improve disclosure about credit derivatives and require more information about the potential adverse effects from changes in credit risk, the FASB issued Staff Positions no. 133-1 and FIN 45-4: 'Disclosures about credit derivatives and certain guarantees' (FASB 2008a).
2. In October 2008, following a joint reminder on this matter by the FASB and the SEC, the FASB issued FSP FAS 157-3, 'Determining the fair value of a financial asset when the market for that asset is not active'. The goal was to clarify the position on fair value measurements in inactive markets and to provide examples of such valuations (FASB, 2008b).
3. In December 2008 the FASB joined the IASB in revising standards for reporting mergers, acquisitions or other consolidations.
4. In December 2008 the FASB issued FSP FAS 140-4 and FIN 46(R)-8, 'Disclosures by public entities (enterprises) about transfers of financial assets and interests in variable interest entities'. The aim was to increase the disclosure requirements of public companies, especially regarding the transfer of financial products. Of special interest are those financial products of variable rate interest held by special-purpose entities (FASB, 2008c).
5. In January 2009 the FASB issued FSP EITF 99-20-1: 'Amendments to the impairment guidance of EITF issue no. 99-20'. The goal was to achieve a more consistent determination of interest income in those cases where an other-than-temporary impairment (OTTI) of income has occurred. This would make the guidelines of securitized financial asset OTTI consistent with that of other debt securities (FASB, 2009a).
6. On 31 March 2009 the IASB issued an exposure draft on the derecognition of assets or liabilities. In particular, focus was given to financial instruments, especially those pertaining to special-purpose entities and whether those entities should be included in consolidated financial statements. The FASB has since joined this project.

Table 5.1   *International Accounting Standards Board recommendations*
            and responses

Recommendation	Measures undertaken by the IASB
1. Reduce the complexity of accounting standards for financial instruments.	The IASB issues IFRS 9, a new standard on the classification and measurement of financial assets. The FASB publishes an exposure draft on accounting for financial instruments, addressing classification and measurement, impairment and hedge accounting.
2. Strengthen accounting recognition of loan-loss provisions by incorporating a broader range of credit information.	The IASB, with the support of the FSB, will establish an enhanced technical dialogue with prudential supervisors and other market regulators. This will include frequent meetings between the IASB and the the Basel Committee on Banking Supervision. The IASB proposes to switch from an incurred loss model to an expected loss model, as relates to the impairment of financial assets. The FASB also proposes switching from an incurred loss model to a more forward looking impairment model, relating to the accounting for financial instruments. The FASB will publish its proposals on accounting for financial instruments in a comprehensive package.
3. Improve accounting standards for provisioning, off balance sheet exposures and valuation uncertainty.	The IASB is undertaking a comprehensive review of off balance sheet financing, in response to the global financial crisis, following the conclusions of the G-20 and in line with the recommendations of the Financial Stability Board. Regarding valuation uncertainty, the IASB has published a staff draft of a forthcoming report on fair value measurement. The proposals would result in a homogenization between IFRS and US generally accepting accounting principles (GAAP) in regards to common fair value measurement and disclosure requirements.
4. Increase efforts to achieve a single set of high quality, global accounting standards, within the context of an independent standard setting process, and complete the board's convergence program by 2011.	In September 2008 the IASB and FASB updated their Memorandum of Understanding. The objective is to achieve convergence of IFRS and GAAP by 2011. In November 2008 the IASB and the FASB reaffirm their commitment to improving IFRS and GAAP convergence. In February 2010 as a result of its consultations on a proposed roadmap for the adoption of IFRS in the US (published in 2008), the US Securities Exchange Commission (SEC) confirms its commitment to a single set of globally accepted accounting standards. The SEC expects to decide in 2011 whether to incorporate IFRS into the US financial reporting system, and if so, when and how.

7. In April 2009 the FASB issued FSP FAS 157, 'Determining fair value when the volume and level of activity for the asset or liability have significantly decreased and identifying transactions'. The objective of this project was to provide guidance for addressing valuation when asset markets are either inactive, or when transactions are undertaken under distressed conditions (FASB, 2009b).
8. In June 2009 the FASB published two statements – 166 and 167 – 'Pertaining to securitizations of special purpose entities' (FASB, 2009c). These projects were initiated at the request of the SEC and the President's Working Group on Financial Markets. The impact of the new standards would be taken into account by regulators conducting 'stress tests' on financial institutions in the future. In particular, the changes were enacted to improve on the existing standards and to address concerns about companies 'stretching' the use of their off-balance sheet entities to the detriment of investors. Improved transparency was a goal.

As an immediate result of the complex interface between the financial crisis and the setting of financial accounting standards, the G-20 created another important short-term institution: the Financial Crisis Advisory Group (FCAG).[2] This internationally chaired group would promote the coordination of the different standards in place in Europe and the US to improve consistency. It was formed to advise the IASB and FASB on the standard-setting implications of the financial crisis, the need for convergence of international standards and to advise on potential changes in the global regulatory environment. In its last report, the FCAG stated: 'Although conditions may have improved somewhat in various markets around the globe, the FCAG believes it remains critically important to achieve a single set of high quality, globally converged financial reporting standards that provide consistent, unbiased, transparent and relevant information across geographical boundaries' (FCAG, 2010, p. 1). Its main focus was on financial reporting issues relating to financial institutions and financial markets because of their central place in the financial crisis.

The FCAG identified three important characteristics that financial reporting should have. First, to be useful, financial reporting must be effective. Financial reporting plays an integral role in the financial system by striving to provide unbiased, transparent and relevant information about the economic performance and condition of businesses. Effective financial reporting depends on high-quality accounting standards as well as the consistent and faithful application through rigorous independent audits and enforcement of those standards. Second, because of the global nature of the financial markets, it is critically important to achieve a single set of high-quality, globally converged financial reporting standards that provide consistent, unbiased, transparent and relevant information, regardless of the geographic location of the reporting entity. Third, in order to develop standards that are both high quality and unbiased, accounting standard setters must enjoy a high degree of independence from undue commercial and political pressures, but they must also have a high degree of accountability through appropriate due process, including wide engagement with stakeholders and oversight conducted in the public interest.

Also, as an admonition to all stakeholders in the financial crisis (and, particularly, to politicians), the FCAG recognized the inherent limitation of even 'unbiased, transparent and relevant information' in providing accounting data to be used to evaluate microeconomic and/or macroeconomic transactions. Even a move toward fair value accounting can only work when 'functioning markets' exist and verification of valuation can occur.[3]

The most important characteristic of financial information in meeting the criteria of the FCAG is the concept of 'unbiased.' By recognizing the plethora of stakeholders in the financial accounting process, the FCAG has effectively negated the concept of 'unbiased.' All information directed toward multiple stakeholders will, of necessity, be biased toward one or more stakeholders at the detriment of others. If on the other hand the FCAG wished to define 'unbiased,' it would need to establish a hierarchy of stakeholders.

LIMITATIONS OF FINANCIAL REPORTING

All users of accounting statements should recognize the limitations of financial reporting: it provides only a snapshot in time of economic performance and cannot provide perfect insight into the effects of future macroeconomic developments. Financial reporting is also dependent on the generation of reliable data by well-functioning markets that have the appropriate infrastructure, and the use by financial institutions and other business entities of proper processes for price verification and other aspects of the valuation of assets and liabilities. Account information is only as reliable as its underlying information – distressed or low-volume markets make base valuations difficult, a problem that is reflected (whether known or not) via accounting statements.[4]

In Europe the response to the G-20 meetings emphasized government intervention in financial institutions, particularly in the area of compensation and bonuses. The US political response, on the other hand, was to stress new accounting rules. During the early stages of the Obama administration, compensation rules and bonus caps were ineffective in stemming the large bonuses paid on pre-crisis contracts. The US government instead directed most of its efforts in re-measuring (through new accounting rules – mark-to-market) the economic effects of derivatives and other financial instruments, leaving the past and present crisis results to stand. Bygones could be bygones, but the hope was that regulatory changes would stop such a situation from arising in the future.

European politicians had a very different perspective. Yes, European politicians do continue to call for amendments to the accounting rules; changes that are considered important for the current recovery. But European politicians – both within the European Commission and the national parliaments – appear to want regulatory reform before accounting reform. In an open letter to the EU before the June 2009 election, French president Nicolas Sarkozy and German chancellor Angela Merkel stated that the politicians of the EU needed

> to ensure genuine European regulation in the financial sector based on coordination and cooperation between regulators. On hedge funds, tax havens and remuneration of executives and traders, we want Europe to be exemplary. We need to set up a financial system which works for our companies and is safe for our savers. (Sarkozy and Merkel, 2009)

The EU politicians understood that accounting reforms alone were not the solution to the financial crisis.

One can see the two different orientations by the EU and US politicians toward the financial crisis. Despite this divergence in opinion and prescription, the common accounting response by both the IASB and the FASB was an implementation of the 'mark-to-market' (a subset of fair value) accounting measures. Under such rules, asset and liability valuations are based on the current market price, or the price of a similar asset or liability. While generally accepted accounting principles (GAAP) have been increasingly incorporating mark-to-market rules since the early 1990s, the crisis marked a turning point in their acceptance and adoption. And while many are seeing such regulatory changes as a panacea to hinder future meltdowns such as the world saw in late 2008, there are reasons to be cautious of such trust.

We argue that any accounting measure will prove to create dysfunctional behavior among companies, individuals and governments. We turn our attention now to the use of these mark-to-market rules as a way to change the underlying economic reality of a situation, and the inherent flaws such an approach will breed.

ACCOUNTING AS A MICROECONOMIC TOOL AND POLICY

One often unheeded caveat of financial accounting is its limited use. Indeed, as Huerta de Soto (2009, p. 76) affirms, the role of accounting is to relay the historical situation to interested parties so that they may make judgments concerning future courses of action. Confusion arises because there is an increasing shift towards having the accounting data already include much that must be judged, for instance, through different measures of accounting for inflation, contingent contractual clauses, and the like. Indeed, the Financial Crisis Advisory Group affirms this prudent belief, stating:

> Financial reporting only provides information about the performance of a business for a finite period and about the condition of a business at a point in time. Especially in turbulent times, financial information may be out of date when, or soon after, it is produced. Accordingly, in making resource allocation decisions, financial market participants should 'look beyond the numbers' in the financial statements that they have before them by also taking into account other relevant qualitative and quantitative information, including performance trends, industry data (national and global), unrecognized intangible assets, risk factors, and information about strategy and the quality of management and governance. (FCAG, 2009, p. 9)

The group goes on to add that it is not the role of the accounting data itself to include 'additional *information*' that is necessary to determine the best course of action. Instead, as accounting's role is fundamentally confined to a reporting of the objective facts, investors, policymakers and regulators must search for the crucial and ancillary information to the financial situation that best complements the information that accountants provide:

> Similarly, while financial reporting provides information that is useful to regulators charged with assessing the financial stability of individual institutions (including such matters as capital adequacy), regulators can and should obtain any necessary additional information directly from the regulated institutions. (FCAG, 2009, p. 9)

Will the new financial crisis accounting rules prove to be microeconomic tools that help solve the European financial crisis? Or should the rules instead serve to keep accounting confined to its role as a financial historian?

Politicians and market regulators would do well to consider the following issues about financial reporting made under any generally accepted accounting standards.

First, accounting is a communicative language for past or present business transactions. Each GAAP has a different representation of the financial position of an entity, its performance, and changes in its financial position. The GAAP chosen is totally arbitrary (hence, merely generally accepted) and represents a philosophical view rather than an economic view of the economic transactions. Politicians and regulators must understand that any new accounting rule put into place will suffer from the same inherent weakness as any previous rule: its inability to represent economic reality will prevent it from becoming a microeconomic tool or mechanism to make microeconomic decisions.

Second, the usefulness of a company's financial reporting depends clearly on its level of accuracy and comparativeness, but also on the ability of GAAP to highlight any differences that exist among economic events. Politicians must understand that the convergence of GAAP on a global basis may only superficially increase the accuracy and comparativeness of different companies' financial statements, but potentially at the sacrifice of really highlighting differences in economic situations that may exist among companies. It has been assumed by the G-20, accounting standard setters and various politicians that convergence is synonymous with accuracy, comparativeness, and most importantly lack of bias.

Third, the primary users of general purpose financial reporting (those financial statements generated under GAAP) have always been understood to be present and potential investors, lenders and other creditors. These groups use this information to make decisions about buying, selling or holding equity or debt instruments and providing or settling loans or other forms of credit. Other groups, such as market regulators and politicians, may not find general purpose financial reports able to meet their needs. However, if the GAAP is changed for the regulators and politicians, will there be a decrease in the usefulness of financial statements for the general user? In other words, each respective group requires something different from the information that it seeks – indeed each group seeks a different set of information. Perverting the existing set of accounting information to suit the needs of regulators will harm those groups that accounting information fundamentally exists to aid – namely, the owners, debtors and creditors to a business. While one aim of accounting rules is to provide a uniform set of standards for comparison, implementing these standards in policy at the hands of a monopolist power (i.e. a governmental regulatory agency) will discourage the discovery and evolution towards better methods of financial reporting (Sunder, 2009).

The IFRS outlines this fundamental divergence between these various groups and the information required of the accounting information in its own framework for financial reporting:

Other parties, including prudential and market regulators, may find general purpose financial reports useful. However, the objectives of general purpose financial reporting and the objectives of financial regulation may not be consistent. Hence, regulators are not considered a primary user and general purpose financial reports are not primarily directed to regulators or other parties. (IFRS, 2010)

Fourth, it seems clear that accounting standards were not a root cause of the financial crisis.[5] The construction of exotic financial instruments and derivatives based on the microeconomic concepts of expected future cash flows and expected risk was one of the root causes of the financial crisis. Gertchev (2009) looks at the role of securitization in promoting an inflationary credit bubble: an occurrence which could not be stopped via accounting methods, and which could not be properly accounted for in any uniform manner. Politicians and market regulators might expect the GAAP rules to in some way 'rebalance' the equation toward an income measurement of performance and valuation, but it will not happen, even with mark-to-market. Financial accounting is still accrual based, while the micro events that make up the economy will always be cash-flow based. It is clear today as in the period leading up to the financial crisis: financial markets are not driven by how an economic event will be accounted for over any number of periods, but economic decisions are made in relation to the life of an economic event. Accounting standards arbitrarily apportioning accounting value to different accounting periods is not, nor should it have, any influence in measuring the economic value of a microeconomic event.

Do regulators or politicians really want (or can they really expect) to change the underlying nature of the economic landscape because financial accounting is incapable of capturing the foundations – complete with all its intricacies – of the economy?

Fifth, for politicians and market regulators to enhance investor confidence in financial markets as a solution to the financial crisis it would be necessary to insure the generation of reliable data. This in turn relies on well-functioning markets that have proper infrastructures for financial institutions and other business entities to use for price verification and other aspects of asset and liability valuation.

The application of fair value accounting standards will be particularly subject to the difficulty of applying mark-to-market accounting in illiquid markets. In the opinion of the Committee on Capital Markets Regulation (2009, p. 183), 'fair value' accounting is a problematic standard in inactive or distressed markets because it conflates the concepts of market value with credit model value and may confuse investors. The SEC (2008) confirms its own ambivalent feelings towards the use of mark-to-market standards. Noting that there are good arguments on both sides of the debate for or against enforcing such norms, it notes that the crisis was probably not caused nor greatly exacerbated by the accounting standards at hand.

Sixth, there is insufficient evidence to conclude that changes in accounting standards will produce, or even promote, functional financial behavior. There is obviously a disconnect (and necessarily so) between the economic decisions made using economic models (Colander et al., 2009),[6] decisions made by market participants (evidently so during the mid-2000s bubble), and the decisions that might have been made based on data generated by any reasonable accounting standard. A lack of homogeneity between decision making in these three realms does not bode well for the use of a homogeneous accounting standard. In fact, it is difficult to see how one non-dysfunctional type of behavior can be promoted through the use of one set of accounting standards when applied to two separate sets of decision-making frameworks (the one that exists in theory and which regulators largely rely on, and the one that exists in practice).

ACCOUNTING AS A MACROECONOMIC TOOL AND POLICY

The six major macroeconomic issues associated with the European financial crisis – price inflation, credit growth, interest rate policy, negative balance of payments, deficit spending, and loan default (especially of the sovereign type) are insignificantly, if at all, related to the issue of financial accounting standards. For the microeconomic policies of the accounting standard setters, specifically the FASB and IASB, to be relevant to macroeconomic events, an assumption would need to be made that the integration of an individual company's accounting data in some way influences the calculation and behavior of these exogenous macroeconomic variables. This is obviously untrue, and in fact, for politicians to believe that accounting standards are a factor (a factor that the market does not already exert) in any exogenous macroeconomic variable is unrealistic.

The one connection between accounting rules and macroeconomic events does relate to the central banking systems, most importantly, the Eurosystem of central banks and the US Federal Reserve System (Fed). What is crucial to the economic landscape through these institutions is how they elect to, ex post facto, account for their own financial events. Fair value accounting and its implementation, exclusively for large companies and especially for financial institutions as called for by the IASB and FASB, has no effect on the accounting that the Eurosystem and the Fed use in their own accounting. To date, no calls have been made for the Eurosystem or the Fed to likewise switch to fair value accounting. Without symmetric accounting by both companies and central banks under fair value GAAP, even more uncertainty will be generated in the financial instruments market.[7]

A larger gap and resulting dissonance will be caused by the asymmetric application of the mark-to-market rules for financial institutions and financial markets and the use of historical (book value) accounting supported today and also likely in the future of the Eurosystem and the Fed. Indeed, given the increasing amounts of illiquid and unmarketable assets that both institutions are purchasing through their open market and refinancing operations (Bagus and Howden, 2009a; 2009b), it is doubtful whether a true mark-to-market value could be obtained for many of their assets.

DYSFUNCTIONAL CONSEQUENCES OF ALL ACCOUNTING MEASURES

Since the early days of administrative science, performance evaluation measures – whether single, multiple, or composite – have all been associated with various forms of dysfunctional behavior.[8] It is our opinion that politicians the world over are seeking ways of integrating performance measures into the accounting standards through mark-to-market accounting standards. Given the historical use of performance measures at both the micro (internal company measures) and macro (financial accounting) levels and the resulting dysfunctional behaviors, an effort by politicians calling for a change to financial accounting standards to eliminate the dysfunctional behaviors by micro players is doomed to failure.

Recent problems arising from the dot.com bust, Enron scandal, and the financial crisis mean that politicians find themselves in need of a supra performance evaluation system which overrides the performance-based incentive systems created in financial institutions such as AIG, Lehman Brothers, and others. Voters find it difficult to reconcile the large incentive costs (bonuses) being paid for such weak performance (at least as represented by financial accounting measures). It appears to the voters, and therefore to the politicians indirectly, that a huge disconnect exists between the micro performance evaluation system and the overall measure of the firm's macro activity (as measured through its financial reports). Politicians, therefore, have only two weapons to eliminate this disconnect. They need to either apply limits to allowable performance compensation (a micro tool) and/or reconcile the micro/macro measures through the establishment of new financial accounting standards.

The European response, particularly as represented by Nicolas Sarkozy and Angela Merkel, has emphasized the micro tool of limiting allowable performance compensation. This response can be attributed, in part, to the more powerful unions and less entrepreneurial nature of Europeans, and the historically closer connection between European businesses and their governments. As previously stated, the IASB has adopted a financial crisis agenda which calls for the changing of the financial accounting standards, but the regulatory process is proving to be extremely slow.

The US response was temporarily to try to restrict performance compensation, but the Obama government did honor compensation contracts at such bailed-out financial institutions as AIG. The rule of law prevailed. After the US bailout, compensation limitations have not been an effective policy in the US. Recent improvements in the performance of financial institutions such as Goldman Sachs have once again led to higher bonuses and compensation for executives, which, if history serves as a guide, will not be impaired from being paid out through either the legislative or executive branches.

The American response, by adhering to the rule of law and allowing the accounting standards to work out a solution to the stickier problems of valuing volatile assets and liabilities will breed a more sustainable future than the European response of intervening to alter the incentives of economic agents directly. By allowing accounting to report on the macro financial landscape, American financial reporting will be able to see the forest through the trees, so to speak, as opposed to the European method of fine-tuning its accounting measures to focus on the micro events at hand.

CONCLUSION

The crisis financial accounting standards agenda as proposed by both the IASB and the FASB will have little impact in preventing future financial crises. Accounting standards are ineffectual microeconomic and macroeconomic tools because of their inherent limitations and totally arbitrary nature. The financial accounting reporting model, however implemented, will lead to dysfunctional economic behavior if used to replace the microeconomic model, in other words, by using some measure of income instead of cash flow to value assets and liabilities.

NOTES

1. The regulatory systems governing the European banking system are primarily undertaken through the Bank of International Settlements (BIS) Basel Accords. The European domiciled insurance industry – which is relatively more important to the European financial landscape than the US one due to its inclusion of many pension activities – is governed via the Solvency Accords as mandated through the European Commission. While the banking industry is regulated through the politically independent BIS, the insurance industry's regulator is the political regime that it is domiciled within – the European Commission. Antonio Zanella's contribution to the present volume assesses the dangers that such a conflict of interest creates for the European insurance industry.
2. The group was originally chartered to conclude after six months. Although issuing its final report on 28 July 2009, the FCAG continues to exist today in its advisory role.
3. The question of how 'functional' the derivatives market is and is likely to be in the near future has recently been raised. ICE Trust, the world's largest derivatives clearing house, has apparently elected not to register with regulators, 'citing concerns over new rules devised to bring transparency to the $600 trillion derivatives market' (Protess, 2010). The importance of ICE Trust becomes apparent because it is closely affiliated with some of American's largest financial institutions: 'On the third Wednesday of every month, the nine members of an elite Wall Street society gather in Midtown Manhattan. . . . The banks in this group, which is affiliated with a new derivatives clearinghouse [ICE Trust], have fought to block other banks from entering the market, and they are also trying to thwart efforts to make full information on prices and fees freely available' (Story, 2010).
4. Not only do distressed markets provide difficulties for valuing assets and companies correctly, but reporting lags of this distress can make accounting statements poor reflections of distressed markets (Whittred and Zimmer, 1984)
5. Although one side of the debate sees the use of fair value accounting as exacerbating valuations in distressed markets (American Bankers Association, 2008), leading some to call for an outright suspension of the practice (Gingrich, 2008), a growing majority is seeing the crisis as being largely exogenous to the accounting system in place. Given that today's recession is mainly a global phenomenon – one that spans a plethora of accounting bodies and standards – we see anecdotal evidence that this is the case. Philipp Bagus' contribution to the present volume looks at the credit markets operating through the ECB during the past decade as a cause of the crisis, a factor which is wholly exogenous to the accounting standards in force. With the interconnectivity of the world's financial markets, it is difficult to see how a domestic regulator could factor for causes of the crisis which largely originate from other countries. Bagus and Howden (2011) provide one indepth look at a country where this was the case – Iceland.
6. This recognition of a body of academic economic theory gone off track has existed for some time now. It is only recent evidence through the financial crisis that has made it apparently so. See Boettke (1997) and Hazlitt (1959), for example.
7. A movement does exist to audit the Federal Reserve through the Federal Reserve Transparency Act of 2009 (H.R. 1207), sponsored by Texas Congressman Ron Paul.
8. One of the most famous and earliest works that V.F. Ridgway (1956) published in *Administrative Science Quarterly* reviewed the nascent discipline's recognition of the dysfunctional consequences of different performance measures.

REFERENCES

American Bankers Association (2008), 'Letter to the SEC, re: SEC Study of Mark to Market Accounting', www.aba.com/NR/rdonlyres/DC65CE12-B1C7-11D4-

AB4A-00508B95258D/56796/ABAletterFairvalueSECstudyNovember132008 final.pdf, 13 November.

Bagus, P. and D. Howden (2009a), 'The Federal Reserve System and Eurosystem's balance sheet policies during the financial crisis: a comparative analysis', *Romanian Economic and Business Review*, **4** (3), 165–85.

Bagus, P. and D. Howden (2009b), 'Qualitative easing in support of a tumbling financial system: a look at the Eurosystem's recent balance sheet policies', *Economic Affairs*, **29** (4), 60–65.

Bagus, P. and D. Howden (2011), *Deep Freeze: Iceland's Economic Collapse*, Auburn, AL: Ludwig von Mises Institute.

Boettke, P.J. (1997), 'Where did economics go wrong? Modern economics as a flight from reality', *Critical Review*, **11** (1), 11–64.

Colander, D., H. Föllmer, A. Haas, M.D. Goldberg, K. Juselius, A. Kirman, T. Lux and B. Sloth (2009), 'The financial crisis and the systemic failure of Academic economics', *Discussion Paper* 09-03, University of Copenhagen, Department of Economics.

Committee on Capital Markets Regulation (2009), 'The global financial crisis: a plan for regulatory reform', www.capmktsreg.org/pdfs/TGFC-CCMR_Report_ (5-26-09).pdf.

FASB (2008a), 'News release', www.fasb.org/news/nr091208.shtml, 12 September.

FASB (2008b), 'FASB staff position no. FAS 157-3', www.fasb.org/pdf/fsp_ fas157-3.pdf.

FASB (2008c), 'News release' 12/11/08', www.fasb.org/jsp/FASB/Page/nr121108. shtml, 11 December.

FASB (2009a), 'FSP No. EITF 99-20-1', www.fasb.org/pdf/fsp_eitf99-20-1.pdf.

FASB (2009b), 'FAS 157', www.fasb.org/project/fas157_active_inactive_dis-tressed.shtml.

FASB (2009c), 'News release', www.fasb.org/cs/ContentServer?c=FASBConten t_C&pagename=FASB/FASBContent_C/NewsPage&cid=1176156240834, 12 June.

FCAG (2009), 'Report of the Financial Crisis Advisory Group', www.fasb.org/cs/ ContentServer?c=Document_C&pagename=FASB%2FDocument_C%2FDoc umentPage&cid=1176156365880.

FCAG (2010), 'Letter to G-20', www.fasb.org/cs/ContentServer?c=Document_C& pagename=FASB%2FDocument_C%2FDocumentPage&cid=1176156594055, 4 January.

G-20 (2008), 'Declaration summit on financial markets and the world economy', meeting held 15 November, Washington, DC, www.g20.org/Documents/g20_ summit_declaration.pdf.

Gertchev, N. (2009), 'Securitization and fractional reserve banking', in J.G. Hülsmann and S. Kinsella (eds), *Property, Freedom and Society: Essays in Honour of Hans-Hermann Hoppe*, Auburn, AL: Ludwig von Mises Institute, pp. 283–300.

Gingrich, N. (2008), 'Suspend mark-to-market now!', *Forbes*, 29 September, www. forbes.com/2008/09/29/mark-to-market-oped-cx_ng_0929gingrich.html.

Hazlitt, H. (1959), *The Failure of the 'New Economics': An Analysis of Keynesian Fallacies*, Princeton, NJ: D. van Nostrand.

Huerta de Soto, J. (2009), 'The fatal error of Solvency II', *Economic Affairs*, **29** (2), 74–7.

IASB (2009), 'Report of the Financial Crisis Advisory Group', www.iasb.org/NR/rdonlyres/2D2862CC.../0/FCAGReportJuly2009.pdf.

IFRS (2010), 'Response to G20 conclusions', http://www.ifrs.org/NR/rdonlyres/511EEE8A-0D58-4C6E-B2E8-64B4DA51ED47/0/G20responseAugust2010.pdf.

Protess, B. (2010), 'Derivatives clearing group decides against registration', *New York Times DealB%k*, http://dealbook.nytimes.com/2010/12/28/ice-trust-pulls-clearinghouse-registration/, 28 December.

Ridgway, V.F. (1956), 'Dysfunctional consequences of performance measurements', *Administrative Science Quarterly*, **1** (2), 240–47.

Sarkozy, N. and A. Merkel (2009), 'Article by Nicolas Sarkozy, President of the Republic, and Angela Merkel, Chancellor of Germany, published in the *Le Journal du Dimanche* and *Welt am Sonntag* newspapers', French Embassy to the United Kingdom, www.ambafrance-uk.org/President-Sarkozy-and-German,15061.html, 31 May.

SEC (2008), 'Report and recommendations pursuant to Section 133 of the Emergency Economy Stabilization Act of 2008: study on mark-to-market accounting', www.sec.gov/news/studies/2008/marktomarket123008.pdf.

Story, L. (2010), 'A secretive banking elite rules trading in derivatives', *New York Times*, http://www.nytimes.com/2010/12/12/business/12advantage.html, 11 December.

Sunder, S. (2009), 'IFRS and the accounting consensus', *Accounting Horizons*, **23** (1), 101–11.

Whittred, G. and I. Zimmer (1984), 'Timeliness of financial reporting and financial distress', *Accounting Review*, **59** (2), 287–95.

6. Solvency II and the European sovereign debt crisis: the case of misplaced prudence

Antonio Zanella

Insurance and reinsurance firms operating in the European Union are regulated by the European Commission through the Committee of European Insurance and Occupational Pensions Supervisors (CEIOPS). Since November 2003 the CEIOPS has strived to imitate the European banking system's regulatory framework (the Basel requirements) by a regulatory standard called the Solvency Requirements. Three fundamental pillars form the base of this new standard: risk measurement and regulatory capital calculation; governance and supervision requirements; and information transparency (Ayadi, 2007).

In order to improve the solvency and liquidity of the insurance market the European Commission developed a parallel standard very similar to the Basel Accords: the Solvency Capital Requirements. Solvency margin requirements have been in place since the 1970s, but in 2002 a limited reform was agreed by the European Parliament, with the main objectives of protecting policyholders and ensuring a level playingfield between insurance undertakings in the EU (Ayadi, 2007, p. 12). This reform, called Solvency I, did not fundamentally change the capital requirements established by the previous system and therefore discussions for a new and wider reform proposal soon began, Solvency II. Having been successfully approved by the European Parliament on 22 April 2009, the new changes will take effect on 1 January 2013 as these regulatory requirements enter their second phase: Solvency II.

The Solvency Capital Requirement (SCR) is the primary tool that Solvency II has to reach its stability objective. The SCR is the capital that an insurance company needs to survive potential losses resulting from an unexpected event occurring on either the asset or liability side of its balance sheet. The SCR is the result of the combination of the Basic Solvency Capital Requirement (BSCR) and the operational risk. The BSCR results from a combination of market, health, default, life, non-life and intangible risk (Doff, 2008; Linder and Ronkainen, 2004).

SOLVENCY II AND THE MARKET RISK CALCULATIONS

In the Solvency II paradigm, market risk 'arises from the level of volatility of market prices of financial instruments. Exposure to market risk is measured by the impact of movements in the level of financial variables such as stock prices, interest rates, real estate prices and exchange rates' (CEIOPS, 2010). Market risk is, therefore, the conjunction of interest rate, equity, property, currency, credit spread and concentration.

Interest Rate Risk

Solvency II considers that interest rate risk affects assets and liabilities whose valuation is sensitive to changes in the term structure of interest rates or interest rate volatility. On the asset side of the balance sheet this type of risk includes fixed-income investments, financing instruments, policy loans, interest rate derivatives (derivatives with an underlying asset sensitive to interest rate volatility) and any insurance asset.

Equity Risk

Equity risk depends on the level of volatility of market prices for equities. To determine the capital requirement, equities are divided in two subcategories: 'global equity' (equities listed in regulated markets in the countries members of the European Economic Area (EEA) or the OECD) and 'other equity' (equities listed in emerging markets or not listed). The shock scenario for global equities is 30 percent, that is, a decrease of 30 percent in the market value of equities, while for other equities a decrease of 40 percent in the market value is the base scenario to determine capital requirements.

Property Risk

Assets affected by property risk are land, buildings, fixed property rights, direct or indirect participation in real estate companies and property investments for the own use of the insurance company. All these assets, in fact, are considered to be sensitive to the level of volatility of market prices of property. The shock considered in the property risk section is a decrease of 25 percent in the value of investments in real estate.

Currency Risk

Currency risk arises from changes in the level of volatility of currency exchange rates. A foreign currency is considered to be relevant for the scenario calculations if the amount of funds depends on the exchange rate between the foreign currency and the local currency (the local currency is the currency used by the firm to prepare its financial statements). The scenario considered in the currency risk is an instantaneous rise or fall in the value of 25 percent of the foreign currency against the local one.

Spread Risk

Spread risk depends on the sensitivity of assets and liabilities to changes in the level or the volatility of credit spreads over the risk-free interest rate term structure. Financial assets such as bonds are subject to this type of risk, especially investment grade corporate bonds, high-yield corporate bonds (junk bonds), subordinated debt, hybrid debt-equity instruments, asset-backed securities, structured credit products and credit derivatives. The spread risk shock on bonds is defined as 'the immediate effect on the net value of asset and liabilities expected in the event of an instantaneous decrease of values in bonds due to the widening of their credit spreads' (CEIOPS, 2010, p. 122). Spread risk is not applied to bonds issued or guaranteed by an EEA country, or by multilateral development banks, while non-EEA countries have a smaller discount factor.[1]

Concentration Risk

The calculation of concentration risk applies to assets included in the equity, spread and property risk sub-modules and considers the accumulation of exposures with the same counterparty. After calculating the excess exposure of an asset, this excess exposure is then multiplied by a factor g that depends on the rating of the asset (or on a solvency ratio in case of non-rated counterparties that are insurance or reinsurance firms). If the asset rating is AAA or AA the parameter g is 12 percent, if its rating is A g is 21 percent, if BBB g is 27 percent, if BB or lower g is 73 percent. In case of a property asset, the factor g is always 12 percent, while EEA government debts do not have any capital requirement. Finally, non-EEA government debt has a lower g than corporate debt with the same rating.

THE EFFECTIVENESS OF REGULATION

Regulation is always problematic, and the regulation of a complex industry such as the insurance market proves no exception. In this section some problematic aspects of regulation will be discussed.[2]

The Lemon Problem

The lemon problem is considered to be a free market failure surging from asymmetric information that shows the need of regulation. This problem has usually been described through the dynamics of the second-hand automotive market and signifies that asymmetric information leads to a lower-quality product. This problem creates a market coordination failure because fewer goods will be sold than the number needed by buyers and, therefore, neither buyers nor sellers are satisfied. It is true that in a variety of market conditions information is asymmetric and sellers have an advantage in the bargaining process. However, even if we admit this problem, it is not an inevitable consequence that regulation is a necessary solution to improve market outcomes. In fact, regulation also comes with a side effect. It blocks one of the most important characteristics of the market process: the human creativity capable of finding solutions to problems in a dynamic environment.[3]

Naturally, if we consider the market as a static snapshot and not as a dynamic process, we find many problems that 'need' intervention and a rapid solution. However, the market is a process in which many individuals exchange goods and services, encounter and face problems and find solutions to them. Problems and solutions, in fact, are the essence of the market and of entrepreneurial function, defined as the innate capacity of humans to discover profit opportunities and consequently act in order to grasp them (Huerta de Soto, 2010, ch. 2). The result of the entrepreneurial action is the coordination of society through a continuous process of Schumpeterian creative destruction (Schumpeter, [1942] 1976, p. 82).[4]

The market process, however, has many ways to self-regulate or solve the lemon problem. Consumers' associations could, for example, gain importance and power in an unhampered market. An exogenously imposed regulatory authority blocks this creative solution as consumers assume their interests to be protected. Moreover, consumers' associations could develop better ways to control sellers and solve the asymmetric information problem because they are explicitly created to serve the consumers' interest. Regulation enacted by authorities removed from the market process are open to alternative, non-consumer welfare enhancing influences – lobbying, rent seeking or skewed interpretation of a cost–benefit tradeoff that consumers face when imposing regulation on an industry (Simpson, 2005).

Licensing and the Feedback Effect

Licensing refers to a guaranteed privilege to a specific firm or group of firms in order to limit the sale of a product. However, licensing requirements also have a side effect that is usually not seen by regulators: they limit the number of providers of a particular good and potentially create an environment of corruption and favoritism (Aidt and Dutta, 2008). This happens especially when licenses are granted to firms or institutions that can positively or negatively affect the issuing authority itself. Rating agencies, for instance, must have a license provided by governments, supposedly because their behavior is fundamental to the correct functioning of financial markets. However, rating agencies themselves have the difficult task of rating governments and assessing the probability of default of the same governments that give them the license necessary to stay in business (Bartlett, 2010; Levy and Peart, 2010). The same happens in the insurance market, as will be seen in a later section where the connections between the regulator, government, rating agencies and insurance companies will be discussed.

Licensing, through the restriction of competition among firms due to the license needed to enter a specific market, can ease the effort made by established firms to search for profit maximizing prices, acting as legal monopolies or oligopolies. In addition, governments could rely on the expertise of established firms in designing an appropriate regulatory standard, giving an advantage to these firms. In fact, some big firms may have strong incentives to recommend low standards for themselves and high ones for prospective competitors that are willing to join the market; or established firms could set requirements that are too restrictive or expensive to crowd out smaller firms. In this case, only larger and more established firms will have access to sufficient capital to face the regulatory costs (such as buying new computer programs, hiring experts in a specific field, etc.). Changes in the composition of the European insurance industry bear this out. In the five-year period from 2004 to 2009, the total number of European insurers declined by 5 percent (CEA Insurers of Europe, 2010, p. 46).

Regulations can prove expensive to implement from the point of view of the government (via taxpayer money) and the individual firms. In the end it is the consumer who is hurt by excessive regulation from both sides. As a taxpayer, the consumer must pay the cost of regulation; as a consumer he will have to buy more expensive products that reflect the cost of regulation assumed by firms.

There is another even more pernicious side effect for consumers. Paradoxically, regulations are set up to increase market efficiency but the result is just the opposite. It is well known that regulation increases costs that are transferred to consumers. But costs also increase the economies of scales and the power of established firms. Therefore regulation can implicitly create legal monopolies, and increase both the size and power of large established firms. This aspect can be called paradoxical because in this way governments can create institutions that subsequently are considered 'too big to fail' and must be saved again with taxpayer money. This is the worst effect of licensing and other pernicious types of regulations. Regulation, in this case, suspends the last check that the market has to test a firm and its products. This check is the bankruptcy of a firm that fails to satisfy its clients. The banking system and the insurance market are clear examples of this fact.

In the free market, consumers are sovereign – they decide where to buy and at what price, and the bankruptcy of a firm is the evolutionary check that the market (or better, individuals that form the market) have in order to guarantee the quality of products and the best allocation of resources. Therefore, consumers become increasingly reliant on regulatory checks and balances as they are implemented. They may think that all products are the same and, as a result, there is a suspension of the process, usually implemented by consumers, of checking themselves the quality of products and creating associations whose task is to do the job for the consumers. The consumer's responsibility is suspended as reliance on the regulatory agency grows; *caveat emptor* is suspended as the regulator is increasingly assumed to remove all caveats from the market. Indeed, as Scott Trask (2003) points out, regarding regulation in the banking sector:

> The American people have not seen widespread bank runs since 1933. In that object at least, the Federal Deposit Insurance Corporation has succeeded. But at what cost? To insure deposits is to invite bad banking—and worse; it is to foster reckless speculation and unsound investments, help make inflation permanent instead of intermittent, obstruct the curative powers of economic contractions, and divorce freedom from responsibility. (Trask, 2003)

In the banking sector, regulation and intervention through the mechanisms of deposit insurance and the lender of last resort (the central bank) are considered to be the only solutions to the problem of asymmetric information between bankers and clients. In fact: 'Depositors are said to be unable to judge adequately the quality of bank assets and thus the default probability of individual banks . . . In banking, this is known as the "too big to fail" problem. In insurance, it forms the basis of the traditional motive for insurance customer protection' (Baltensperger et al., 2008, p. 6).

The effect of regulations such as the deposit insurance and the lender of last resort can result in a worse situation for the depositors. In fact, as Trask points out, depositors no long feel that it is their duty to check the product that they are buying (a deposit in a bank) and there is no discrimination between good and bad banks. As a solution, depositors could rely on professional investors to investigate the solvency and liquidity of a particular bank, or could create a depositors' association whose task would be the continuous monitoring of bank reserves and investments. In the market, in fact, the situation of asymmetric information is common. A consumer who buys a personal computer is usually not a software or hardware expert, but through competition, price differentiation and information available in the market, consumers can decide the type and quality of product that they want. Computer firms that offer a bad product can (and often do) go bankrupt.

This mechanism is suspended in the banking and insurance sectors. While Trask speaks about regulation in the banking sector, the same pernicious effects of regulation can be found in the insurance market. In fact, in the insurance business another problem arises: the 'inversion of the production cycle.' This means that insurance services are produced and delivered many years after they are purchased and paid for by the policyholders. This is usually used as an example of the need of regulation, because of the difficulties that policyholders have in monitoring the financial condition and solvency of insurance companies over a long period of time (Plantin and Rochet, 2007). However, many solutions to these problems can be found in the market, solutions similar to the ones proposed before for the banking sector. Moreover, the side effect of regulation is that depositors do not check bank reserve requirements any longer and policyholders do not check solvency requirements of insurance companies, given that there is no risk of bankruptcy thanks to the deposit insurance and the 'too big to fail' philosophy.

Even if regulators supposedly act in favor of consumers' interests, the reality is that special interest groups and lobbies will try to influence the regulator's decision and tend to succeed in their effort. Behind the Solvency II standard, powerful interest groups are pressing for its implementation: groups such as auditors, investment banks and stock market speculators. As Jesús Huerta de Soto points out, 'when models become fashions . . . an attempt is made to implement them using the force of law' (2009a, p. 74). In order to fulfill the regulatory requirements, firms have to hire professionals with specific knowledge and expertise, purchase or lease equipment to calculate solvency requirements, or hire external consultants. Therefore, costs increase and bigger firms have a competitive advantage and can create entry barriers that block competition arising from smaller ones; economies of scale magnify.

Regulation can harm consumers while generating higher prices and fewer product choices. Producers benefit by reduced competition allowing for higher profits. Finally, regulation can block product innovation and quality differentiation.

THE CONFUSION BETWEEN RISK AND UNCERTAINTY

The fundamental flaw of the Solvency II approach is the confusion between risk and uncertainty (Huerta de Soto, 2009a, p. 75). In fact, risk is measurable and insurable (i.e. it can be treated probabilistically) while uncertainty is its immeasurable (and uninsurable) counterpart. This is a fundamental difference, especially relevant to the insurance business, because insurance companies can only insure risky events, that is, events of which there is enough statistical information to build stable probability distributions. For example, the risk of old age death can be insured because a mortality table can be calculated and insurers can extrapolate the probability of death for an individual of a definite age. Deviations from the forecast can arise, but under the law of large numbers and assuming that insurance companies charge a sufficient premium, such deviations will not have a significant effect on the solvency of the insurance company. Actually, deviations will have a mean of zero, so positive deviations cancel with negative ones. Therefore, risk is measurable and is so because the actions of an individual cannot influence the behavior of the larger population.

Uncertainty is a completely different epistemological problem. It cannot be measured and cannot be modeled with probability distributions and confidence intervals. Historical knowledge cannot be extrapolated and projected into the future to assess the probability of future events given the probability of past ones. Uncertainty is the inevitable effect of purposeful human action and the past cannot be identical to the future because human beings act and create the future through their own actions. The essential characteristic of human beings is their ability to learn and change their ideas and actions given new information available in the market process. In addition, information is not an object that can be written and objectively copied from one source to another one (Hayek, 1972). Information relevant to human beings is always subjective and has to be interpreted before it is learned (Huerta de Soto, 2010, ch. 10). Therefore, given the same information, every human being will come to a different conclusion, depending on their mood, previous knowledge, personal history, prior education and so on. All of these factors, together with the innate creativity of human

Table 6.1 Case and class probability

The field of natural science (class probability)	The field of human action (case probability)
1. *Class probability*: The behavior of the class is known or knowable, while the behavior of its individual elements is not.	1. *Probability of a unique case or event*: class does not exist, and while some of the factors which affect the unique event are known, others are not. Action itself brings about or creates the event.
2. A situation of *insurable risk* exists for the whole class.	2. Permanent *uncertainty exists*, given the creative nature of human action. Thus uncertainty is not insurable.
3. Probability can be expressed in *mathematical terms*.	3. Probability cannot be expressed in *mathematical terms*.
4. Probability is gauged through logic and *empirical research*. Bayes's theorem makes it possible to estimate class probability as new information appears.	4. It is discovered through insight and *entrepreneurial estimation*. Each new bit of information modifies *ex novo* the entire map of beliefs and expectations (concept of *surprise*).
5. It is an object of research to the natural *scientist*.	5. It is a concept typically used by the *actor-entrepreneur* and by the historian.

Source: Huerta de Soto (2006, p. 388).

brain, will result in different actions and an uncertain future. Because of this uncertainty, the notion of probability and probabilistic tools cannot be applied to the field of human action (Huerta de Soto, 2009a, p. 75). Probability theory needs a stable underling distribution in order to apply its theorems (Mises, 1957). The field of human action is completely different because of its dynamism, the learning capacity of individuals and the subjectivity of the information typical of the economic process.

Ludwig von Mises distinguished between two concepts of probability: class probability and case probability (Mises, [1949] 1998, pp. 107–15). Class probability can be applied to the field of natural sciences, while case probability is the only one that can be applied to the field of human action. Table 6.1 shows the five essential differences between class and case probability.

As Huerta de Soto points out:

the insurance sector covers technically insurable risks, because it has at its disposal sufficient statistical information concerning the behavior of a class of homogeneous phenomena . . . (such as the risk of death per age group as listed in a mortality table, the number of homes with certain characteristics that catch fire each year, the frequency and average cost of traffic accidents, etc). (Huerta de Soto, 2009a, p. 75)

Moreover, Huerta de Soto points out that insurance companies find themselves caught between the two fields. On the one hand, especially on the liabilities side of the balance sheet, they work in the field of the natural sciences and with insurable risks. But on the other side, the asset side (especially financial investments), they work in the field of human action and uncertainty. This is why the accounting principle of prudence is especially important for an insurance company to face uncertainties. Given that insurance companies' liabilities are more predictable and tractable in mathematical terms, while assets and especially investments in financial assets have more unpredictable cash flows to match with the cash outflows of the liabilities side, the solvency margin and the capital required to face possible losses must be conservatively calculated and the principle of prudence of accounting statements that assets be understated, while liabilities overstated, is fundamental to improving the solvency of firms.

The major part of the liability side of an insurance company's balance sheet is composed of the possible future policyholder claims that will become effective if the event covered by the insurance contract happens. At the beginning of the contract the insurance company must estimate the liability it incurs: the contingent cash outflow weighted by its probability of occurrence. The disbursement agreed on is data, but its probability of occurrence must be calculated using mortality tables. The probability of death is an insurable risk that can be expressed in mathematical terms because the behavior of the class is known (or knowable). Therefore, the probability of death, together with the capital agreed upon, form the liability incurred by the insurer, a liability that can be estimated with a high level of confidence, given the applicability of the law of large numbers.

The situation on the asset side of an insurer's balance sheet is different. When, for example, a life insurance contract is formed, the insurer assumes the liability and earns a premium that must be sufficient to cover the risks insured and to earn a profit on the operation. The insurer invests this premium, usually in assets such as real estate, stocks and bonds. However, the returns of these assets belong to the field of case probability or human action, where permanent uncertainty exists, given the innate creativity of human beings. In this field there is no class with a homogeneous behavior and probability cannot be expressed in mathematical terms. Probabilistic theorems cannot be applied to this field in order to forecast future returns of the assets. The only forecast that can be done is the uncertain forecast of entrepreneurial estimation (Howden, 2009). Therefore, the estimation of liabilities with class probability is more reliable than the estimation of assets that must cover these liabilities, given the fact that these assets belong to the 'different' world of human action and case probability, where only entrepreneurial estimation is possible and probability cannot be expressed in mathematical terms.

Solvency II tries to overcome the traditional principle of prudence that recognized this fundamental difference between the asset and liability side of an insurance company's balance sheet, in an attempt to find a more modern and perfect mathematical system to calculate capital requirements. The objective of this new approach is to reach the perfect (i.e. minimum) quantity of capital that each firm needs in order to face future possible losses, without having too much capital. Having too much capital is considered unproductive and inefficient. The ultimate goal of this new capital requirement calculation is to make the 'risk' of insolvency almost null and to put unnecessary capital to work to earn better returns that can be remitted to policyholders through lower premiums.

The problem with this new approach is that it is based on a confused conception of risk and uncertainty. In the field of human action, a class composed by homogeneous members does not exist. Only unique events exist – events that cannot be repeated and cannot be treated with concepts taken from numeric probability theory. Hans Hermann Hoppe (1995, p. 36) proposes a philosophical argument against the use of probability in the field of human action. Every deterministic theory of human action (such as the probabilistic) falls into an irresoluble contradiction. This theory, in fact, must presuppose constant relations between the action (stochastically explained events) and its preconditions (stochastic distributions). This implies that individuals cannot learn, because every new idea would change the way individuals act under unchanging circumstances. However, the fact that people cannot learn goes against the necessary assumption of every scientific program intended as a means to improve human knowledge, which is that the scientific program has a meaning that can be learned by individuals. The future is always uncertain and has to be determined by individuals' actions and one can have only ideas and expectations about this undetermined future.

At this point, another error of modern finance strictly connected with the confusion between risk and uncertainty must be pointed out: the concept of time used in financial models. Modern financial theory that lies behind the Solvency II project treats time in a deterministic way. Thus, time is objective – a spatial concept that can simply be modeled as t_1, t_2, t_n and so on. This concept of time is built on an analogy between the passage of time and its spatial expression such as the movement of a hand in a mechanical watch.

However, in the field of human action time is subjective and not a mere sequence of events. Time is Bergsonian in the sense that it has to be felt by individuals during their actions, and its length depends on the context and duration of the specific action in which the individual is involved (Bergson, 2007).[5] Therefore, in the field of human action, the future is not just some point t_n, but it is the creation of action and interaction between individuals during some previous moment in time. As Huerta de Soto explains,

> Bayes' theorem (and the notions of objective and subjective probability) requires a stable, underlying stochastic structure which is incompatible with the creative capacity of human beings. This is not only because one does not know even all of the possible alternatives or cases, but also because the actor possesses merely certain subjective beliefs or convictions . . . which, as they are modified or expanded, tend to change by surprise, in a radical, divergent manner, the actor's entire map of beliefs and knowledge. In this way, the actor continually discovers totally new situations he had not been able to even conceive of before. (Huerta de Soto, 2009a, p. 75)

It is, therefore, impossible to insure against uncertainty arising from running a business such as an insurance company, because there is not the necessary stochastic independence between the existence of the insurance (the Solvency II capital requirement) and the concrete actions of entrepreneurs which create the event that the insurance tries to cover, such as the bankruptcy of an insurance company. This kind of insurance increases the chances of a bankruptcy, creating a moral hazard from the point of view of the entrepreneur. Lulled into complacency, these insurance companies believe that their assets are sufficient to meet adverse risks from future contingent liabilities. They will be surprised when the true uncertain events that they did not, indeed, could not plan for unmask themselves.

THE FLAWED USE OF VAR IN SOLVENCY II

We have seen that one 'fatal error' of Solvency II is the confusion of risk and uncertainty. Even if we accept the fundamental flaw of confusing uncertainty for risk, the acceptance of risk as volatility of return still poses additional problems. The past mean return cannot be seen as the expected future return of an asset because in the investment field (that belongs to the field of human action) the future is not equal to the past. The future is always the result of individuals' actions and reactions to a changing environment. The past mean return is the result of past actions that there is no guarantee that will be repeated in the future, especially given the innate creativity of human beings and their capacity to learn and act differently in a changing world. The same critique can be applied to the concept of volatility as a measure of risk. Given that the mean does not have a significant meaning in forecasting future returns, the volatility around the mean cannot be a good measure for risk.

The capital requirements of Solvency II rely on three pivotal concepts: volatility, correlation and value at risk (VaR). Value at risk was developed after the market crash occurred in 1987.[6] Other risk management techniques (such as GAP analysis, duration analysis, statistical analysis and scenario analysis) have being developed before, techniques that apply statistical concepts to the problem of risk measurement (Dowd, 1998, pp. 9–10). However, all these techniques fail to grasp the uncertainty connected to human behavior that affects financial assets. Instead of posing serious doubts on the foundations of risk management (such as the confusion between risk and uncertainty), the huge losses incurred during the financial crisis of the late 1980s were interpreted as the fault of these simplistic models. The proposed solution was a more complex and refined model capable of better assessing financial risks.

What is VaR? 'VaR is a statistical measure of downside risk . . . VaR measures the *total* portfolio risk, taking into account portfolio diversification and leverage' (Jorion, 2003, p. 243). That is, VaR is a tool to measure market risk, a tool that attempts to quantify the risk of losses caused by movements in financial market variables, such as interest rates, equities and foreign exchange rates. The great advantage of VaR when compared to other risk management tools is that it measures the downside risk of the total portfolio, taking into account the correlation that exists among the assets within it. To put it simply, VaR is just a new charming name to indicate the standard deviation of a portfolio of assets for a given confidence level. The confidence level itself depends on the probability distribution that best fits the data.

There are six significant shortcomings of the value that VaR specifies as being 'at risk.' First, Solvency II assumes that returns are normally distributed and uses a 99.5 percent value-at-risk measure for net assets over one year, meaning that the probability of losing more than the VaR measure is only 0.5 percent, in a definite period of time (for example one day or one month). However, asset returns almost never follow a normal distribution and the tails of the distribution are usually fatter than the ones described by it. This means that extreme price movements are much more probable than normal distribution predicts. Indeed, as early as 1965 Eugene Fama noted: 'if the population of price changes is strictly normal, on the average for every stock . . . an observation more than five standard deviations from the mean should be observed about once every 7000 years. In fact such observations seem to occur about once every three to four years' (1965, p. 50). During Black Monday in 1987 (19 October), stocks plunged 23 percent, a fall that cannot be even considered using modern risk management tools, especially if these models assume normally distributed returns.

The assumption of normality is used because the normal distribution is the easiest to manage from a mathematical point of view. However, investments' returns are not normally distributed (Taleb, 2005; 2007). Taleb outlines that the world in which human beings act in general and the financial one in particular, are not Gaussian (i.e. normal) and the normal distribution is not a good description of reality. The tails of distributions that better fit the data are usually much fatter than is assumed by a Gaussian world. In financial terms, there is a small, but not infinitesimally so, probability of quickly losing or winning large sums of money, as often does happen during a financial crisis. Normal distributions, at best, describe 'normal' situations but fail to be useful when really needed. In a risk management context the normal distribution is of limited use in assessing risk, because large volatility around the mean is so improbable that is not accounted for.

Anecdotal evidence suggests that financial crises occur every few years. Large-scale losses that are supposed to be almost impossible according to risk models occur more frequently than the underlying (normal) statistics suggest. This is the fundamental paradox of the VaR concept. In fact, VaR is defined as the maximum loss over a target horizon but normal distribution cannot really consider situations with large losses because of their almost-zero probability of occurrence.

Second, in order to calculate volatility, an asset's historical returns must be serially independent. The statistical concept of variance can be applied only to a so-called random variable – each observation of the sample must be independent and no causal relation can be established between two distinct observations. However, today's return of a definite asset seems to be connected with yesterday's return of the same asset (Lo and Mackinley, 1988). Therefore, this important assumption that makes possible the application of abstract statistical theorems to reality seems not to hold in the financial environment. This is a paradox of modern risk management: one of the fundamental assumptions of VaR is that historical returns are mutually independent. However, these historical returns are then used in order to forecast future returns, as if future returns were dependent on past ones. There is an internal contradiction in assuming that past returns are mutually independent and then using these returns to forecast future returns as if they were dependent from the past.

Third, even if VaR is considered to be an objective and precise tool of risk management, there is a high degree of subjectivity in selecting the sample size and the probability distribution that best fits the data. The size of the sample is crucial because different sample sizes can follow different distributions and can result in different mean and volatility calculations. For example, the distribution followed by asset returns in the last three years (during the financial crisis) is markedly different from the distribution followed by the returns of the same asset if a longer timeframe is taken into account; the recent short-term returns are much more volatile. The correct timeframe depends on the risk manager's subjective view of the present and future market conditions. Therefore, the capital requirement prescribed by a VaR calculated with a shorter timeframe can be very different from the capital requirement prescribed by a VaR calculated with a longer one. This aspect is important because it adds subjectivity to the calculation of a supposedly objective risk management tool. It is not only that the holding period of the asset is important in deciding the VaR timeframe (a daily VaR measure is more accurate if the asset is held for trading, but if the asset is held to maturity an annual VaR measure is better), but also that different timeframes will result in different risk measures. Different sample sizes, in fact, can result in different distributions and different volatility estimations. The objective of VaR as a risk management tool is to state the maximum possible future loss, given a confidence interval. To obtain this objective, a data sample must be chosen but which is the best choice? Daily or yearly data? How many years of data? There is no correct answer to these questions – they depend on the subjective view of present and future market situation that the risk manager has. In fact, the point is to figure out future risk of loss (that is volatility), given past volatility. But past volatility depends on the past data chosen. If risk managers expect a period of high volatility, they should collect data from a sample with correspondingly high volatility.

The fourth aspect is the aforementioned confusion between risk and uncertainty. In fact, Taleb's critique of the Gaussian world is correct but fails to grasp the real problem of applying statistics to the field of human action. The fundamental fallacy is the confusion between class and case probability.

Fifth, projecting the past into the future in a forecasting effort is wrong when intelligent and creative human beings are involved in the process. In fact, as pointed out before, human beings can learn and when given new information they can act in different and unexpected ways. Even if there is no change in the environment or information, they can act differently because they interpret old information differently.

Sixth and finally, one of the largest perils of VaR is its apparent simplicity and certitude. Being a complex mathematical model that can be explained through simple concepts, managers using this tool feel increasingly confident in assuming an incremental quantity of risk, given that VaR is supposedly able to assess the worst possible losses. Therefore, risk managers feel more comfortable with a given risk-holding even if their portfolio risk is increasing in a way that cannot be grasped by these models.[7]

Due to these six points, the VaR model is not a good measure of the optimal capital requirement for banks, mutual funds and insurance companies. The calculation of the Solvency Capital Requirement implemented by the Solvency II paradigm is based on VaR and poses serious problems to the future solvency of the entire insurance sector. In fact, insurance companies may believe themselves well capitalized because they fulfill the regulatory capital requirements and in response assume an increasing level of risk (or better stated, uncertainty). They become overconfident about the maximum loss that they can face given the assets and liabilities held on their balance sheet. However, because of the six shortcomings explained here, these regulatory capital requirements cannot really assess the level of risk that companies are assuming. The result can be that companies assume more and more risks, falsely believing that their risks are much lower than they really are, and find themselves in a situation of undercapitalization or, worse, insolvency. In conclusion, the Solvency II standard can have the paradoxical effect of increasing the possibility of insolvency of insurance companies.

POSSIBLE EFFECTS OF THE EUROPEAN SOVEREIGN DEBT CRISIS ON SOLVENCY II

The insurance market is one of the largest financial markets in Europe. As of year end 2009 the European insurance industry had more than €6800 billion invested in a variety of assets (CEA Insurers of Europe, 2010). The largest share of insurance company assets are investments composed of fixed-income securities (40 percent), followed by shares and other variable yield securities (26 percent), land and buildings (17 percent), and other investments such as investments in affiliates, loans and deposits (17 percent). Total gross written premiums in 2009 amounted to €1057 billion, after a decade of average growth of 3 percent per year.

The sovereign debt of European Union member states receives special treatment under Solvency II, directing large amounts of financing to European member states. For example, consider three different bonds with the same modified duration.[8] The first bond is sovereign, the second one is an AAA corporate bond and the third one is a BB corporate one.

Considering only credit spread risk, Solvency II does not require insurers to hold any capital against the first bond. The capital required for the second is 9 percent, while the capital required for the third is 45 percent. There is a large incentive for insurance companies to hold substantial amounts of sovereign debt on their balance sheets.

Moreover, corporate rating agencies (CRA) play an important role in the corporate and sovereign debt market. CRAs such as Moody's, Standard & Poor's and Fitch specialize in assessing the risk of many different corporate bonds and sovereign debt. Setting aside the theoretical flaws of their models, based on modern financial theory, their functioning faces big problems given the enormous interests in play.[9] In fact, the CRAs are very important in increasing market efficiency because they alleviate investors' apprehension of the risks attached to their investments. In a free market there is no reason to suggest that the rating system would work any differently than any other business based on trust and reputation. Investors that need to know the financial situation of a particular firm would pay an expert, the CRA, in order to investigate and make a judgment on the level of risk of the firm. The CRA would be paid by readers of their reports and by firms that agree to be rated, because having a good rating can help firms to raise capital at a lower cost. Moreover, firms that do not want to be rated would be pressured by the market because investors could believe that their financial position is poor, or that that these firms have something to hide. The fact that part of their salary is paid by firms rated by them should not raise a conflict of interest because if the rating agency issues a positive report on a firm that later faces financial distress, its reputation would be at stake. For a business based on reputation this is a detrimental situation (Cantor and Packer, 1995; Hill, 2004; Levy and Peart, 2010).

This system works only if the CRA market is contestable. This is not currently the case. As it stands now, the CRA market is heavily regulated, with regulators restricting the entrance to this market. In order to stay in business a CRA must be licensed. This aspect decreases the reputational feature of the rating market. Even if this market is still reputation based, the effect of an erroneous judgment is diminished because there is no competitor ready to enter the market and build a strong reputation.

Consequently, rating agencies depend heavily on licenses given by the same governments that they have to rate. This vicious circle is reinforced by the fact that governments base their financial regulations on ratings assigned by these same rating agencies. In Solvency II, for example, the capital requirement for many assets depends on the rating attached to them. Therefore, it is not surprising that these agencies experience difficulties in downgrading governments who give them the license to stay in the business. One does not bite the hand that feeds it. Downgrading a sovereign bond, in fact, can have important effects on government finances, on the financial system as a whole and especially on the insurance market's solvency. A rating downgrade increases the cost of borrowing for the affected state, consequently increasing its debt burden. Moreover, insurance and bank balance sheets are hit hard because they require more capital to cover possible losses on their assets.

In the present crisis, a downgrade of some debt issued by distressed countries such as Greece, Ireland or Spain could trigger a downward spiral in which insurance companies and banks try to reduce their positions in such bonds in order to decrease their losses. This sell-off would cause more losses on these bonds and new sales, resulting in the skyrocketing of interest rates that these governments pay to investors to obtain financing. The end of this spiral could be a default of one or more European states and an insolvent banking and insurance system. The European Union cannot allow this, and rating agencies do not want to be the cause of this spiral, given their connections with regulatory agencies. In particular, a downgrade of some bonds would trigger a huge amount of sales by the insurance companies, because below a BBB rating, capital requirements are very high and some bonds would not be eligible to calculate the solvency margin of insurance companies.

Following Solvency II regulation, there is a large incentive for insurance companies to increase their European Sovereign debt holdings, given the privileged situation of this type of asset in the solvency capital requirement calculations. Insurance companies could desire a more diversified portfolio of assets (assets such as equities or real estate), but Solvency II is increasing the need of concentration in just one type of asset: sovereign debt.

As sovereign debt is considered a risk-free asset under Solvency II, spread and concentration risks do not affect European member state debts and no capital is required to back it. However, there is non-EU sovereign debt that is considered less risky than European sovereign debt, but Solvency II actually treats it as more risky in order to guarantee greater financing to EU members. This may be considered as a protectionist measure even if it is a largely hidden from view.

As Figure 6.1 below shows, the European insurance industry manages a large amount of capital – €6.4 trillion as of the end of 2008 (CEA Insurers of Europe, 2010). The fact that there is no capital requirement on European sovereign debt guarantees an increased amount of financing to EU member states to the detriment of non-European states and private firms. Therefore, if non-European states need to raise capital from European insurance companies, they must pay a higher 'premium' than the one they would have paid without this hidden tariff.

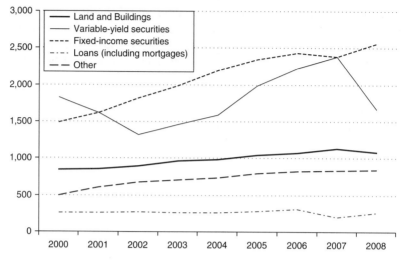

Source: CEA Insurers of Europe (2010, p. 45).

Figure 6.1   Structure of insurers' portfolios (in billions of Euros)

Additionally, we can see that while insurance industry holdings of other asset classes – land or equity, for example – have declined or plateaued over the past decade, fixed-income debt holdings have enjoyed a steady increase. Indeed, while insurance industry investments increased by 31 percent over the eight-year period ending 31 December 2008, fixed-income investments grew by over twice as much: 73 percent. Such rapid growth and asset class shift is attributable in part to the preferential treatment of fixed income assets, especially sovereign ones, under the Solvency requirements.

The effects of this special treatment of European sovereign debt are multiple and often pernicious. Fiscally unsound countries such as Greece or Ireland can find cheaper financing because their debt has the same capital requirement as German bunds. This is one of the reasons why the spread between German and Greek bonds in the last years was so narrow, before the European sovereign debt crisis. Moreover, this preferential treatment helped to decrease interest rates all around Europe, fueling several asset bubbles, especially in the peripheral states. Given that sovereign bonds have inferior reserve requirements, more insurance companies will buy them, further increasing their price and decreasing their yields.

It must be considered that the sovereign debt curve is the risk-free curve used to discount the future value of insurance liabilities. The decreasing pattern of the yield curve continually increases the liabilities of insurance companies. This happens because liabilities are calculated via the discounted cash flow method. The risk-free curve used to discount these liabilities is the sovereign debt curve of European countries and a lower discount curve increases the present value of future liabilities of insurance companies. Therefore, a lower discount rate lowers insurance companies' solvency ratio and this, in turn, causes more bond purchases that further lower the discount rate triggering a downward spiral.[10]

Furthermore, insurance companies of peripheral states have incentives to give financing to their own states. At the moment, yields on Greek, Irish, Portuguese, Spanish and Italian bonds are higher than BBB corporate bonds in core European countries, creating an incentive to purchase these bonds. Given that insurers guarantee a return of around 2 percent to policyholders and earn at least 5 percent on their sovereign debt, the incentive to buy other assets is very low.

At this point one question arises. What happens if one of these peripheral states cannot service its debt and declares default? Default can happen in two ways: either through a debt restructuring in which just a fraction of the nominal amount is paid back to bondholders, or through a monetary inflation in order to pay back the same nominal amount of debt with a devalued currency. A debt restructuring would increase the financing costs and, therefore, it could be more viable for a country to default via inflation, thus spreading the cost of the default over the country's greater population. At the moment inflation is not an option because of the monetary union.

An individual country could, however, leave the Euro and return to its previous monetary system. Obviously this would have a big impact on future government finances, but it remains one potentially politically viable solution. In this situation, insurance companies would have their assets and liabilities redenominated in the new currency and therefore no loss would be recognized on their balance sheet. One could think that in this situation capital ratios could change and a situation of undercapitalization would arise, given that the debt held by these companies would no longer be from a Eurozone country. This is true from the point of view of insurers of countries that are still in the monetary union and hold sovereign debt of the country that is leaving the monetary union. The insurer that operates in a country that is no longer in the monetary union would not recognize significant losses if it held debt of its own country. In fact, this debt would simply be redenominated in the new currency. This insurance company would be under the new regulatory institution of this country and it is quite improbable that this regulator would force bankruptcy on its entire insurance market by making higher capital requirements to back the country's debt. Moreover, if the regulator applies stricter regulatory standards

and higher capital requirements to the country's debt, the result would be
a huge wave of selling of this debt, and an increase in the financing costs of
the state. It is more probable that a member state that leaves the monetary
union would set new capital requirements granting a privilege to its own
debt through lower capital requirements, in order to secure financing at a
lower cost.[11] This aspect increases the connection between a government
and its financial system – particularly its capital and insurance industries.

The fact that Solvency II does not require insurance companies to hold
any capital against EU government bonds has another important and
hidden effect. As pointed out before, this rule guarantees huge amounts
of financing to governments and a relative decrease in financing available to private corporations. This is especially dangerous in times of crisis
when many malinvestments have been made by entrepreneurs misguided
by compromised interest rate signals. In fact, this is the precise time when
more capital is needed because much of it has been thrown away in misguided entrepreneurial projects. Therefore the lack of capital available
for corporations increases the interest rate of corporate debt and renders
impossible those projects that otherwise could have been profitable at a
lower interest rate.

These events aggravate the situation of the private sector. The effect can
be more bankruptcies and less investment, leading to an increase in unemployment. This increase in bankruptcies and unemployment increases
public expenditure (for example in unemployment benefits) and decreases
public revenue (fewer taxes collected because of reduced profits in private
firms and the increase in unemployment). In the end, the draining of
capital from the private to the public sector leads to an increase in public
deficits and a worsening of the financing situation of governments.

In conclusion, the new Solvency II capital requirements can have significant negative effects not only on the insurance market through the increase
of possible insolvencies, but also on the present European sovereign debt
crisis and on the formation of future asset bubbles in the European monetary union. Through granting new financing options to European governments, Solvency II can, in fact, only postpone the inevitable deleveraging
process of European states. Many European states are already in a heavily
indebted position. The debt to GDP ratio of Greece (127 percent) and Italy
(116 percent) in 2009 is already much higher than the 70 percent permitted by the European Union.[12] Moreover, in 2009 countries such as Spain
(11.1 percent), Ireland (14.4 percent) and Greece (15.4 percent) had budget
deficits higher than the 3 percent permitted by the Maastricht Treaty.
The budget deficit situation of these countries indicates that they will
need more financing through debt issuances and the result will be higher
debt levels. However, increasing debt levels will result in higher financing

costs. This increase in borrowing costs would worsen the debt situation of these countries. It is therefore illogical to try to solve a situation of heavy indebtedness with increasing amounts of debt. Solvency II, increasing the incentives for insurance companies to invest in European sovereign debt, would succeed only in postponing the much-needed process of deleverage in the European Union.

CONCLUSION

Solvency II has already been approved by the European Parliament and will be effective by 2013. Its implementation has been widely received as an improvement in the foundation of the insurance business, given that it is based on the most advanced tools of finance theory and risk management. However, this enthusiasm should be appeased and a new discussion based on the correct apprehension of the problems should be started.

New is not always a synonym for improvement. In the last 200 years, insurance companies have survived wars, economic crises and all kinds of calamities thanks to a set of customs evolved in order to face uncertainties successfully – customs such as 'historical cost accounting, the passive highly conservative management of investments, the use in life insurance of technical interest rates with no inflation component, the introduction of contractual clauses aimed at eliminating moral hazards, etc.' (Huerta de Soto, 2009a, p. 76).

Until 1997, liabilities were held in the balance sheet at their historic values. Solvency II changed this as historical cost accounting supposedly failed to show the real value of an insurance company and was unable to measure risks.[13] However, accounting standards are not designed for valuation purposes but only to guide the entrepreneur in the decision-making process and in economic calculation toward the preservation of capital. The Solvency II paradigm, with its sophisticated risk management tools, tries to eliminate these traditional principles in favor of more complex and supposedly scientific management tools. As Huerta de Soto points out: 'The traditional principles are to be replaced with a "post-modern" ad hoc management which is supposedly more scientific . . . However, if the new postulates end up prevailing in practice . . . clearly the effects will be quite the opposite of those allegedly sought' (2009a, p.76.).

The unseen effect of the new regulation is an increase in the insolvency risk of European insurance firms. The full effects of the implementation of Solvency II are, in fact, even more dangerous and widespread than currently thought. Through the permanent financing of public debt and the commensurate decrease in interest rates, Solvency II has lent a hand in causing asset bubbles, malinvestments and the waste of the already scarce capital that is necessary for the recovery from recession.

NOTES

1. The fact that spread risks do not apply to bonds issued or guaranteed by an EEA country and that these bonds are practically considered risk free within the solvency standard is particularly important and will be discussed later.
2. An insightful discussion of some of the shortcomings of regulation can be found in Miller (2008).
3. The dynamic environment typical of the free market is well described in the second chapter of Huerta de Soto (2010).
4. Alternatively, Huerta de Soto (2009b) has an insightful look into the market process through the theory of dynamic efficiency.
5. Bergson (2007) distinguishes between two different concepts of time: pure time that is of real duration and mathematical time that is of measurable duration. Bergson describes pure time as indivisible and continuous while mathematical time is divisible into units and intervals.
6. The interested reader can consult Holton (2002) for a brief history of VaR.
7. A clear example of the shortcomings of the VaR model is the story of the hedge fund Long Term Capital Management (see, for example, Lowenstein, 2001).
8. Modified duration is a measure of the sensitivity of a bond to interest rates.
9. All the critiques made to the solvency criteria in this chapter can be applied to CRA models in general. Particularly present in the models is the confusion between risk and uncertainty. In this section only the operational functioning of rating agencies will be criticized, not the flawed or erroneous assumptions behind their models.
10. Jensen, in the article 'Insolvency II' (2010), states that in the first half of 2010 solvency fell by 13 percent on average as a result of falling bond yields.
11. This actually happened in Spain in 2010 in relation to the banking sector. Due to the high interest rates of the Spanish sovereign debt, Spanish banks increased their exposure to it. However, in November, when the credit crisis worsened and banks should have recognized huge losses due to the decrease of the prices of these bonds, the Spanish central bank decided that the banking system could postpone the recognition of these losses. It could happen also in the insurance sector (Martinez, 2010).
12. Debt to GDP accounts for not only public, but also private debt.
13. Maria Alvarado, Laura Muro and Kirk Lee Tennant's chapter in the present volume assesses the reaction to the crisis by the European accounting authorities. In a similar vein, a shift from historical cost to fair value accounting was thought by policymakers to be a panacea for 'overvalued' assets during the boom. What regulators did not understand was that a change in the standards used for accounting would also alter (detrimentally) the relevance of the accounting data available.

REFERENCES

Aidt, T.S. and J. Dutta (2008), 'Policy compromises: corruption and regulation in democracy', *Economics and Politics*, **20**, 335–60.
Ayadi, R. (2007), 'Solvency II: a revolution for regulating European insurance and re-insurance companies', *Journal of Insurance Regulation*, **26** (1), 11–36.
Baltensperger, E., P. Buomberger, A.A. Iuppa, B. Keller and A. Wicki (2008),

'Regulation and intervention in the insurance industry: fundamental issues', *Geneva Reports, Risk and Insurance Research 1*, February, 1–55.

Bartlett, B. (2010), 'The corruption of the rating agencies: is AAA junk?', www.thefiscaltimes.com/Issues/The-Economy/2010/10/01/The-Corruption-of-the-Rating-Agencies.aspx.

Bergson, H. (2007), *The Creative Mind: An Introduction to Metaphysics*, New York: Dover Publications.

Cantor, R. and F. Packer (1995), 'The credit rating industry', *Journal of Fixed Income*, December, 10–34.

CEA Insurers of Europe (2010), 'European insurance in figures', CEA statistics 42, www.cea.eu/.

Committee of European Insurance and Occupational Pensions Supervisors (CEIOPS) (2010), 'Quantitative impact study 5', www.ceiops.eu/en/consultations/qis/quantitative-impact-study-5/index.html.

Doff, R. (2008), 'A critical analysis of the Solvency II proposals', *Geneva Papers of Risk and Insurance*, **33**, 193–206.

Dowd, K. (1998), *Beyond Value at Risk. The New Science of Risk Management*, West Sussex: John Wiley & Sons.

Fama, E. (1965), 'The behavior of stock-market prices', *Journal of Business*, **38** (1), 34–105.

Hayek, F.A. (1972), *Individualism and Economic Order*, Chicago, IL: Henry Regnery.

Hill, C.A. (2004). 'Regulating the rating agencies', *Washington University Law Quarterly*, **82** (43), 43–95.

Holton, G.A. (2002), 'History of value-at-risk: 1922–1998', working paper.

Hoppe, H.H. (1995), *Economic Science and the Austrian Method*, Auburn, AL: Ludwig von Mises Institute.

Howden, D. (2009), 'Single trial probability applications: can subjectivity evade frequency limitations?', *Libertarian Papers* **1** (42), 1–12.

Huerta de Soto, J. (2006), *Money, Bank Credit and Economic Cycles*, Auburn, AL: Ludwig von Mises Institute.

Huerta de Soto, J. (2009a), 'The fatal error of Solvency II', *Economic Affairs*, **29** (2), 74–7.

Huerta de Soto, J. (2009b), *The Theory of Dynamic Efficiency*, London: Routledge.

Huerta de Soto, J. (2010), *Socialism, Economic Calculation and Entrepreneurial Function*, Cheltenham, UK and Northampton, MA, USA: Edward Elgar.

Jensen, N. (2010), 'Insolvency II', *Absolute Return Letter*, October, 1–7.

Jorion, P. (2003), *Financial Risk Manager Handbook* (2nd edn), New Jersey: John Wiley & Sons.

Levy, D.M. and S.J. Peart (2010), 'Prudence with biased experts: ratings agencies and regulators', working paper.

Linder, U. and V. Ronkainen (2004), 'Solvency II: towards a new insurance supervisory system in the EU', *Scandinavian Actuarial Journal*, **6**, 462–74.

Lo, A.W. and A.C. Mackinley (1988), 'Stock market prices do not follow random walks: evidence from a simple specification test', *Review of Financial Studies*, **1** (1), 41–66.

Lowenstein, R. (2001), *When Genius Failed*, New York: Random House.

Martinez, M. (2010), 'Respiro para la banca española', Expansion.com, www.expansion.com/2010/11/14/opinion/editorialyllaves/1289768768.html.

Miller, R.L. (2008), *Economics Today*, Boston, MA: Addison Wesley.

Mises, L. von ([1949] 1998), *Human Action: A Treatise on Economics*, Auburn, AL: Ludwig von Mises Institute.

Mises, R. von (1957), *Probability, Statistics and Truth* (2nd edn), New York: Macmillan.

Plantin, G. and J. Rochet (2007), *When Insurers go Bust: An Economic Analysis of the Role and Design of Prudential Regulation*, Princeton, NJ: Princeton University Press.

Schumpeter, J.A. ([1942] 1976), *Capitalism, Socialism and Democracy*, New York: Harper Perennial.

Simpson, B. (2005), *Markets Don't Fail!*, Lanham, MD: Lexington Books.

Taleb, N.N. (2005), *Fooled by Randomness*, New York: Random House.

Taleb, N.N. (2007), *The Black Swan*, London: Penguin.

Toke, S.A. and J. Dutta. (2008), 'Policy compromises: corruption and regulation in a democracy', *Economics and Politics*, **20**, 335–60.

Trask, S. (2003), 'In defense of bank failure', Ludwig von Mises Institute, daily article, http://mises.org/daily/1389, 5 December.

7. The Eurosystem: costs and tragedies

Philipp Bagus

The institutional setup of the Eurosystem brought the system close to collapse in May 2010. The Greek government had to be rescued by a €110 billion loan package. The Spanish, Portuguese and Irish governments only stabilized after the introduction of a €750 billion loan facility.

Member states of the Eurozone are in the process of reforming the Stability and Growth Pact (SGP) in order to prevent a future sovereign debt crisis and a collapse of the Euro. The future of the Eurozone depends on a reform that enforces meaningful penalties on fiscal irresponsibility. In this chapter I explain why the current institutional setup of the Eurosystem provoked a sovereign debt crisis and demonstrate that the institutional structure resembles a classic tragedy of the commons.

In addition to the tragedy of the commons of the Eurosystem, we will find several other layers of negative externalities in the monetary sphere. We will analyse which circumstances have limited the exploitation of the commons and how the limits have been insufficient to prevent the sovereign debt crisis. Finally, we will set out several reforms that may alleviate the situation or even totally eliminate the culpable negative externalities. The more externalities a reform eliminates the more difficult tends to be its introduction politically, that is, there is a trade-off between political feasibility and reduction of negative externalities. We will rank reforms starting with the more politically moderate and hence more feasible ones, before ending with the more ambitious, thorough ones.

TOWARD A USEFUL DEFINITION OF EXTERNALITIES

Orthodox textbooks often define externalities as uncompensated effects of actions on third parties, bystanders not participating in a particular action or exchange. Examples given are a person smoking next to you in a restaurant (in the case of negative externality), or a neighbor planting flowers in his garden (in the case of an appeasing positive externality). The literature goes on to distinguish between psychic, pecuniary and technological (or real) externalities (Prest and Turvey, 1965).

Psychological externalities result from the internal feelings that a particular action evokes in third persons, such as the good feeling that the view of the beautiful neighbor's garden provokes. Pecuniary externalities result when actions affect third parties indirectly through the price system. When a new restaurant opens in a neighborhood it tends to have negative pecuniary effects on competing restaurants. Real or technological externalities are defined as the direct effects that actions of some firms have on the output of other firms. The pollution of a farmer's field by a factory harms the farmer's crop production.

Unfortunately, the mainstream taxonomy of externalities is confused and not useful to analyze problems of the real world. First, the definition of externalities is too broad. Any action may have psychological, pecuniary or technological externalities. In a society with a high degree of division of labor, a consumer buying chewing gum in China may have a pecuniary external effect on all other producers world-wide as the money spent on chewing gum cannot be spent on other goods. By implementing scarce resources in an investment project the 'production function' of all other firms may be directly affected; if I convince Celion Dion to sing for free at a charity event, no other producer can use this resource at the same day in his 'production function.'

Moreover, any action may affect the subjective well-being of any other human being exercising a psychological externality.[1] The planting of flowers by the neighbor may exert negative or positive externalities on all passersby. If the neighbor announces his action on the internet and puts pictures on his blog all internet users may be affected positively or negatively in their well-being. In fact, any action announced over the internet may exert such effects. In other words, any action that is known to third parties may affect their well-being. As such, the definition of externalities is too broad to be useful as an analytical tool.

Second, the distinction between real, pecuniary and psychic externalities seems to suggest that there are both objective and subjective externalities. Yet, externalities are only relevant for actors if they affect the subjective well-being of individuals. It is not the objective changes that are relevant but the subjective perception of them. Thus, there is no clear-cut distinction between real, pecuniary and psychic externalities. Take an example of supposedly 'real externalities.' Goods affected by pollution provide services that are appreciated subjectively. When a farmer produces fewer crops due to pollution his well-being is affected subjectively. If he wanted to produce fewer crops and restrict supply to increase prices, he may actually welcome the pollution. In the same way, flowers planted by the neighbor given as an example for 'psychological externalities' affect the subjective well-being of passersby. Lastly, pecuniary externalities are relevant to actors only if they affect their subjective well-being. It is not the higher or lower monetary income that is important to actors, but their subjective valuation of these changes. Thus, the subjective well-being of individuals may be increased or lowered when a new restaurant opens in a neighborhood. Why distinguish between pecuniary, real and psychological externalities if all externalities affect the subjective well-being in the end? Why not only refer to psychological externalities?

This leads us to the third critique. As all externalities are 'psychological' or subjective and individually experienced by actors, mainstream classification puts aside or does not mention the true and only meaningful distinctive characteristic of externalities: the poor definition and defense of private property rights.[2] The poor definition and defense of private property rights is objectively discernable. In fact, effects resulting from actions where property rights are not violated are relatively uninteresting, because all actions have effects or 'externalities' in the sense that they may affect the well-being of third parties positively or negatively.

Actions violating property rights inflict damages on the property or health of third parties and pose important theoretical questions. Actions that do not respect property rights may be called irresponsible as they do not account for the effects resulting from ill-defended property rights. Consequently, we will define externalities as effects of actions that affect third parties and that do not respect private property rights. The distinctive characteristic of externalities is the respect of private property rights as explained by Ludwig von Mises: positive and negative externalities (or external benefits and costs) occur when a proprietor does not assume the full advantages or disadvantages of employing property because of ill-defined or defended property rights (Mises, [1949] 1998, p. 651).[3]

Negative externalities may be due to privileges and ill-defended property rights such as the potential to pollute a privately 'owned' field, or common property resources when the property rights are ill-defined. The result of negative externalities often generates perverse incentives that increase the harm for third parties. Some people do act because of the costs they inflict upon others.

NEGATIVE EXTERNALITIES IN THE MONETARY SPHERE

Base Money Production

In a gold standard base money production respects private property rights. The gold money producers assume the full costs of money production. Even though prices tend to increase due to the money production, there is no violation of property rights or ill-defined property rights. No one has to accept newly minted coins. People will only accept these coins if they expect to benefit from their acceptance. Third parties do not have to use the inflated money supply either, but are free to use alternative currencies. Consequently, there are no negative externalities.

In our modern monetary system, however, base money production implies negative externalities because it is not free and competitive. A single institution produces base money. The money monopoly implies a privilege violating private property rights as no one is allowed to use their own property to produce base money. This privilege is normally combined with legal tender laws. People have to accept the legal tender in settlement of all contracts, even if they want to contract in another currency. The legal tender money is often also privileged by authorities as it is the only currency in which taxes can be paid.

Legal tender laws present a violation of the freedom of contract and also, thereby, property rights. People cannot use their property in the way they want but must accept the legal tender in exchanges. As private property rights are violated, negative externalities may evolve.[4] When the monopolist produces base money and uses it to buy goods and services, the prices of these goods and services are bid up. The price increase harms third parties, which see the monetary costs of goods and services increase. Damage is inflicted on the purchasing power of money that people hold through a violation of property rights.[5] Money that is held renders fewer services than it otherwise would have yielded. The reduced services present the negative externalities in the same way in which the poorly defined property of a farmer's field which is polluted yields fewer services in the form of a reduced crop.

There results a redistribution in favor of the first receivers of the new base money to the detriment of the last receivers. As the redistribution results from a violation of private property rights we are faced with negative externalities. The money producer does not assume all costs of his action and will try to maximize his income out of the money production, at the same time attempting to avoid a breakdown of the monetary system. In our modern monetary systems, central banks are the monopolist producers of legal tender base money.

Fractional Reserve Banking

Another area where private property rights in the modern monetary economy are ill-defined and ill-defended is banking. In a deposit contract, the depositor entrusts to the depositary a good for the depositary to guard, protect and return on demand at the depositor's request. The fundamental purpose of a deposit contract is the custody and safekeeping of the good deposited (Huerta de Soto, 2009, ch. 1). When a person deposits money at a bank, the bank is obliged to guard and protect the money and to return it when the depositor should ask for it. The bank's duty is to hold 100 percent reserves on these deposits to meet this contractual obligation.

Consequently, it is both a privilege and a violation of private property rights if banks are allowed to expand credit and hold fractional reserves. When banks appropriate the money entrusted to them as deposits and loan it out to other persons, they not only violate the property rights of the depositors; they also create new fiduciary media, which in turn creates negative externalities.

Governments have granted the privilege to banks to hold fractional reserves, in other words, they have not defended the property rights of depositors. The results are negative externalities. The creation of fiduciary media by fractional reserve banks leads to upward pressure on prices. The services from money held are reduced. Existing depositors lose purchasing power as the privileged banks have created new money. The first receivers of the new money profit at the cost of the last receivers of this same money, who see prices rise before their incomes increase. A negative externality is imposed on the innocent depositors by the fractional reserve banking system.

Another negative externality is that the quality of money is reduced. The quality of money is its subjectively perceived capacity to fulfill its functions as a medium of exchange, store of value and unit of account (Bagus, 2009a). By credit expansion the reserve ratio of deposits is reduced. Banks expand credits to grant loans for long-term investment projects. As a result, the average quality of assets that might be used to redeem deposits falls because banks acquire illiquid assets with the newly created money. The credit expansion also distorts relative prices. Economic calculation becomes more difficult. A resulting intertemporal discoordination in society constitutes another negative external effect.[6]

One may make the argument that in the case of our present fractional reserve banking systems we are not faced with ill-defended property rights of depositors but rather with ill-defined property rights. In fact, it may not be clear for many parties involved whether they deal with a deposit contract. Probably many depositors want complete availability of their money, which is the characteristic of a deposit contract. However, it is not clear who really owns the 'deposited' money. The bankers and recently also the positive legal system tend to regard deposited money as 'loans' granted to bankers. At the same time depositors tend to regard the deposited money as their own and want it fully available. Bankers fail to make clear whether they have been authorized or not by the 'depositor' to use the money.[7] As Huerta de Soto states:

> To fail to clarify or fully specify these details indicates a remarkable ambiguity on the part of bankers, and in the event that adverse legal consequences result, their weight should fall on the bankers' shoulders and not on those of the contracting party, who with good faith enter into the contract believing its essential purpose or cause to be the simple custody or safekeeping of the money deposited. (Huerta de Soto, 2009, p. 145)

It is not clear what kind of contract is entered into with a fractional reserve demand deposit contract – whether it is a loan or a deposit. Without clear and unambiguous contracts, property rights are ill-defined, resulting in negative externalities as banks use the money as if it would be theirs and depositors simultaneously regard it as their own. Thus, we may interpret modern fractional reserve banking in basically two ways. First, we may regard deposits as ill-defended because banks have the privilege to use genuine deposits. Second, we may regard the property rights of demand deposits as ill-defined because it is not clear what kind of contract is actually being signed. With both interpretations, modern fractional reserve banking leads to negative externalities.

We are faced with a special case of negative externalities, namely a tragedy of the commons – a term coined by Garrett Hardin (1968). A tragedy of the commons is defined by two aspects: rivalrous use of the resource, that is the benefits from the use of the resource accrue to its user, and nonexcludability in the access of the resource, that is many persons may exploit it. A tragedy of the commons occurs in the case of unowned or common property resources. It is an extreme instance of negative externalities (Mises, [1949] 1998, p. 652). Not only one actor but several actors can exploit a resource due to ill-defined or ill-defended property rights. An example is the harvesting of fish in the ocean, depleting the stock of available fish. As property rights on fish swarms are not defined, anyone can harvest fish, thus reducing the stock. All fishermen bear the burden of the reduced stock of fish, while the advantage of increased fishing is fully absorbed by the individual fisherman. There is the incentive to fish as many fish as possible, because otherwise other fishermen may deplete the stock. A tragedy of the commons, thereby, leads to the destruction of the common property resources. If property rights were defined and defended well, the owner would bear the full costs of fishing and reducing the stock. He would take these costs into account and most probably refrain from immediately depleting the resource, in order to preserve its capital value.

We can apply the concept of the tragedy of the commons to banking (Huerta de Soto, 2009, pp. 666–9). Fractional reserve banks can exploit the common property resource, that is the deposits of their depositors. Any bank that expands credit reaps the full benefit of the money creation. Yet, it does not assume the full costs, which are borne by all money holders and also all other fractional reserve banks. Banks see the possibility of benefiting from credit expansion reduced as the purchasing power of money falls. All banks can profit from the ill-defended and ill-defined property right by expanding credit and reducing the purchasing power of money. In fact, the higher the expansion, the higher may be the profits. There is an incentive to exploit the commons as fast as possible, because otherwise other banks will exploit it. If a bank does not participate, it suffers costs if other banks exploit the commons and expand credit.[8]

Nevertheless, competition and the interbank clearing mechanism are checks on the exploitation of deposits. Fractional reserve banking, therefore, is no pure tragedy of the commons without any limits on the exploitation of the common resource.[9] A bank that expands credit faster than other banks will lose reserves to the more conservative banks, and might fall into severe liquidity and ultimately solvency problems. Only when all banks expand in the same rhythm are there no reserve losses due to the clearing mechanism. Thus, there is an incentive for banks to collude and coordinate credit expansion.

Banks have traditionally pushed for an institutionalization of the coordination of credit expansion through the introduction of a central bank. A central bank can coordinate the credit expansion of the banking system, prevent reserve losses and ensure a controlled exploitation of the commons. The central bank, by regulating the exploitation of the deposits, may prevent the total destruction of the resource and the purchasing power of money. The tragedy of the commons would be averted, and converted to a managed commons. Regulation prevents the immediate destruction of the resource by imposing certain quotas on its exploitation.

A Tragedy of the Commons in Base Money Production

Beside the tragedy of the commons implied in fractional reserve banking in the Eurozone, there is an additional tragedy in the monetization of government debts via the production of base money and the fractional reserve banking system.[10] This tragedy is a unique feature of the Eurozone.

Institutions in crisis

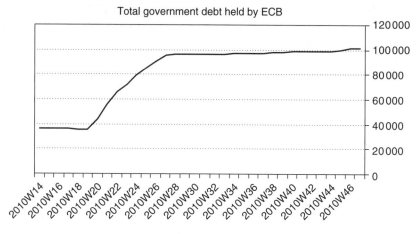

Source: ECB.

Figure 7.1   Total government debt held by ECB (in millions of Euros)

Several governments can use one banking system to finance their debts by increasing the money supply.

Traditionally, there have been several instruments by which central banks monetize government debts. In fact, one purpose of central banks is to make the finance of government expenditures more easy (Rothbard, 1994).[11] Central banks buy government bonds from the banking system or accept them as collateral in their loans to the banking system.[12] The difference between the two instruments is more legal than economic in nature. When the government spends more than it receives through taxes, it issues bonds. The fractional reserve banking system buys a not insignificant part of these bonds because these bonds receive a favorable treatment in the open market operations of central banks. Indeed, both the ECB and the banking system hold a substantial amount of government debts, as can be seen in Figures 7.1 and 7.2. In Figure 7.3, we can see the percentage of Euro area government debts held by the banking system and the ECB.

Central banks purchase government bonds and accept them as collateral of the highest quality, applying the lowest haircut.[13] When a central bank purchases bonds from a bank, the bank's reserves held in its account at the central bank increase. Base money increases and the bank may expand credit on top of its increased reserves. Similarly when a central bank grants a loan to a bank and accepts government bonds as collateral, the reserves of the bank held in its account at the central bank increase. Base money increases and the bank may expand credit as long as the loan

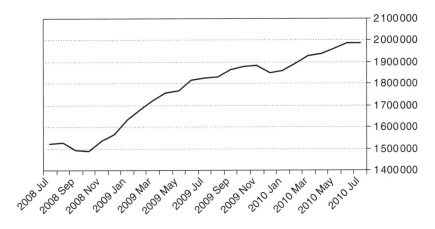

Source: ECB.

Figure 7.2   *Eurozone bank holdings of government debt (in millions of Euros)*

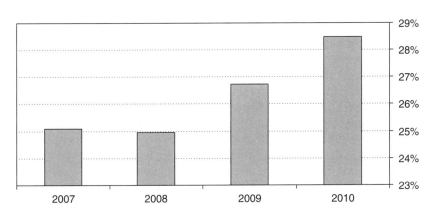

Source: ECB and AMECO.

Figure 7.3   *Euro area debts held by the banking system and the ECB (as percentage of Euro area government debts)*

is renewed. The difference between these two methods is mainly legal. In the case of the outright purchase the central bank owns the bonds and increases the base money until it sells the bonds. In the case of the collateralized lending the central bank holds the bonds as collateral and increases base money until it stops rolling over the loans. In both cases, central banks effectively monetize government debts. They increase base money to hold the government bonds outright or as collateral, thus indirectly financing the government's deficit.

In addition to the outright monetization of government bonds there is an indirect monetization occurring in the financial system. Market participants know that central banks buy government bonds and accept them as the preferred collateral. Thus, banks buy the bonds due to their privileged treatment, ensuring a liquid market and pushing down yields. On another level, knowing that there is a very liquid market in government bonds and a high demand by banks, investment funds, pension funds, insurers and private investors buy government bonds. Government bonds become very liquid and almost as good as base money. In many cases they serve to create additional base money. In other cases they stand as a reserve to be converted into base money if necessary. As a consequence, new money created through credit expansion often ends up buying liquid government bonds, indirectly monetizing the debt.

Imagine that the government has a deficit and issues government bonds. A part of it is bought by the banking system and used to get additional reserves from the central bank who buys the bonds or grants new loans, accepting them as collateral.[14] The banking system uses the new reserves to expand credits and grant loans to, for example, the construction industry. With the new loans the construction industry buys factors of production and pays its workers. The workers use part of the new money to invest in investment funds. The investment funds then use the new money to acquire government bonds. Thus, there is an indirect monetization. Part of the money created by the fractional reserve banking system ends up buying government bonds because of their preferential treatment by the central bank, that is its direct monetization. We have already seen that an increase of fiat legal tender money leads to negative externalities and that fractional reserve banking implies a (managed) tragedy of the commons. In the European Monetary Union (EMU), several governments may use the direct and indirect monetization mechanisms of the Eurosystem to finance their expenditures and please voters. Any government in the Eurosystem may do the following: the government issues bonds to pay for its deficit; fractional reserve banks buy these bonds and use them as collateral to receive loans from the ECB in their lending operations; the new reserves may be used to expand credits on top of these reserves. A tragedy of the commons develops because any government may use banks and the ECB to monetize their debts. There exists the incentive to have higher deficits and print relatively more government bonds than the other governments and to use the Eurosystem to finance these deficits. As printing bonds is almost analogous to printing base money, those governments that print bonds faster than other governments of the Eurosystem profit because they receive relatively more new money than other governments. There is a redistribution from the slower printing governments (i.e. those that undertake the least debt financing) to the faster printing governments (i.e. those that undertake the most debt financing). Through the redistribution system of the national governments part of the advantages and disadvantages are transferred to the general population in the respective countries.[15]

Take the example of Greece. Important parts of the Greek economy are not competitive at prevailing wage rates and other factor prices. Yet, prices are maintained high by government spending. The Greek government maintains high deficits to pay the unemployed, to pay high pensions, sustain a large public sector and other social expenditures. Thereby, the income of many Greeks is raised above the level that would have obtained on the free market. Greeks use the income to import goods and services from abroad where they are less costly. A trade deficit is maintained by government deficits. In order to pay for these deficits, the Greek government prints bonds that are purchased by the banking system in order to use them to obtain funds from the Eurosystem. New money is created and tends to bid up prices. While the purchasing power of the Euro affects all users of the currency, the printing of the Greek government bonds benefits the Greek government and special-interest groups that receive their income from it. The Euro is a legal tender fiat money, and represents an infringement on property rights. Printing government bonds, therefore, leads to negative externalities in the form of the lower purchasing power of the Euro imposed on all other users of the currency.

Imagine the following case to visualize the redistribution. The Greek government prints government bonds that are bought by the banking system that uses them to increase base money to expand credit on top of. The government uses the money to pay a public servant. The public servant buys a German car. Prices of German cars tend to be bid up. The money supply is increased, bidding up prices, while goods flow toward Greece. Slowly the new money spreads throughout the Eurozone. The purchasing power of the Euro has fallen and a Greek trade deficit has developed. There is a redistribution in favor of the first receivers of the new money – the Greek governments and its public servant – other people faced with the rising prices of German cars are the losers in this redistribution.[16]

Of course, it is not only the Greek government that may use this mechanism for its own advantage and that of its population, but the other governments of the Eurozone may do so as well. A government is on the winning side of the redistribution scheme if it prints government bonds faster than other governments. If a government prints its bonds at a pace of 3 percent of GDP but the rest of the governments print them at a pace of 10 percent of GDP and the purchasing power of the Euro falls at 8 percent per year, prices rise faster than the government prints bonds. Even though government spending increases by 3 percent (financed by deficit spending), real government spending may actually fall. The incentives resemble a tragedy of the commons: the incentive is to print faster than your peers. In fact, the system resembles a situation where several actors may use a commonly owned printing press. While the analogy is close, it is no pure tragedy of the commons. There are some differences between the Eurosystem and a commonly owned printing press. Indeed, if it were equal the Euro would have already disappeared via hyperinflation.

Limitations, or Why the System is Not a Pure Tragedy of the Commons

The differences result from the fact that governments cannot directly print Euros but can only issue their own government bonds.[17] Banks might not buy these bonds or might not use them as collateral for new loans from the ECB.

There are several reasons why this might happen. First, collateralized lending with government bonds may be unattractive for banks. If the interest rate offered for the government bonds is lower than the interest rates banks must pay for loans from the ECB, lending will be unattractive. The danger of this happening is not too high because central banks tend to be accommodating to fiscal policies. Especially in the Eurozone, a too-restrictive monetary policy may trigger fiscal problems for member states and thereby a general sovereign debt crisis. Alternatively, governments have to offer higher yields to attract bank buyers.

Second, governments may default on their bonds. The default risk may deter banks from purchasing the bonds. In the Eurozone the default risk was and still is reduced by (implicit) bailout guarantees. Market participants and the media interpreted the single currency as coming with a bailout guarantee from other member states (Arghyrou and Tsoukalas, 2010; Browne, 2010; Samuelson, 2010). Once a country introduced the Euro, it was understood that it would never leave the EMU. An exit was politically unthinkable and the Maastricht Treaty does not provide for an exit of the monetary union (Bandulet, 2010, p. 57).

The Euro is a political project.[18] It is conceived as a further step toward the unavoidable political integration of the European Union. Politicians imply that there can only be progress via increased European political integration. Any regress would imply a defeat of European politicians and put into doubt the whole project of European political integration.

Consequently, a default by a member state that might force the country to exit the Eurozone would not only be regarded as a failure of the Euro but also of the greater project of the European Union. Thus, for a long time market participants regarded a default as politically next to impossible. The expectation was that in the worst case the fiscally stronger member states would support the weaker ones. Countries such as Germany would guarantee the bonds of the Mediterranean nations (Portugal, Italy, Greece and Spain – the PIGS) and prevent a default. As Tarullo (2010), member of the board of the Federal Reserve, states: 'For years many market participants had assumed that an implicit guarantee protected the debt of euro-area members.'

The political guarantees reduce the default risk of government loans issued by member states. The market's expectations were accurate. Implicit guarantees have now become explicit. Greece was bailed out in spring 2010 by the rest of the Eurozone. The Greek government has been granted a rescue package of €110 billion from the governments of the Eurozone and the International Monetary Fund (IMF) (Thesing and Krause-Jackson, 2010). The danger of contagion obliged the Eurozone in May 2010 to pledge €750 billion for further bailouts of other member states (Nazareth and Serkin, 2010).

Third, banks are faced with a liquidity risk when they use the ECB to refinance themselves and pledge government bonds as collateral. The term of government bonds is in most cases longer than the term of the loans granted by the ECB. The term of government bonds ranges from three months to 30 years. The ECB lending operations have traditionally consisted of one-week and three-month loans. In response to the financial crisis the ECB increased the maximum term to one year. Nevertheless, most government bonds are still of a longer term than the available ECB lending channels. There is a consequent risk that the rating of the bonds is reduced over their lifetimes and that the ECB stops accepting them as collateral in their lending operations. When the ECB stops rolling over the loan collateralized by the government bonds, banks may suffer severe liquidity problems. The risk of such rollover problems is reduced because the ratings of the government bonds are supported by the formerly implicit – now explicit – bailout guarantee.[19] The political willingness to save the Euro project supports the ratings.

The liquidity risk is also expressed by the risk of a change in interest rates that may make the operation unattractive. The ECB might increase its interest rates in the future until they are, finally, higher than the fixed rate of a longer-term government bond. The risk is alleviated by a sufficient interest spread between the yield of the government bonds and the interest rates applied by the ECB. With interest rates currently charged by the ECB at 1 percent and Greek yields over 10 percent, the spread is highly attractive (German bund yields are also more than 100 percent higher than ECB rates).

Fourth, the ECB might refuse to accept certain government bonds as collateral. The ECB demands a minimum rating for bonds to be accepted as collateral. Before the financial crisis of 2008 the minimum rating was A−. In order to support the banking system during a period of falling ratings, the ECB reduced its minimum rating to BBB−. If government bonds fall below the minimum rating they cease to be acceptable collateral. This is not a very great danger either, as the ECB, as other central banks, will tend to be accommodating. Indeed, the ECB has been accommodating in respect of its collateral rules for government bonds. Initially, the ECB planned to cease the reduction of the minimum rating to BBB− after one year. Yet, when markets started to doubt that Greece would maintain at least an A− rating, the ECB extended the rule for another year. Even though the ECB stated that it would not apply special rules to a single country, it announced at the height of the sovereign debt crisis of 2010 that it would accept Greek debt even if rated junk (Jones, 2010). A precedent was set. Governments from now on can expect that collateral rules will be changed to support their deficits and that the ECB will be accommodating.

Fifth, the ECB applies haircuts. When a bank offers €1000 worth of government bonds as collateral it will receive a loan of less than €1000 from the ECB. The difference depends on the haircut applied to the collateral. The ECB distinguishes five different categories of collateral. The ECB demands different haircuts depending on the category of collateral. Haircuts for government bonds are the smallest. The central bank, thereby, subsidizes the use of government bonds as collateral vis-à-vis other debt instruments. The application of the haircut implies that the scheme of printing bonds increasing the amount of base money is hampered by a reduced base money production as a consequence of the haircut.

Lastly, the ECB might just not play the game. It may choose not to accommodate all demands for new loans. Banks may offer more government bonds as collateral than the ECB makes available through loans. By applying a restrictive monetary policy, not every bank that offers government bonds as collateral will receive a loan. Yet, again the ECB can be expected to be accommodating as it has been in the past. Political reasons, especially the will to continue the Euro project, reduce this risk for banks. A non-accommodating monetary stance may lead to both a banking crisis and a sovereign debt crisis that could trigger the default of member states, banking systems and the end of the Euro. The ECB has already proved how accommodating it can be. In late 2008 in response to problems in the financial system the ECB started to offer unlimited liquidity to markets. Any demand for a loan is satisfied, provided sufficient collateral is offered.

Limiting the Commons

Despite these frictions, the potential to finance government deficits indirectly through the ECB constitutes a traditional tragedy of the commons. The problems of the setup were known in the beginning, even though it has (to my knowledge) never been called a tragedy of the commons. On behalf of Germany and its allies in favor of relatively low inflationary policies, the Stability and Growth Pact (SGP) was enacted in 1997, with the intention of limiting the debts and deficits of member states. According to the SGP, government debts should be below 60 percent of GDP and deficits below 3 percent of GDP.

The SGP acts thereby as a managed commons imposing quotas on the exploitation of the commons, namely the common currency. The incentive in such a case is to exploit the quota to the maximum, that is 3 percent of GDP, if the quota is enforced. However, the SGP was never enforced. Automatic sanctions as proposed by the German minister of finance, Theodor Waigel, were not instituted. To impose sanctions and penalties against governments that repeatedly violated the 3 percent limit is a political decision. Governments themselves are the guardians of the pact that limits their fiscal options. Infringing nations may then collaborate to get away without penalties. Thus, France and Germany grouped together in 2003 to prevent sanctions from being imposed. The SGP utterly failed in its purpose of effectively limiting fiscal spending because governments themselves decided on the very sanctions that they would have to enforce on themselves. The system resembles a cartel where cartel members promise not to exceed a quota of 3 percent of GDP. Thus, the price of the exploited 'resource' (the purchasing power of money) is kept from falling fast. Yet, the cartel is not enforceable and the incentive for members is to exceed the quota to benefit at the cost of members fulfilling the quota. In 2010 all but one country is expected to have a deficit higher than 3 percent of GDP.

The financial crisis accelerated the tendency to excessive deficits implied in the institutional setup of the Eurosystem. Governments generously increased spending to bail out failing banks and struggling industries. Spending on unemployment went up and tax revenues decreased. The financial crisis accelerated a development that is implied in the institutional setup of the Euro. Markets started to doubt the implicit bailout guarantee and yields on bonds of periphery countries soared. The sovereign debt crisis of 2010 forced Eurozone governments to make the implicit guarantee explicit.

REFORM THE EUROPEAN MONETARY SYSTEM AND REDUCE NEGATIVE EXTERNALITIES

There are several possibilities to alleviate the incentives for excessive deficits implied in the Eurosystem; we will now look at several options. We will start with the less ambitious, more superficial options, which are less thorough but more politically feasible because they get rid of fewer privileges and advantages of the political class than the more thorough and complete reforms. The more ambitious reforms are more disruptive to the existing economic structure and eliminate more state-granted privileges. They eliminate more negative externalities in the monetary sphere. They close more loopholes in the defense and definition of property rights in the monetary system.

A Monetary Growth Rule

The fixed increase in base money as proposed by Milton Friedman (1960) would limit tragedy of the commons of the monetization of deficits. Governments could use only a limited increase in base money to finance their deficits. Fractional reserve banks would expand credits on top of the increase in base money. Governments would have the incentive to direct the credit expansion of the entire European banking system to finance their own deficit. The tragedy of the commons remains as governments would try to ensure that the newly created money ended up financing their deficits. The tragedy would be limited through the growth rule for base money and minimum reserve requirements for banks. Politically, the reform does seem feasible.

A Reform of the Stability and Growth Pact

A reform of the SGP could limit the externalities implied in the tragedy of the commons of the Eurozone.[20] The ECB, the European Commission and especially Germany opted for this alternative to limit the tragedy. They proposed more automatic penalties not dependent on political negotiation, the freezing of voting rights and an orderly default process. The European Commission demanded an analysis of competitiveness. With credible penalties, the tragedy can be limited. Nevertheless, on a summit in October 2010 the proposals were not successful and decisions to sanction violators of the SGP continue to be left to political hands (Neuger and Buergin, 2010). Naturally, governments that expect to exceed the 3 percent limit did not agree to more automatic penalties. The decision on sanctions remains in the hands of EMU governments. The main change under discussion is the introduction of orderly defaults in which private investors bear part of the losses. This change would mean only a partial bailout of governments. The reform of the SGP was, however, unsatisfactory as the main institutional setup would not change. A thorough reform of the SGP would have been quite unambitious compared to other reforms, but even this one failed in the face of political resistance.

A Return to National Currencies

A return to the national currencies such as the Deutschmark, the lira, the peseta or the French franc would eliminate the externalities implied in the tragedy of the commons of the Eurozone. By eliminating a common central bank for several currencies, the tragedy of the commons on the level of the Eurozone disappears. Nevertheless, negative externalities in base money production and the tragedy of the commons implied in fractional reserve banking remain. A return to national currencies would still be relatively simple, because it does not depend on the approval of all member states. For example, Germany might leave the Eurozone unilaterally. Moreover, such a reform maintains the advantages for governments that they can keep their gains from monopolistic base money production and the fractional reserve banking privilege. Yet, disruptions could be substantial because over-indebted governments may have to default, leading to problems in the financial system. This is so because the interest rates that governments in the Eurozone pay on their debts is artificially lowered by the bailout guarantee that the Euro carries. A return to national currencies would lead to a surge in yields of government bonds and buyers of new debts would be hard to find. Interest payments would most likely become unbearable.

Abolition of National Central Banks

The abolition of central banks would open the way for currency competition. Proponents of the abolition of central banks and competing currencies include fractional reserve bankers such as White (1984) and Selgin (1988), as well as Hayek (1990) or Vaubel (1986). In such proposals, legal tender laws are abolished and no one is forced to accept any specific currency. As a consequence, the external effects of monopolistic base money production disappear. The only negative externalities remaining result from the privilege of fractional reserve banking.

In White and Selgin's proposals the issuers of money may hold fractional reserves on demand deposits. Credit expansion is, however, limited through adverse clearing and competition between banks. A drawback of the system is its inherent tendency toward credit expansion and the interests of individual banks to introduce a coordinating central bank (Huerta de Soto, 2009, pp. 669–70). This reform is more radical, disruptive and politically more difficult than the aforementioned options. The abolition of central banks violates vital interests of governments and the banking system that is restricted in its credit expansion.

Abolition of the Fractional Reserve Privilege

The introduction of a 100 percent reserve commodity standard has been defended by authors such as Mises ([1953] 1981) (for all newly issued money substitutes), Reisman (2000), Rothbard (1983; 1991) and Huerta de Soto (2009). A 100 percent reserve commodity standard would eliminate all negative externalities in the monetary sphere. There would be no apparent tragedy of the commons in base money production. Property rights in the production of money would be completely restored. There would be no tragedy of the commons resulting from credit expansion, as all banks would have to hold 100 percent reserves for deposits and respect the property rights of depositors. Only then would all negative externalities be eliminated and complete freedom would be restored. Property rights in the production and depositing of money would be clearly defined and defended.

There are several ways to get to such a system. Mises makes a proposal for the situation of the 1950s when the US was on a gold exchange standard. His goal was to freeze the amount of fiduciary media issued, and back all new money substitutes 100 percent with gold. Rothbard, Reisman and Huerta de Soto advocate the use the gold held by central banks to back banknotes and demand deposits 100 percent. Huerta de Soto's plan includes the choice of depositors to get either their deposits 100 percent backed by gold or to exchange them for participation in an investment fund formed out of the assets of banks. His plan involves the use of unclaimed participations in the investment funds to cancel public debts. My own plan (Bagus, 2009b) involves an immediate abolition of all government interventions in money.[21]

These ultimate proposals are the most thorough, ending all negative externalities in the field of money by closing all loopholes against the protection of property rights. As the viability of many economic structures currently depends on one of the negative externalities in the monetary sphere, these reforms would be disruptive and hurt the vital interests of many influential groups ranging from big business, the financial industry and politicians. Therefore, the political resistance to such reforms will be substantial. Nevertheless, it is important at least to offer such alternatives.

Table 7.1   Negative externalities of different monetary system alternatives

	Monetization of government deficits	Production of fiduciary media	Monopolistic base money production
Current Eurosystem	High	High	High
Eurosystem with reformed and enforced SGP	Limited	High	High/Limited
System of national currencies	None	High	High
Fractional reserve free banking	None	Limited	None
100 percent commodity standard	None	None	None

Their viability in the end depends on public opinion, which can be influenced by proposing and consistently defending such reforms. Any of the aforementioned reforms is a step in the right direction of eliminating negative externalities. How far a reform may go depends on the political circumstances. The negative externalities of the resulting monetary systems are shown in Table 7.1.

As Table 7.1 summarizes, a 100 percent commodity standard is the only monetary system that fully eliminates and removes the three detrimental aspects of the current monetary regime: 1) a tragedy of the commons in the monetization of government deficits; 2) a tragedy of the commons in credit issuance; and 3) the negative externalities stemming from a monopoly issue of base money. Thus, if the root monetary problems of today's recession in Europe are to be fully avoided in the future, painful reform must be enacted today to prohibit the forces that brought the recession on. Only a return to a fully backed commodity standard will achieve such an ambitious and essential goal.

CONCLUSION

In the Eurosystem there exist several layers of negative externalities due to poorly defined and defended property rights. Monopolistic base money production and legal tender laws violate the property rights of currency holders. Negative externalities consist mainly of a tendency toward a lower purchasing power for actors who must use the Euro (enforced through legal tender laws). On top of the base money production, fractional reserve banks hold the privilege of creating Euros by credit expansion. The property rights of depositors are both ambiguously defined and poorly defended. Negative externalities result when banks violate traditional legal properties and appropriate the deposited money for their own use. The purchasing power of money is lower than otherwise would be the case, negatively affecting all money users. As all banks can expand credit to exploit the purchasing power of money, a tragedy of the commons develops that is limited only by the central bank. These two layers exist in all industrialized nations that share this particular monetary regime: a fractional reserve banking system coordinated by a centralized monetary authority, the central bank.

The peculiarity of the Eurosystem that brought the system to the verge of collapse and unleashed powers that led to its self-destruction is a third layer of negative externalities in the form of a tragedy of the commons in the monetization of government deficits. Governments of the Eurozone may use a single central banking system to finance their deficits. Banks buy government bonds and the ECB accepts them as collateral for the creation of new base money. Bonds are monetized, increasing the money supply and thus leading to higher prices in the whole Eurozone than otherwise would have been the case. Governments spending faster than others profit from the redistribution of the new money first flowing into their coffers. The initial plan was to curb the tragedy of the commons by the SGP that imposes quotas on the deficits of countries at 3 percent of GDP. As the sovereign debt crisis of 2010 shows, the SGP has failed to restrict deficits. In its current form, the Eurosystem incentivizes the Eurozone member states to incur higher deficits than fellow governments. These incentives will ultimately lead to hyperinflation or massive redistributionist policies.

I have proposed several reforms to alleviate or completely eliminate negative monetary externalities in Europe. A reform and strict enforcement of the SGP would alleviate, and a return to national currencies would eliminate, the tragedy of the commons in the monetization of government deficits. The abolition of central banking would eliminate the externalities of monopolistic base money production. Finally, only a 100 percent commodity standard money would end the tragedy of the commons of fractional reserve banking and close all loopholes in the protection of property rights in money and banking.

In its current form, the Eurosystem is unsustainable and will lead to its own destruction. The monetary future of Europe depends on how far-reaching reform can go.

NOTES

1. As Hoppe (1989, p. 30) points out, all goods are more or less public goods affecting third parties. The degree to which they affect third parties is also constantly changing. Positive effects may even become negative if a person suddenly starts to dislike the flowers planted by the neighbor.
2. For a similar view see Barnett et al. (2010). They define negative externalities as property rights violations. We more precisely define it as effects on third parties resulting from property rights violations or insufficient defined property rights.
3. Note that our definition does not coincide with the orthodox definition of real or technological externalities. Real externalities occur when the action of one individual directly (not through the price system) affects the output of other individuals. Yet, this may happen with or without the defense of private property rights that is the distinctive mark of our definition. If I convince the owner of a scarce resource to give it to me for free or if I get someone's permission to pollute his property, the output of a competing firm is directly affected, even though property rights are not violated.
4. It is true that in a free society no one owns the value of a property, as Rothbard (2001, p. 157) points out in his discussion of external costs. No one owns the value of one's cash balance. Nevertheless, there can be violations of property rights in the monetary realm that affect the value of cash balances and therefore constitute negative externalities. One must not forget that it is the services of a good that make it valuable for an actor. When property rights to money are not defended, the services it provides are affected negatively. Hoppe (1994, pp. 70–71), Hoppe et al. (1998, p. 23 fn. 6) and Huerta de Soto (2009, p. 668) refer to negative externalities resulting from property rights violations in money. The distinction between the value of a property and physical property may explain why the externalities resulting from meddling with property rights in the monetary sphere are sometimes neglected.
5. It is true, as Rothbard argues, that people do not have a right in the value of their money. However, their property rights are violated if they have to obey to legal tender laws and if monopolistic money production exists. These property rights violations cause negative externalities or damage in the form of reduced services that their money yields. The violation of property rights in the monetary sphere reduces the value of their money.
6. Hoppe (1994, pp. 70–71) also points to these negative externalities of fractional reserve banking. When banks expand credits, all depositors are harmed because the likelihood of a successful withdrawal of their deposits is reduced. Furthermore, all borrowers are harmed because credit expansion increases the likelihood of business failure via an Austrian business cycle. In addition, negative externalities of fractional reserve banking concern creditors. When banks violate property rights and expand credits, creditors are hurt as the monetary units they receive will have a lower purchasing power than otherwise. Possible other external costs include menu-costs and coping costs. Actors spend more resources to change prices or to anticipate, influence and deal with the inflationary effects of the property rights violations.
7. One example of this ambiguity are so-called 'time deposits.' In time deposits the saver renounces the availability of the money for a certain term in exchange for interest. Time deposits are loans to the bank; they are not deposits. It adds to the confusion to call them 'time deposits.' The clear distinction between demand deposits and time deposits becomes blurred (Bagus and Howden, 2009a).
8. The two aspects of a tragedy of a commons are fulfilled. There is rivalrous use of the deposits. A bank that does not appropriate and use deposits gives up possible profits out of credit expansion. Any bank that expands credits, thereby leading to a tendency for a lower purchasing power of money, reduces the benefits that other banks can reap from a use of 'their' deposits because the purchasing power of these deposits has fallen. Moreover, no bank can be excluded from the exploitation of the commons because any bank may expand credits legally up to the limit set by the minimum reserve ratio or

other regulation. The tragedy is exacerbated because legal tender laws force people to accept the fiduciary media at par. Even banks must accept deposits created through the credit expansion of rival banks.

9. On the incentives of actors to remove the limits on a tragedy of the commons and convert them into pure tragedy of the commons, see Bagus (2004).

10. The Eurosystem consists of the European Central Bank (ECB) and the national central banks forming part of the Eurozone. The national central banks carry out the policies determined by the ECB.

11. The ECB was modeled after the Bundesbank with the official purpose of being an independent central bank. The sovereign debt crisis of 2010 has severely compromised that original goal as the ECB has changed collateral rules in order support troubled governments and monetizes directly more and more peripheral Euro area debt.

12. Traditionally, central banks have used both ways in financing government debt. America's Federal Reserve System places emphasis on the purchase of government bonds in its open market operations. It also accepts government bonds as collateral in repurchase agreements. Repurchase agreements and other loans in which government bonds were accepted as collateral rose in importance during the financial crisis of 2008. The ECB, on the contrary, has put more emphasis on accepting government bonds in collateralized loans in its lending operations to the banking system. Only during the sovereign debt crisis of 2010 did the ECB start buying government bonds outright. On these central bank policies in the wake of the financial crisis, see Bagus and Howden (2009b) and Bagus and Schiml (2010).

13. In this way we see some similarities between the crisis facing the European insurance industry via the new Solvency II proposals and that facing the ECB via its collateral rules. As Antonio Zanella's chapter in this book argues, Solvency II limits the haircuts that the insurance companies domiciled in the EU must apply to EU member state debt, thus creating an incentive to overload their balance sheets accordingly. Likewise, we see that the ECB has the same incentive – member states' bonds are purchased with the lowest haircut, under the pretense that these are the 'safest' assets that could be held. In both cases the result is the same – an artificially high demand for Euro area government debt.

14. We implicitly assume that the central bank is accommodating and supports the government by monetizing at least a portion of the deficit. There is an inherent tendency for central banks to be accommodating. They are connected with the government – at least through the legal privilege as the monopolist provider of base money politically endowed in them. Their staff is usually appointed by the government. Parliaments may change their legislation and end the banks' 'independence.' As Mankiw makes clear, 'independence was created by Congress, and it can be taken away by Congress' (2007, p. 183). Moreover, one of the official functions of central banks was to stabilize the financial system, i.e. to support the banking system. If a government runs deficits and the central bank does not accommodate them, government bonds will lose value. As banks hold large amounts of government bonds, the banking system may consequently be troubled. When the government finally defaults (because the central bank was not accommodating enough), the banking system is bound to fall.

15. Howden (2010) identifies another aspect of this redistribution. As it cannot continue unheeded forever, knowledge of the extent that it has been undertaken in the past is essential for the successful exit from a credit-induced boom. A hierarchy develops concerning who received the new credit, and when this is occurs a hierarchy also develops concerning who will be most likely to realize when the debt pyramid has become unsustainable and susceptible to collapse. Individuals and small businesses, typically the last in line to access the fresh fractional reserve credit, suffer in a twofold way: first through the reduced purchasing power of their monetary units, and second through their relative lack of knowledge as to whether the situation is sustainable or not.

16. These 'other people' could be German, or even other Greeks who did not originally have access to the new credit.

17. See for these differences also Bagus (2011).
18. See Marsh (2009) for the political road toward the Euro.
19. Bailout guarantees for the banking system increase the amount of undertaken maturity mismatching, as banks are lulled into thinking that the necessary funds to roll over their investments will be forthcoming in the future – whether via a fiscal bailout or an accommodative monetary authority (Bagus, 2010; Bagus and Howden, 2010).
20. Both a monetary growth rule and a reformed SGP would limit the tragedy of the commons. The difference between the two is that in Friedman's proposal a government has a stronger incentive to go directly to the limit. In the SGP, if a government has a deficit below 3 percent it does not mean that other governments can have a deficit higher than 3 percent. The limit is the same for all. Under a monetary growth rule, the fact that one government has no deficits implies that other governments can incur higher deficits. Thus, there is an incentive to incur deficits faster than others to enjoy a higher 'quota'.
21. I have criticized Mises', Rothbard's and Huerta de Soto's plans for being interventionist (Bagus, 2008). All these plans try to avoid a deflation of the money supply and preserve the status quo as much as possible to minimize disruptions. These disruptions will be, nevertheless, of a greater extent than in the aforementioned reforms because companies depending on credit expansion will have to restructure. The government plays a vital role in directing the reform, which gives it the option of revising the reforms at any moment with each new 'problem' that occurs. I also maintain that these reforms are unethical in that they try to maintain the status quo and impose a gold standard, while market participants might prefer other commodities. I develop my own proposal as a way of arriving at such a monetary system free of externalities faster and more efficiently in Bagus (2009). By eliminating all government interventions in the monetary sphere, by getting rid of central banks, the fractional reserve privilege and legal tender laws market participants can choose the money that they prefer. This contains the advantages of being ethical, quick, does not impose the final result, leaves room for entrepreneurial creativity and is not based on an irrational fear of deflation. For a critique of Austrian views on deflation see Bagus (2003).

REFERENCES

Arghyrou, M. and J. Tsoukalas (2010), 'The escalating Greek debt crisis: what has been happening and where is it going?', Roubini Global Economics, www.roubini.com/euro-monitor/258838/the_escalating_greek_debt_crisis__what_has_been_happening_and_where_is_it_going_, 6 May.

Bagus, P. (2003), 'Deflation: when Austrians become interventionists', *Quarterly Journal of Austrian Economics*, **6** (4), 19–35.

Bagus, P. (2004), 'La tragedia de los bienes comunales y la escuela austriaca: Hardin, Hoppe, Huerta de Soto y Mises', *Procesos de Mercado: Revista Europea de Economía Política*, **1** (2), 125–34.

Bagus, P. (2008), 'Monetary reform and deflation: a critique of Mises, Rothbard, Huerta de Soto and Sennholz', *New Perspectives on Political Economy*, **4** (2), 131–57.

Bagus, P. (2009a), 'The quality of money', *Quarterly Journal of Austrian Economics*, **12** (4), 22–45.

Bagus, P. (2009b), 'Monetary reform: the case for button-pushing', *New Perspectives on Political Economy*, **5** (2), 111–28.

Bagus, P. (2010), 'Austrian business cycle theory: are 100 percent reserves sufficient to prevent a business cycle?', *Libertarian Papers*, **2** (2), 1–18.

Bagus, P. (2011), 'The tragedy of the Euro', *Independent Review*, **15** (4), 563–76.

Bagus, P. and D. Howden (2009a), 'The legitimacy of loan maturity mismatching: a risky, but not fraudulent, undertaking', *Journal of Business Ethics*, **90** (3), 399–406.

Bagus, P. and D. Howden (2009b), 'The Federal Reserve and Eurosystem's balance sheet policies during the subprime crisis: a comparative analysis', *Romanian Economic and Business Review*, **4** (3), 165–85.

Bagus, P. and D. Howden (2010), 'The term structure of savings, the yield curve, and maturity mismatching', *Quarterly Journal of Austrian Economics*, **13** (3), 64–85.

Bagus, P. and M. Schiml (2010), 'A cardiograph of the dollar's quality: qualitative easing and the Federal Reserve balance sheet during the subprime crisis', *Prague Economic Papers*, **19** (3), 195–217.

Bandulet, B. (2010), *Die letzten Jahre des Euro. Ein Bericht über das Geld, das die Deutschen nicht wollten*, Rottenburg: Kopp Verlag.

Barnett II, W., W. Block and J. Dauterive (2010), 'Negative externalities of government', *Procesos de Mercado – Revista Europea de Economía Política*, **7** (1), 215–38.

Browne, J. (2010), 'Euro fiasco threatens the world', Triblive, www.pittsburghlive.com/x/pittsburghtrib/opinion/columnists/s_690819.html, 18 July.

Friedman, M. (1960), *A Program for Monetary Stability*, New York: Fordham University Press.

Hardin, G. (1968), 'The tragedy of the commons', *Science*, new series **162** (3859), 1243–8.

Hayek, F.A. (1990), *Denationalisation of Money: The Argument Refined. An Analysis of the Theory and Practice of Concurrent Currencies* (3rd edn), London: Economic Affairs.

Hoppe, H.-H. (1989), 'Fallacies of the public goods theory and the production of security', *Journal of Libertarian Studies*, **9** (1), 27–46.

Hoppe, H.-H. (1994), 'How is fiat money possible? or, the devolution of money and credit', *Review of Austrian Economics*, **7** (2), 49–74.

Hoppe, H.-H., J.G. Hülsmann and W. Block (1998), 'Against fiduciary media', *Quarterly Journal of Austrian Economics*, **1** (1), 19–50.

Howden, D. (2010), 'Knowledge shifts and the business cycle: when boom turns to bust', *Review of Austrian Economics*, **23** (2), 165–82.

Huerta de Soto, J. (2009), *Money, Bank Credit, and Economic Cycles* (2nd edn), Auburn, AL: Ludwig von Mises Institute.

Jones, M. (2010), 'EU will accept even junk-rated Greek bonds', Reuters, http://in.reuters.com/article/idINIndia-48186920100503, 3 May.

Mankiw, N.G. (2007), 'A letter to Ben Bernanke', *American Economic Review*, **96** (2), 182–4.

Marsh, D. (2009), *Der Euro – Die geheime Geschichte der neuen Weltwährung*, trans. F. Griese, Hamburg: Murmann.

Mises, L. von ([1953] 1981), *The Theory of Money and Credit*, Indianapolis: Liberty Fund.

Mises, L. von ([1949] 1998), *Human Action: Scholar's Edition*, Auburn, AL: Ludwig von Mises Institute.

Nazareth, R. and G. Serkin (2010), 'Stocks, commodities, Greek bonds rally on European loan package', Bloomberg, http://noir.bloomberg.com/apps/news?pid=newsarchive&sid=albR_vFvAad4, 10 May.

Neuger, J.G. and R. Buergin (2010), 'EU leaves Euro deficit penalties in political hands', Bloomberg, http://noir.bloomberg.com/apps/news?pid=newsarchive&si d=aohFfddJKSpk, 19 October.

Prest, A.R. and R. Turvey (1965), 'Cost–benefit analysis: a survey', *Economic Journal*, **75**, 683–735.

Reisman, G. (2000), 'The goal of monetary reform', *Quarterly Journal of Austrian Economics*, **3** (3), 3–18.

Rothbard, M.N. (1983), *The Mystery of Banking*, New York: Richardson & Snyder.

Rothbard, M.N. (1991), *The Case for a 100 Percent Gold Dollar*, Auburn, AL: Ludwig von Mises Institute.

Rothbard, M.N. (1994), *The Case Against the Fed*, Auburn, AL: Ludwig von Mises Institute.

Samuelson, R. (2010), 'Greece and the welfare state in ruins', Real Clear Politics, www.realclearpolitics.com/articles/2010/02/22/greece_and_the_welfare_state_ in_ruins.html, 22 February.

Selgin, G. (1988), *The Theory of Free Banking*, Totowa, NJ: Rowman and Littlefield.

Tarullo, D.K. (2010), 'International response to European debt problems', testimony before the Subcommittee on International Monetary Policy and Trade and Subcommittee on Domestic Monetary Policy and Technology, Committee on Financial Services, US House of Representatives, Washington, DC, www. federalreserve.gov/newsevents/testimony/tarullo20100520a.htm, 20 May.

Thesing, G. and F. Krause-Jackson (2010), 'Greece gets $146 billion rescue in EU, IMF package', Bloomberg, http://noir.bloomberg.com/apps/news?pid=newsarc hive&sid=alJWdKeR1TDU, 3 May.

Vaubel, R. (1986), 'Currency competition vs. government money monopolies', *Cato Journal*, **5** (3), 927–47.

White, L. (1984), *Free Banking in Britain: Theory, Experience, and Debate, 1800– 1845*, New York: Cambridge University Press.

8. Fiscal stimulus, financial ruin

Fernando Ulrich

With few exceptions, the current European sovereign debt ordeal is a direct consequence of Keynesian policies aimed at tackling the financial crisis. The wrong medicine can not only be ineffective, but also, in many cases, fatal.

Before attempting to demonstrate why and how the Keynesian fiscal stimulus is a misconceived idea and a recipe for disaster from the onset, we must put matters into context. With that in mind, let us understand the sequence of events that led to the current predicament. Triggered by the subprime crisis and the eventual burst of the housing bubble in the US in 2007, the financial turmoil soon spread to Europe and the whole world, leading central bankers to unprecedented measures to avoid a total economic collapse. By late that year, the credit crunch had forced monetary authorities to take immediate actions to safeguard liquidity.

At the next G-20 meeting, world leaders reached a consensus with regards to the need for additional measures to avert a global economic collapse. The Washington Summit's declaration suggested the 'use of fiscal measures to stimulate domestic demand to rapid effect' (G-20, 2008).

The then British prime minister Gordon Brown was heeding the advice of Paul Krugman, that year's Nobel economics prize winner, and leading the world to take appropriate and immediate fiscal measures. Professor Krugman in turn praised the prime minister's leadership stance as a probable 'savior' of the world's financial system while urging world leaders to avoid 'thinking too small' with respect to fiscal stimulus packages (Parker, 2008).

Keynesian economics was definitely alive and well. The policy recommendations of the most well-known British economist of the 20th century culminated in a communiqué issued by the Commission to the European Council on 26 November 2008 delineating its European Economic Recovery Plan, in which it essentially recommended that member states embarked on budgetary stimulus packages in order to boost aggregate demand in the short term and avoid further deterioration of unemployment and GDP growth rates (Commission to the European Council, 2010). Despite being already in breach of the European Union's (EU) fiscal rule book, which sets limits to budget deficit to GDP ratio at 3 percent and debt to GDP ratio at 60 percent, several countries embraced the Keynesian budgetary impulse recommendations, jeopardizing their fiscal sustainability. At the end of 2008 budget deficits in Spain, Ireland, France, Poland, and the United Kingdom were all above the 3 percent limit established by the Maastricht Treaty. Public indebtedness in Italy, Belgium, Hungary, France, Germany, Portugal and Austria was also exceeding the 60 percent of gross domestic product rule.

By May 2009 monetary policy's room for maneuver was virtually non-existent. The federal funds rate had been set a few months before at the range between zero and 25 basis points, the Bank of England's official bank rate was defined at 0.5 percent and the European Central Bank (ECB) set its target for the main refinancing operations rate at 100 basis points. In its entire history, the Bank of England had never before lowered its official rate below 2 percent, not even in times of crisis such as World Wars I and II or the Great Depression. In a scenario of unprecedented near-zero interest rates, deficit spending seemed to be the sole means of reviving an ailing economy – at least in the eyes of Keynesian economists.[1]

According to the Public Finances in EMU Report of 2009 the scale of the measures varied strongly from one member state to another. Adopted or announced fiscal stimulus packages by member states amounted to 1.1 percent of EU GDP. Spain headed the list of budgetary expansion in that year, reaching 2.3 percent of GDP in stimulus spending, while outside the Euro area the United Kingdom took the lead, adding 1.4 percent of its gross domestic product in additional deficit spending. Approximately a year after the fiscal measures were adopted in the EU, the solvency of some member states was already being questioned by the financial markets, especially in Greece, where the official figures were pending validation from Eurostat. In its 2009 autumn economic forecast the European Commission raised concerns about the increasing likelihood of deteriorating public finances in the EU. Such concerns were duly deserved; according to Eurostat, the Euro area general government deficit in 2009 was 6.3 percent of GDP. Apart from Luxembourg and Finland, all Euro area countries reported a deficit in excess of 3 percent of GDP. In addition to exceeding the deficit rule, indebtedness ratios were markedly high too. The general government debt for the Euro area stood at 78.7 percent of GDP in 2009. Ten Euro area countries out of 16 surpassed the 60 percent of GDP reference value, and it was well above 100 percent of GDP in the cases of Greece and Italy. In particular strong increases in government indebtedness were witnessed in Ireland, Greece and Spain, which recorded budget deficits above 10 percent of GDP in 2009.

The sovereign debt crisis in Greece was intensifying in 2010 and by April of the same year Greek bond spreads (vis-à-vis Germany) and credit default swaps spreads were already widening as negotiations between the European Union and International Monetary Fund (IMF) were taking place. In order to avoid contagion to other peripheral European countries such as Ireland, Portugal, and Spain, a rescue package of €110 billion was unveiled by both organizations. A week after Greece's bail-out, on 10 May 2010, the EU and the IMF announced a further €750 billion in rescue funds for fear that Spain, Portugal and Ireland might go the way of Greece. It soon became evident that European sovereign debt was on a dangerous trend and unless governments resorted to fiscal responsibility backed by credible austerity measures, the erosion of confidence in financial markets could further hamper the economic recovery. Greece was just the trigger of an already worrying situation, namely, fiscal sustainability.

FISCAL STIMULUS: A RECIPE FOR DISASTER

Before answering the question of why Keynesian fiscal stimulus is a road to poverty, it is expedient to understand how Keynesians see the world and why this view is simply fallacious. In most modern mainstream economics textbooks one will encounter the following definition of national income, that is, a nation's total output.

$$Y = C + I + G$$

where Y stands for national income, C for private consumption, I for investment and G for government purchases (Krugman, 2003, p. 300). Gross domestic product is the equation above plus exports minus imports.

The standard national income equation is outright erroneous. Governments do not add to a nation's economy since each and every resource the government spends or transfers has to be either taxed or borrowed from its citizens, namely the private sector. Therefore, one cannot simplistically add government expenditures to a nation's total output; public spending is actually a subtraction of private sector consumption or investment. Given their monopolistic nature, government services are not tested in the free market, thus it is not possible to estimate the government's actual contribution to the economy. Additionally, the government's tax revenue and deficit revenue both burden the production capacity of a society. Therefore, public expenditures are more likely to be depredations upon, rather than contributions to, production. Consequently, in order to estimate an economy's total output correctly, it would be more appropriate to deduct government purchases from total national income (Rothbard, 2009, p. 1293).[2]

With regards to gross domestic product (GDP) accounting it is crucial to note that current methods of calculation exclude a significant part of a nation's economic activity, that is, the intermediate stages of production. As a result consumption represents a substantial amount of modern GDP metrics, overestimating its relative importance in the economy. Thus, economists and politicians alike tend to exaggerate the essential role consumption plays in an economy. The current national statistics neglect the effects that monetary expansions and contractions have on the productive stages furthest from consumption. In contrast to what is commonly understood, gross national product statistics are actually 'a net figure that excludes the value of all intermediate capital goods which at the end of the measurement period become available as inputs for the next financial year' (Huerta de Soto, 2006, pp. 418–20). Hence, a substantial part of the entrepreneurial efforts dispensed in the productive stages of the economy are miscomputed. Consumption is then exaggerated in gross national product figures, implying that society can in fact consume more than is produced. It inverses the cause-and-effect relationship of production and consumption, fitting perfectly the Keynesian focus on aggregate demand and its flawed national income equation.

HOARDING AND THE PARADOX OF THRIFT

Keynes was unable to understand the structure of production and its different stages. Lacking an adequate theory of capital, the Keynesian system cannot conceive how an initial increase in savings would add to the pool of loanable funds decreasing the rate of interest and thus causing changes in relative prices, enabling a lengthening of the structure of production. Garrison provides an adequate definition, clarifying that 'in its strictest interpretation, the structure of production is conceptualized as a continuous-input/point-output process' (2001, p. 46). This is shown in Figure 8.1.

Contrary to the Keynesian doctrine, hoarding, that is, saving, does not constitute a sociological problem in need of correction. It is in fact the prerequisite for investment and the ensuing capital accumulation, which increases the productivity of the economy, leading to a higher standard of living. Huerta de Soto further clarifies:

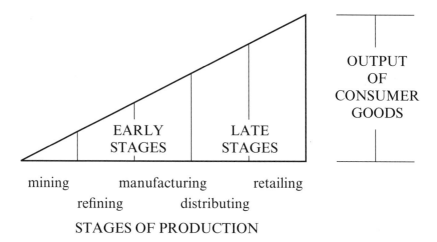

Source: Garrison (2001, p. 47).

Figure 8.1   The structure of production

the main error in the theory of the paradox of thrift consists of the fact that
it ignores the basic principles of capital theory and does not treat the productive structure as a series of consecutive stages. Instead it contains the implicit
assumption that only two stages exist, one of final aggregate consumer demand
and another made up of a single set of intermediate investment stages. (Huerta
de Soto, 2006, p. 343 fn. 58)

When individuals change their time preferences and increase their
savings, that is, reduce present consumption patterns in order to consume
more at a later stage, it causes a lengthening of the structure of production,
as can be seen in Figure 8.2.

Keynesian theory provides a different assessment, though. Since the
production structure is not part of its capital theory, Keynesians see
only half of the picture, literally. They only draw attention to the fall in
consumption, but not the eventual effects in the stages of production, as
depicted in Figure 8.3.

It is wrongly assumed that no change in the capital stock or configu-
ration takes place, causing a decrease in 'aggregate demand'. Given the
Keynesian framework, one can easily understand why a decrease in consumption poses a grave torment for policymakers.

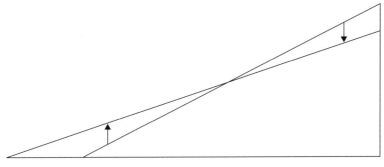

STAGES OF PRODUCTION

Source: Garrison (2001, p. 62).

Figure 8.2   Savings-induced capital restructuring

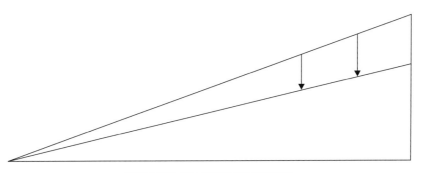

STAGES OF PRODUCTION

Source: Adapted from Garrison (2001, p. 163).

Figure 8.3   Keynesian view of increase in savings

THE MULTIPLIER

The multiplier concept developed by Keynes is one of the widely used 'theoretical justifications' for public investment. Although it is a highly dubious concept, as we shall analyse, there has been ample literature on the multiplier's magical effects, which for policymakers is a blessing, since it enables them to substantiate the public works' alleged benefits to society. In the words of Keynes: 'Let us call *k* the investment multiplier. It tells us that, when there is an increment of aggregate investment, income will increase by an amount which is *k* times the increment of investment' (1936, p. 115).

According to Keynes, consumption is a stable function of income. Therefore, we can infer that, for the sake of simplicity, that consumption will always be 0.80 (income). The equation would be as follows:

$$\text{Income} = 0.80\,(\text{Income}) + \text{Investment}$$
$$0.20\,(\text{Income}) = \text{Investment; or}$$
$$\text{Income} = 5\,(\text{Investment}).$$

The '5' is the 'investment multiplier'. Consequently, all we need to increase social income by a desired amount is to increase investment by 1/5 of that amount; and the multiplier should take care of the rest. As will be developed further below, Keynesians realized that to rely on a volatile factor, such as private investment, was too uncertain, concluding that government should step in to provide the extra spending when the private sector failed to do so. The optimal solution would be by means of credit creation so that governments would not need to resort to private funds. Hence, as Rothbard asserts (2009, p. 867), the basis for calling all government spending 'investment': it is 'investment' because it is not tied passively to income.

What Lord Keynes suggests is that the more people spend, the more their income will grow, leading the reader to conclude that if a community spends none of its additional income but saves all of it,

> then the public works will give only the additional employment that they themselves provide, and that will be the end of it. But if a community spends all of the additional income provided by the public works, then the multiplier is infinity. This would mean that a small expenditure on public works would increase income without limit, provided only that the community was not poisoned by the presence of savers. (Hazlitt, 1959, pp. 135–55)

In the end the investment multiplier concept is in fact nothing but a subterfuge for justifying further government spending (Hazlitt, 1959, p. 148). A diligent analysis reveals that Keynes is not preoccupied with real investment aimed at increasing productivity and reducing costs. What he really means is any spending regardless of an economic justification. Through the use of subtle and indirect language, Keynes skillfully advocates more public spending. Although he never really explicitly linked the investment multiplier with government spending, it is nowadays commonplace to associate the multiplier effect with public spending.[3] In fact, multiplier, investment multiplier, fiscal multiplier, government multiplier and spending multiplier are terms used interchangeably even in academia.

Recently there have been several studies and researches attempting to quantify the multiplier in our present context. In a scenario of near-zero interest rates, different papers have been put forward in order to estimate the multiplier effect generated by fiscal stimulus. Fujiwara and Ueda (2010) have found that the fiscal multiplier exceeds one in a global liquidity trap, that is, near-zero interest rates. Eggertsson (2009, p. 19) on the other hand strives to analyse not only fiscal stimulus, but also different kinds of tax cuts which can positively or negatively impact the multiplier. Nevertheless, the conclusions go along the same Keynesian theory: lack of sufficient aggregate demand requires government spending, and maybe 'a commitment to inflate'.

We must ask ourselves: can the models be relied upon for policy-making? When one understands government can only acquire resources from the private sector either through borrowing or taxation (inflation being a hidden tax), one presupposes the 'fiscal' multiplier must contemplate the loss of the private sector. If we take into consideration the fact that public spending takes the form of projects with questionable economic content, the multiplier calculations should also include such wasteful spending.

By employing mathematical models economists try to find direct connections between government expenditure and private investment and consumption. Those models struggle to define functions of government spending with business activities. Companies do not take decisions; behind every enterprise there are real-life entrepreneurs and managers who act according to price signals provided by the market and a multitude of other factors which no single model can contemplate in their entirety. In other words, these models attempt to find constancy in the field of human action, where we only find infinite variables, but certainly no constants (Mises, 1998, p. 103). Conclusively, the multiplier concept lacks a sound theoretical foundation, rendering any attempt to rationalize fiscal stimulus through the use of multiplier estimates highly questionable, if not useless.

WHY FISCAL STIMULUS IS NOT THE ANSWER

Synonyms for fiscal stimulus include 'contracyclical policies', 'budgetary impulse', 'budgetary expansion' and 'deficit spending'. In simple language it is additional government expenditure financed with borrowed money. By definition a stimulus is something that rouses or incites activity; it is something that has an impact, impulse or influence on a system.[4] If an object needs stimulation, it follows that it is simply not responding in accordance to its normal functioning. If stimulation is needed in an economy, one infers that it is not responding the way it should, prompting action by government. The economy is lethargic. So goes the traditional thinking.

One of the main flaws in Keynesian and mainstream economics is an inadequacy to understand what is causing an economy to be in such a mode. As exposed previously in this chapter, in the absence of a correct and sound theory, the answers never point to the appropriate solution. Actually, not only are the wrong answers put forward, but irrelevant questions are also raised.

Why is consumption falling? This question is neglected and focus is instead turned toward the prescription. Government must step in to revive total aggregate demand in support of a falling private demand. So advise the Keynesian experts. Contracyclical policy means policy aimed at countering the cycle. Keynesian and mainstream economists alike do recognize that there is a business cycle; they fail to understand, however, why there is a cycle.[5] This is a key point. It is as if business cycles were a given in Keynesian theory: they simply exist. It is hardly surprising that the prescriptions focus on the symptoms rather than on the underlying causes, reinforcing the problems instead of alleviating them.

Credit expansion not backed by a commensurate increase in real savings sends false signals to entrepreneurs who are misled to embark in investment projects as if the necessary resources were actually available for their completion. Consumption patterns have not changed, that is, time preference has not been altered, but credit creation masks precisely this fact. Fiduciary media have increased, while the pool of loanable funds remains unchanged. This phenomenon causes an inflationary boom which brings about large-scale malinvestments, since not all projects can come to fruition because there are insufficient resources. Eventually, unviable businesses will have to be liquidated, turning the previous boom into the inevitable recession.

During this phase all unprofitable ventures are liquidated so the economy can reassign the resources to viable businesses once again. Although the public at large would like to avoid unwanted suffering, the inescapable outcome of an unsustainable boom is malinvestment, that means, businesses which should not have been even initiated. Therefore, redundancies and bankrupt firms are inherent to a boom and bust cycle. Allowing for an as frictionless process as possible is all that is required from governments, as it will accelerate the profitable reallocation of resources, ensuring a solid and sustainable recovery.

The conventional wisdom sees the recession as the stage of the business cycle where all the misfortune takes place: lay-offs, bankruptcies, debt defaults, among others. Depressions are inherent to the market economy, Keynesian economists contend. Governments are supposedly responsible for restoring 'economic stability'. This is where monetary policy and fiscal policy should intervene and guarantee economy activity do not recede.

Considering the theoretical background explained above, one can already sense how deficit spending may in fact only worsen the predicament, as we will attempt to demonstrate next. If governments are only able to employ resources previously appropriated from the private sector (via taxation or borrowing) it is simply not possible to invest without divesting from somewhere else in the economy. Public investment necessarily entails private divestiture. Consequently, the much sought after 'increase in aggregate demand' is nothing but a misconceived notion. Egger exposed further how it is a wholly fictitious concept:

> Aggregate demand is an unintended result of individuals' actions and has no causal role in determining them. But if aggregate demand is irrelevant to action and has no meaning in an analysis of the functioning of a market system, there can be no standard for determining that it falls short of some ideal, and there can be no such thing as unemployment caused specifically by this shortfall. (As quoted in Skousen, 1992, p. 43)

Entrepreneurship and profits have no place in Keynesian economics. As the title of his notorious work denotes, his main concern is employment. Thus, it is of little significance, according to Keynes, if public investment is in fact productive and resources are efficiently utilized. What matters first and foremost is whether people are employed.

As Egger succinctly explained, it is essential to understand that 'all unemployment is caused by mispricing, and none by insufficient aggregate demand' (ibid.). Profits arise from the differential between revenue and costs. Entrepreneurs are concerned with the differentials in relative prices and not with an increase or fall in the general level of prices. Any attempt to expand the money supply by means of extra central bank liquidity will only aggravate the distortions, preventing companies from adjusting their businesses and correcting the aforementioned mispricing. 'This, in turn, implies that a policy designed to reduce unemployment by bringing aggregate demand closer to its ideal is fundamentally misconceived from the start. The result is typical of well-intentioned efforts to solve problems that do not exist: the problems that do exist are made worse', concludes Egger (as quoted in Skousen, 1992, p. 43).

In addition, government expenditure and investment contributions to society are at the very least highly questionable, since there is no rational way for governments to base their investment decisions. Moreover, the whole process tends to be excessively politicized (Rothbard, 2009, p. 938).

Without the profit motive, government employment of resources is by definition inefficient. According to Mises: 'While government has no power to make people more prosperous by interference with business, it certainly does have the power to make them less satisfied by restriction of production . . . Spending and unbalanced budgets are merely synonyms for capital consumption' (1998, pp. 737 and 845).[6] The only viable contracyclical policy is to refrain from monetary expansion at the outset. All other attempts will only attenuate the crisis, attacking symptoms but not the root cause of economic cycles.

A NOTE ON MONETARY POLICY

It is important to understand the distinction between monetary and fiscal policy and how each affects the economy. Monetary policy is the management of the money supply by the monetary authority. Usually this function rests with the central bank. Among other methods, a central bank manipulates interest rates to effect its policy targets. Monetary policy finds its way to the economy through the banking system. When the central bank lowers interest rates below what the free market would otherwise have set, it generates a credit-induced boom. Private business and consumers borrow cheap money to embark in seemingly viable projects, which turn out to be unprofitable once inflation sets in, raising prices throughout the economy.

Fiscal policy, though, is government expenditure financed either by taxation or borrowing. Consequently, public spending is often voted through congress in democratic countries. It is political rather than economical, as is the case in the private sector. Governments can spend regardless of profitability, whereas the private businesses must make a minimum of economic calculation prior to employing its resources in order to ensure they are efficiently used. Despite having this 'advantage', governments cannot spend at will; their spending depends on their capacity to tax and borrow. When the former seems to have no room left for maneuver, the latter is resorted to. Governments will be able to keep borrowing as long as financial markets remain confident the ability to service the debt is unshaken. As will be developed further below, 'PIIGS' countries (Portugal, Italy, Ireland, Greece and Spain) appear to have approached this limit.

Monetary policy effects are not immediately perceived in the real economy, since it involves banks lending to worthy borrowers, who in turn must borrow based on the expected profitable use of those funds. Banks cannot force businesses to borrow, just as the latter cannot force the former to lend. If both banks and businesses are reluctant to lend and borrow, monetary policy loses its effectiveness. Thus, if risk and uncertainty become so pervasive the private sector will come to a halt.[7] Public and private indebtedness have reached such colossal levels that attempting to reflate a bubble with an even more aggressive monetary policy might not work.[8]

This is the exact moment where Keynesians claim that fiscal policy can 'do the trick', and rightly so. Fiscal policy can indeed put 'idle resources' to work on shorter notice than monetary policy. However, that rests on the government's monopoly in the use of force with regards to appropriation of resources. It can tax, it can borrow and it can resort to the printing press. In other words, the damage can be done much sooner. Though it may appear that the economy is 'moving', the malinvestments are being intensified, ensuring an even worse recession thereafter. Hence, Keynesians are right to proclaim that deficit spending can boost aggregate demand in the short term, but this is at the expense of more misallocation of resources, wasteful spending, and ultimately a compounded recession.

EUROPE'S TREATIES AND INSTITUTIONS

The EU Treaty and Price Stability

Before analysing the European System of Central Banks (ESCB) and the ECB, it is expedient briefly to outline the main articles and clauses which institute, delineate and establish the workings of the financial system in the European Union.

Among several other objectives, Article 3 of the Lisbon Treaty states

> the Union shall establish an internal market. It shall work for the sustainable development of Europe based on balanced economic growth and price stability, a highly competitive social market economy, aiming at full employment and social progress, and a high level of protection and improvement of the quality of the environment. It shall promote scientific and technological advance.

On the Treaty's establishment, it was resolved that monetary policy for member states whose currency is the Euro would be conducted by the Union, which delegated this power to the ECB, the main institution in the European System of Central Banks.

Abdicating control over monetary policy deserves special attention, since it directly affects how individual government finances are run. Prior to the creation of the Euro, each member state functioned with its own central bank or a similar body in charge of monetary policy, which inevitably provided an implicit guarantee that its government could be bailed out in times of need, that is, the national currency could be inflated to avoid outright default. Under the present arrangement, governments face stricter budget constraints enforced by a supranational body. Logically, by being signatories of the treaties which established the system, they were well aware of the consequences. However, the reality now imposed by the ESCB may have been tougher than initially anticipated.

According to Article 127 of the Treaty on the Functioning of the European Union, the primary objective of the ESCB shall be:

> to maintain price stability. Without prejudice to the objective of price stability, the ESCB shall support the general economic policies in the Union with a view to contributing to the achievement of the objectives of the Union as laid down in Article 3 of the Treaty on European Union. The ESCB shall act in accordance with the principle of an open market economy with free competition, favoring an efficient allocation of resources, and in compliance with the principles set out in Article 119.

It is worth examining one specific paragraph of the aforementioned Article 119, which prescribes that the economic policies 'of the Member States and the Union shall entail compliance with the following guiding principles: stable prices, *sound public finances* and monetary conditions and a sustainable balance of payments' (emphasis added).

Ample independence was granted to the ECB for achieving the Union's objective of price stability, as set out in Article 130:

> When exercising the powers and carrying out the tasks and duties conferred upon them by this Treaty and the Statute of the ESCB, neither the ECB, nor a national central bank, nor any member of their decision-making bodies shall seek or take instructions from Community institutions or bodies, from any government of a Member State or from any other body. The Community institutions and bodies and the governments of the Member States undertake to respect this principle and not to seek to influence the members of the decision-making bodies of the ECB or of the national central banks in the performance of their tasks.

Since the Lisbon Treaty does not give a precise definition of what is meant by *price stability*, the ECB's governing council assumed responsibility and clearly and quantitatively defined it as 'a year-on-year increase in the Harmonised Index of Consumer Prices (HICP) for the euro area of below 2%'. Moreover, the ECB clarifies: 'By referring to "an increase in the HICP of below 2%" the definition makes clear that not only inflation above 2 percent but also deflation (i.e. price level declines) is inconsistent with price stability.'[9] It also underlines the ECB's commitment to:

provide an adequate margin to avoid the risks of deflation. Having such a safety margin against deflation is important because nominal interest rates cannot fall below zero. In a deflationary environment monetary policy may thus not be able to sufficiently stimulate aggregate demand by using its interest rate instrument. This makes it more difficult for monetary policy to fight deflation than to fight inflation.[10]

The European Economic Recovery Plan

As of late 2008, the consensus among policymakers was that they needed to prevent 'aggregate demand' from falling further and avoid a deflationary scenario at all costs. Bearing this in mind, the European Commission set out to design an emergency plan to stimulate demand and boost consumer confidence in the Eurozone, under the title of European Economic Recovery Plan. Though it did contain important measures with a view to promote entrepreneurship, such as tax reductions and fewer bureaucratic requirements, it was extremely ambitious. In one shot, the plan was aiming at: reducing unemployment, fostering entrepreneurship, increasing world trade, tackling climate change, and, of course, promoting social justice.

Its commissioners, headed by José Manuel Durão Barroso, wanted to show leadership and courageousness amid the worst financial crisis since the Great Depression. Unfortunately, it was an ill-conceived plan, recommending that member states expand their budgets at an approximate level of 1.5 percent of GDP, which would result in a total impact of €200 billion. Obviously, some countries were already so fiscally constrained that they simply lacked any room for maneuver in order to comply with the Maastricht Treaty. Others, however, were still able to embark on deficit spending despite risking surpassing the limits in the Union.

Despite any good intentions it might have contained, the plan was contradictory and would result in further misallocations of scarce resources, precisely the opposite of what the economy needs during a recession. The plan intended to direct action to 'smart investment', which meant 'investing in energy efficiency to create jobs and save energy; investing in clean technologies to boost sectors like construction and automobiles in the low-carbon markets of the future; and investing in infrastructure and interconnection to promote efficiency and innovation'. Diverting resources to 'green' investments does not render them more efficient. When projects are artificially brought about – that is, they are being subsidized – it necessarily deprives other lines of businesses of those very same resources. The profit and loss system is the yardstick which measures efficiency. If we need to consume more resources in order to produce the same output of energy we promote the opposite of what is intended: efficiency.

Investing for the sake of investing; that is the classic Keynesian recipe for curing unemployment. The underlying rationale is to get people to work immediately, regardless of profitability. A project which consumes the least amount of resources possible is the actual environmentally friendly investment. Only the profit and loss system can really gauge how energy efficient a project is. Subsidizing an 'eco-friendly' venture to create jobs in a given field ultimately means destroying jobs elsewhere in the economy.[11]

Infrastructure is always the obvious choice for politicians, after all: roads, bridges, broadband internet connection, ports, railroads, among others, are always needed in the economy. The main problem, however, is that governments cannot calculate economically in order to decide rationally where to invest resources; the decision is to a great extent driven by politics, not economics. Therefore, although enlarging an important street in the city centre might be extremely useful, resources might be more urgently needed in other branches of business. Government cannot discriminate which investments are more appropriate; only entrepreneurs competing for resources in a free market can. Hence, a recovery plan which aims to direct investment to chosen lines of the economy, stimulating 'green' projects, promoting social justice, and simultaneously reducing unemployment is theoretically impossible.

One must at least wonder whether governments are indeed able to cure the economy 'surgically'. The Commission recommended a budget stimulus package 'which should be timely, targeted and temporary, to be implemented immediately', and 'member States should commit to reverse the budgetary deterioration and return to the aims set out in the medium term objectives'. That means the right amount of projects, directed at the right sectors, at the right time and immediately. And the final ingredient – governments should be in charge of executing them. If governments do have this ability, why were they shelving such beneficial projects until now?

The plan also advised countries to engage in structural reforms to enable them to return to indebtedness levels consistent with the Stability and Growth Pact over the medium and long term. Additionally, the plan would ensure the reversibility of measures increasing deficits in the short term. In other words, spend now and deal with deficits later. The political process is intricate and complex; approving public expenditure and increasing deficits is relatively uncomplicated. Removing expenditure, reducing subsidies, cutting benefits and promoting structural reforms are extremely lengthy and strenuous undertakings. Advising countries to spend now and save later is simply disingenuous.

In conclusion, it was an overly ambitious plan, based on false premises with contradictory objectives and disastrous fiscal and economic consequences.

Implications for and Independence of the ECB

The dangerous loophole of not precisely defining what price stability means allows for a clever artifice which the ECB can use should the financial crisis intensify. Ben Bernanke, chairman of the US Federal Reserve (Fed), has already started to revise the Fed's own price stability definition, affirming that higher inflation rates might be pursued by the American monetary authority (Harding, 2010).

Furthermore, current price stability is measured by a consumer price index, which excludes important asset classes such as real estate and the stock market. Actually, it is an ongoing debate among central banks throughout the globe whether monetary policy should also target these other classes to prevent asset bubbles from forming (Smaghi, 2009). The pre-crisis consensus was that focusing on consumer prices provided an adequate and sufficient means of maintaining price and economic stability. In hindsight, it is undeniable that central banks failed miserably in this task.

In fact, the debate on monetary stabilization and prevention of cycles, presently referred to as price stability, dates back a couple of centuries, with the banking and currency school as protagonists. Attempting to bring about price stability, that is, stable purchasing power, through price indices is an extremely difficult task since there is no perfect and accurate method for measuring changes in the purchasing power. It is impossible to realize the ideal of either a monetary unit of unchanging value or economic stability (Mises, 2006, pp. 137–9). By focusing on an aggregate level of prices, monetary authorities miss the really crucial effect of monetary expansion: changes in relative prices throughout the economy. Monetary stabilization is theoretically not sufficient for the prevention of economic crises. Empirically, central banks cannot deny this conclusion either.

The European Central Bank specifically, and central banks in general, ironically strive to fight the two outcomes of their own policies: inflation and deflation. A monetary expansion not backed by real savings will eventually turn a boom into a bust. A previous inflation, that is, credit expansion, must inexorably lead to a deflation, namely, credit contraction. This contraction causes a fall in the general level of prices. In order to combat deflation the ECB is forced to pursue a further inflationary policy by lowering interest rates. Nonetheless, the central bank is limited by the zero lower-bound of interest rate setting. Unfortunately, it does not mean that the monetary authority options are immediately exhausted; the bank can still directly purchase assets in the open market, such as government or private bonds, among other asset classes. By focusing on an inflation

target the ECB must expand the money supply. It then attempts to manipulate it, utilizing as a yardstick the consumer price index, thus permitting
asset bubbles to form elsewhere in the economy. When the unsustainable
asset prices burst, an eventual contraction in the money supply ensues,
lowering the general level of prices. Decreases in prices will soon be verified in the consumer price index. Thus, to bring the inflation target in line
with its mandate, the ECB must expand the money supply. This is the
vicious circle story of central banks. The Keynesian faulty concept of
aggregate demand permeates not only the ECB's policies, but also almost
every monetary authority in the Western world.

With regards to its autonomy and independence, we must ask ourselves,
is the ECB genuinely independent? Can it exercise its mandate while avert-
ing any influence from Community institutions or bodies, from any government of a member state or from any other body?

On 10 May 2010 the ECB announced it would 'conduct interventions
in the Euro area public and private debt securities markets (Securities
Markets Programme) to ensure depth and liquidity in those market seg-
ments which are dysfunctional'.[12] In layman's terms, it will step in and buy
securities if nobody else is willing to purchase them. Logically, the recent
change in stance by the ECB was contingent on countries taking 'all measures needed to meet their fiscal targets this year and the years ahead in line
with excessive deficit procedures'. It is significant that directly intervening
in bond markets had been avoided by the ECB since its inception, as it
did not want to compromise its independence nor confuse monetary with
fiscal policies.

Although being certainly independent on the surface, the ECB's decisions are affected by the economic policies and public finances of member
states.[13] Furthermore, through its interventions in public securities
markets, it does blur the line dividing monetary and fiscal policy, precisely
what was to be avoided. Besides jeopardizing its independence, the purchase of government bonds by the ECB adds another ingredient to the
predicament – moral hazard. Frugal countries are encouraged to incur
in deficit spending once they perceive that the monetary authority will
accommodate any fiscal constraints.[14]

A NOTE ON FISCAL DEFICITS

The current deterioration in the public finances of European countries
does not indicate, however, the extent of the necessary structural adjustments required. As lucidly explained in an IMF working paper, by April
or May 2010 financial markets:

began to question the ability of some euro-zone members to make good on their debt payments to creditors. This resulted in temporary panic, with spiking spreads on government bonds. What this episode reflected was a manifestation of the unyielding force of what economists call 'the intertemporal budget constraint,' which requires governments to be able to generate enough fiscal surpluses in the future (in excess of their interest payment needs) to meet their current (net) debt obligations. Often thought of as a mere theoretical concept that only applies in the long run, this constraint can become binding much sooner, if fiscal imbalances, coupled with a weak outlook, become so large that they are no longer thought of as sustainable, thus telescoping problems seemingly operating on a long-term horizon back into the present. (Velculescu, 2010, p. 3)

Under the Excessive Deficit Procedure, countries are required to undertake large fiscal reforms in order to return to the limits prescribed by the Maastricht Treaty. Deficits and indebtedness measured by traditional indicators lack a highly important quality: they are not forward looking. Unfunded liabilities such as pension schemes are not reflected in the commonly used indicators such as budget deficits (overall, primary and structural), gross debt and even public sector financial net worth. Demographics will weigh heavily in member states which have not yet engaged in structural reforms, increasing their long-term fiscal gap.[15] Consequently, while countries may be embarking on budget constraints on the short term, their efforts might not be sufficient to meet liabilities over longer horizons. Conclusively, as the IMF paper suggests, efforts required to satisfy the Maastricht deficit procedure by 2012 would be inadequate and insufficient to eliminate the long-term liabilities and the subsequent fiscal needs.

In a recent interview for the Council of Foreign Relations (CFR), Alan Greenspan uttered a few words which should be analysed, for their implications are not wholly appreciated by politicians and Keynesian economists alike (CFR, 2010). Asked to comment on debt to GDP forecasts by official agencies which indicate serious concerns on the long-term sustainability of fiscal deficits, the former Fed chairman answered that he feared 'we are running out of real resources'. Underlying Greenspan's statement, which has passed largely unnoticed by economists and the media, is the fact that money is nothing but a medium enabling exchanges between real goods and services. As long as it is still being commonly accepted by market participants, its main purpose, among others, is to serve as a medium of exchange. It facilitates and eases transactions. When a venture is incurring losses, monetarily it means the intake of money units is lower than the expended money units. Non-monetarily, it is the signal that more resources are being consumed than produced.

When actuarial estimates indicate that there is a funding gap in social security, public pension schemes, healthcare and similar programs, it means there are not enough resources to meet all the commitments pledged by various governmental agencies. Production is not sufficient to front these programs' entitlements. Increasing the nominal money supply via the ECB will not produce the necessary real resources to sustain these programs. Hence, regardless of the intensity of monetary expansion, real resources will not emerge ex nihilo. The longer structural reforms are postponed, the more drastic the eventual measures will be. Despite being a truism, it urges close consideration more than ever.

CONCLUSION

What was initially a contained subprime mortgage crisis rapidly contaminated the banking system through securitization. The world suddenly awoke to a major financial crisis, not just a local housing bubble restricted to the US. European and global banks soon realized they too would be affected. In haste, central banks and governments took unprecedented actions to avoid a financial calamity. Monetary policy swiftly reached its limits and it was now up to the states to unload heavy fiscal ammunition. Public finances in Europe were certainly not on a sustainable path, although budgetary impulses may have precipitated the day of reckoning, turning a financial crisis into a severe sovereign debt debacle in Europe less than two years after the announcement of fiscal stimulus packages.

The fiscal situation was already precarious and the universal recommendation was to indebt oneself even deeper in order to revive the economy. It was assumed the Keynesian multiplier would take effect once the spending started restoring growth and economic activity, thus increasing tax receipts, enabling governments to stabilize deficit and debt to GDP ratios close to EU targets, ensuring long-term fiscal sustainability. Attempting to stimulate growth, the European Economic Recovery Plan caused more unemployment, price instability, permeating uncertainty and forcing more resources to be squandered. Besides crowding out private investment, further deficit spending and balance-budgets-later recommendations endangered EU member states' long-term solvency. Fiscal stimulus, thus, brings us a step closer to the edge of the precipice.

Regrettably, it is not a matter of choice. Eventually, unfunded liabilities must be confronted in order to ensure long-term sustainability. At present it seems the United Kingdom is determined to reduce its deficits and force controversial structural reforms into a vote. Peripheral European countries are destined to follow suit, or financial market will punish profligate states with higher interest rates and risk premiums. Debt cannot be rolled over indefinitely. Sooner or later it must be either repaid or defaulted. Historically low interest rates are postponing this day.

As per the October 2010 notification for countries under the Excessive Deficit Procedure the estimates for next year are alarming. The so-called PIIGS countries are estimated to reach deficit levels of at least 5 percent or more of GDP, with Ireland on top of the list with 32 percent due to its recent national banks bail-out. Indebtedness levels are also seriously off the mark. Spain has the lowest debt to GDP ratio of the PIIGS at 62.8 percent while Italy and Greece are expected to be well above 110 percent of their gross domestic product. The United Kingdom does not fare any better, with deficit at 10.6 percent and indebtedness at 76.4 percent. Nevertheless, its current government stance seems determined to remedy the predicament.

With regards to the future of the Union, the Commission will have to address decisively how it will penalize member states that breach deficit and debt limits, otherwise it will keep ignoring Article 125 and continue instituting moral hazard as the norm. Ultimately, any eventual reform of the financial system must endeavor to tackle its interventionist nature. Article 127 of the Treaty on the Functioning of the EU stipulates that 'the ESCB shall act in accordance with the principle of an open market economy with free competition'. Unless free competition is indeed extended to the financial system, we will keep experiencing disastrous economic crisis.

Excessive credit creation caused by a fractional reserve system masks structural deficits and prolongs the imbalances, but it cannot continue indefinitely. Only real savings can be loaned. Under a fiat money and fractional reserve system, countries can inflate their way out of their obligations, socializing the losses through inflation. Economic laws teach us we can either save or spend. But not both simultaneously, as Keynes (and many modern-day Keynesians) would have wished.

NOTES

1. One does not have to be a Keynesian economist to favor deficit spending, even though it is a typical Keynesian policy. Moreover it is important for us to identify a few names who have been traditional advocates of Keynesian economics, especially in the current financial crisis: Paul Krugman, J. Bradford DeLong, Joseph Stiglitz, Robert J. Schiller, N. Gregory Mankiw, among others. Making a group is fraught with peril, as it will always overstate some people's opinions in the group, and understate others'.
2. For a detailed account of how government expenditures should be accounted for in GDP calculation see Rothbard (2009, p. 1293).
3. In his General Theory, Keynes never employed the expressions 'fiscal nor spending multiplier'.
4. From the Merriam-Webster Online Dictionary.

5. Randall Parker's book on the Great Depression offers an interesting illustration of how economists failed to understand the root causes of the bust and even dismissed them as not so relevant. Morris Adelman provides a telling answer when asked on the causes of the Great Depression and the reasons for its long duration: 'I don't know what the initial impetus was, and I can't account for how deep it went except I would say that the second question is much more important than the first' (Parker, 2002, p. 162).

6. Jörg Guido Hülsmann's chapter in the current volume also deals with this capital problem, to which we add the following passage from Mises: 'The fundamental error of the interventionists consists in the fact that they ignore the shortage of capital goods. In their eyes the depression is merely caused by a mysterious lack of the people's propensity both to consume and to invest. While the only real problem is to produce more and to consume less in order to increase the stock of capital goods available, the interventionists want to increase both consumption and investment. They want the government to embark upon projects which are unprofitable precisely because the factors of production needed for their execution must be withdrawn from other lines of employment in which they would fulfill wants the satisfaction of which the consumers consider more urgent. They do not realize that such public works must considerably intensify the real evil, the shortage of capital goods' (1998, p. 793).

7. Both the financial and non-financial sectors come to a halt. Not only will companies refrain from borrowing to continue their investment and expansion plans, but financial institutions will also cease lending and will actually insist that outstanding loans are paid back.

8. Indebtedness of enterprises (OECD data) verified in France, Germany, Italy and the United Kingdom have constantly risen since 1995 when this indicator was first disclosed. Since 2000 only Germany managed to reduce its enterprise indebtedness slightly. The very same pattern can be noticed in the indebtedness of households (OECD). With the exception of the German state, all countries mentioned above have witnessed dramatic increases in household leverage. Eurostat too provides an alarming picture. While special attention should be given to the United Kingdom, Spain, Ireland and Portugal specifically, gross debt to disposable income ratios have been on a worrying trend in virtually every European nation. Thus, to prescribe as a remedy against excessive leverage even greater levels of debt simply defies logic and common sense.

9. European Central Bank, www.ecb.europa.eu/mopo/strategy/pricestab/html/index. en.html.

10. Ibid.

11. Calzada Álvarez (2009), 'Study of the effects on employment of public aid to renewable energy sources', concluded that the Spanish experiment with subsidies aimed at stimulating the green energy sector had the unintended result of actually destroying 2.2 jobs for each green job created.

12. ECB, www.ecb.europa.eu/press/pr/date/2010/html/pr100510.en.html.

13. While there have been studies on the subject of independence it is rather complex to gauge objectively how independent a central bank is; neither is it simple to compare different central banks. Nonetheless, a March 2007 paper (at www.ecb.int/pub/pdf/scpwps/ecbwp742.pdf) by members of the ECB attempted to answer this inquiry through the analysis of the personal, functional and financial independence of the ECB, the Federal Reserve and the Bank of Japan, concluding that the European monetary authority presented the most independent structure of all.

14. Philipp Bagus' chapter in the current volume derives the same conclusion.

15. As the abovementioned IMF paper suggests, estimated population growth for 2008–2060 in the EU-27 states is less than 5 percent, whereas the percentage of population over 65 years old will increase from less than 20 percent in 2008 to more than 30 percent in 2060.

REFERENCES

Calzada Álvarez, G. (2009), 'Estudio de los efectors del apoyo publico a las energias renovables' www.libertaddigital.com/doc/estudio-de-los-efectos-del-apoyo-publico-a-las-energias-renovables-sobre-el-empleo-15849401.pdf, March.
Commission to the European Council (2010), 'A European Economic Recovery Plan', http://ec.europa.eu/economy_finance/publications/publication 13504_en.pdf.
Council of Foreign Relations (CFR) (2010), 'A conversation with Alan Greenspan', www.cfr.org/publication/22947/conversation_with_alan_greenspan_video. html?cid=rss-fullfeed-a_conversation_with_alan_green-091510, 15 September 2010, 50th minute onwards.
Eggertsson, G. (2009), 'What fiscal policy is effective at zero interest rates?', Federal Reserve Bank of New York staff reports 402.
Fujiwara, I. and K. Ueda (2010), 'The fiscal multiplier and spillover in a global liquidity trap', Federal Reserve Bank of Dallas Globalization and Monetary Policy Institute working paper 10-E-03.
G-20 (2008), 'Declaration Summit on Financial Markets and the World Economy', www.g20.org/Documents/g20_summit_declaration.pdf, 15 November.
Garrison, R.W. (2001), *Time and Money: Macroeconomics of Capital Structure*, London: Routledge.
Harding, R. (2010), 'Buck stops with Bernanke in QE2 debate', *Financial Times*, 28 October, www.ft.com/cms/s/0/7cf440d8-e2bb-11df-8a58-00144feabdc0.html.
Hazlitt, H. (1959), *The Failure of the 'New Economics'*, New Jersey, London and Toronto: D. Van Nostrand.
Huerta de Soto, J. (2006), *Money, Bank Credit and Economic Cycles*, trans. M. Stroup, Auburn, AL: Ludwig von Mises Institute.
Keynes, J.M. (1936), *The General Theory of Employment, Interest and Money*, London: Macmillan.
Krugman, P. (2003), *International Economics*, New York: Addison Wesley.
Mises, L. von (1998), *Human Action: A Treatise on Economics*, Auburn, AL: Ludwig von Mises Institute.
Mises, L. von (2006), *Causes of Economic Depressions*, Auburn, AL: Ludwig von Mises Institute.
Parker, G. (2008), 'Brown calls for "urgent" global stimulus', *Financial Times*, 12 September.
Parker, R. (2002), *Reflections on the Great Depression*, Cheltenham, UK and Northampton, MA, USA: Edward Elgar.
Rothbard, M.N. (2009), *Man, Economy, and State with Power and Market*, Auburn, AL: Ludwig von Mises Institute.
Skousen, M. (ed.) (1992), *Dissent on Keynes: A Critical Appraisal of Keynesian Economics*, Auburn, AL: Ludwig von Mises Institute.
Smaghi, L.B. (2009), 'Speech at Freiburg', www.ecb.int/press/key/date/2009/html/sp091014.en.html, 14 October.
Velculescu, D. (2010), 'Some uncomfortable arithmetic regarding Europe's public finances', IMF working paper 10/177, www.imf.org/external/pubs/ft/wp/2010/wp10177.pdf.

9. From German rules to European discretion: policy's slippery slope

Malte Tobias Kähler

The German Deutschmark was long considered to be among the strongest currencies in the world. In its statutes, the emitting central bank (the Bundesbank) confirmed price stability to be its main goal and managed to '[establish] its reputation as one of the most successful central banks in the world' (Beyer et. al., 2009, p. 1). Indeed, from the end of Bretton-Woods until one year before the German reunification (1973–89), average annual inflation was lower in West Germany than in any other OECD country (Clarida and Gertler, 1996, p. 1). Furthermore, monetary policy was embedded in a general framework of economic policy that sought a viable equilibrium between four policy tasks that are believed to be conflicting: price stability, low unemployment, a low trade deficit and continuous growth.[1]

Price stability aims at maintaining a moderate inflation rate, which is believed to provide guidance to the public in forming expectations of future price developments. Low unemployment is beneficial for the overall economy as unemployed people mean idle resources not used in the economy. Maintaining a low trade deficit ensures that no imbalance will endure and inflation is thus neither imported nor exported. Within this framework, the Bundesbank was committed to maintaining a policy of low inflation. This rule-based mandate[2] of the German monetary authority served as the role model for the European System of Central Banks (ESCB) in its early years. In order to safeguard the currency, the Bundesbank was freed from the demands of fiscal policy as it was guaranteed that the institution was not allowed to finance government deficits (Clarida and Gertler, 1996, p. 5). This principle of independence from political influence was later applied to the ESCB. However, the economic crisis that hit the world in 2007 led to a course of events that resulted in the softening of the rules and increased doses of discretion. If this development is not dealt with, it may eventually threaten the survival of the common currency.

This chapter analyses the development that led to this situation and comments on the future of the Euro. The second section deals with the historical background of the Eurozone. The third section seeks to give a theoretical rationale for the monetary integration that took place in Europe. The next section outlines some effects that the financial crisis had on Germany and the political reaction to it. The last section discusses the issue of rule-based vs. discretion-based monetary policy and its importance for the future of the Eurozone.

CREATING THE EUROPEAN CURRENCY UNION

From the beginning of the European Union's integration process, a fundamental aim has been the removal of trade barriers to goods, labor and capital. As the abolishment of these obstacles gave space for freer and increased trade, the uncertainty-creating effects of fluctuating exchange rates for intra-European trade became more evident. The first attempt at coordinating exchange rates and keeping them within certain bands was the agreement to the European Monetary System (EMS) in the 1970s. Yet, the ultimate foundations for the common monetary union were established in the 'Delors Report', by European Commission President Jacques Delors in 1989. He envisioned an economic and monetary union progressing in three stages.

Delors' proposal ultimately resulted in the Maastricht Treaty of 1992, which sowed the seeds of European monetary integration. The Treaty established the criteria that those states wanting to adopt the Euro had to fulfill. Great Britain, followed by Denmark and Sweden, opted out of this project, preferring not to give up their monetary policies. The remaining states agreed to reduce budget deficits below the critical acceptance level of 3 percent of GDP necessary to be considered for admittance. Additional limits were placed on the levels of total sovereign debt allowable: a maximum of 60 percent of GDP would be placed on any accepted country. National European monetary authorities were urged to target low convergence levels of inflation (Baylis and Smith, 2001, pp. 505–6).

In 1999 the Euro became the official, yet still virtual, currency used for bank transfers and, since 2002, Euro coins and notes have replaced the national currencies in 16 countries. The agreement to join the Currency Union is remarkable, for it incurs high 'political costs', as national governments not only had to give up important policy instruments such as devaluation, but had to agree to comply with the strong stability criteria set by the European Union. So, the question is raised: why did European politicians accept this new institutional framework that undermined their own domestic political power?

WHY WAS THERE A POLITICAL TENDENCY TOWARD A COMMON CURRENCY?

Among the theories that aid our understanding of the European integration process is the theory of liberal intergovernmentalism, developed by Moravcsik (1993). In a nutshell, his theory is based on two assumptions: states are collective agents that act rationally and are self-interested; and states base the decisions they make in the international arena on a cost–benefit analysis, giving special attention to national interests.

This interest or 'preference scale' of a state is not treated as a given 'black box'. Instead, as the liberal theory bases itself on methodological individualism, the needs of decision makers are explained by internal (or endogenous) processes of preference formation and bargaining between a variety of actors and individuals. Interest groups, executive and legislative members and political parties try to influence the domestic policy process in their favor. Governments thus face pluralistic domestic competition, while at the same time retaining reelection as their major concern.

Government action in the international arena, and especially the integration process in Europe, can then be explained by a combination of two forces: the intention of governments to deliver to their electorate a policy that ensures their reelection and the intention to implement this policy on an international level through bargaining with other states. Since each government bases its foreign policy proposals on self-interest and the desire to be reelected, agreements on the international level can only occur if common desires are shared, or if bargaining allows for equitable agreements to be reached. From the perspective of liberal intergovernmentalism the European Union itself does not possess a common interest; rather it serves as an 'international regime for policy co-ordination' (Moravcsik, 1993, pp. 498–9).

If we are to apply this theory to the process of creating the Currency Union, we need to identify three factors: 1) the relevant actors and their preferences; 2) the options available to them; and 3) the structural environment in which the decisions are undertaken. Following Kohler-Koch et al. (2004), who take a similar approach, one can describe the structure of interests that finally led to the implementation of the Euro. The authors divide the different players into two coalitions: France led the 'southern coalition' (of Spain, Portugal and Greece), joined by Ireland and Belgium; Germany headed a group that had concerns about the sacrifice of conservative (i.e. low inflation and stabilizing) monetary policy. This latter group also included the Netherlands, Luxembourg, Denmark and in some respects also the United Kingdom. These countries wanted to prevent a system in which a centralized monetary policy would become a vehicle for more interventions similar to the French *planification*. By refraining from joining the Union, these countries introduced the implicit argument that Italy and France wanted to establish a common European economic policy, one which they wanted no part of (Kohler-Koch et al., 2004, pp. 95–6).

A common currency was one important vehicle to establish, or at least further this goal. Moreover, after the breakdown of the Soviet Union and Germany's reunification, fears of a powerful revival in Germany grew afresh among European countries and with it the desire to include the Federal Republic in a strict institutional structure. On the other hand, Germany's preferences were split. The Bundestag's foreign ministry and Chancellor Helmut Kohl desired, along with the French, a rushed integration of the newly united Germany into a new pan-European framework to calm the concerns of their neighbors regarding a new Germany longing for power. Domestically, however, the support for the European project was much more restrained. For the first time since the foundation of the European Economic Community (EEC) in 1957, there were growing concerns in Germany against further European integration (Kohler-Koch et al., 2004, p. 97). Only a minority of Germans supported joining a single European currency. The majority of Germans still favored retaining their stable Deutschmark amid fears that the Euro would lead to higher inflation.

Eventually the debating parties agreed to monetary union, but Germany's coalition insisted on including the stability criteria. In order to calm the fears of German voters, former German President Horst Köhler, then still a government secretary in the Ministry of Finance, made clear that each member state would have to deal with its own deficits and that there would never be any aid obligations for the European Community. He went further to assure German voters that 'it won't happen that the South cashes in on the so-called rich countries [Germany included], as then Europe would fall apart' (as quoted in Fischer, 2010, p. 1).

A compromise was reached whereby the German monetary policy model was exported to the rest of Europe. The European System of Central Banks (ESCB) was designed to be politically independent and to target low inflation (below but close to 2 percent per year), just as the Bundesbank did before. Unlike the Federal Reserve in the United States, the ECB focuses solely on the objective of price stability and is not responsible for pursuing low unemployment by means of expansionary monetary policy. This singular objective of price stability implies a more dedicated response, with fewer conflicts of interest disrupting the decision-making process.

THE EFFECTS OF THE CRISIS ON GERMANY

Most economists seem to agree that the ECB's policy of low interest rates between 2002 and 2005 fostered an 'irrational exuberance' in both the housing and the capital markets (Goodhart, 2008, pp. 331–46). According to Austrian business cycle theory (ABCT) the natural rate of interest established by market participants ensures the intratemporal as well as the intertemporal compatibility of the entrepreneurs' plans of action. In other words, the market interest rate brings together real savings and investment in a way that all projects undertaken can be completed with sufficient savings.[3] Any disruption to this natural rate of interest will disrupt entrepreneurs' plans, and lead to widespread discoordinations throughout the economy.

If a central bank lowers the market interest rate through an expansion of the money supply, it becomes too low compared with the preferences of market agents.[4] Erroneous signals concerning savings levels lead investors to both more numerous and more time-intensive investment projects than can be finished with the available funds. The owners of the factors of production receive the newly created income and spend it according to their old consumption–savings ratio (since this ratio does not change if merely the money supply increases and no real savings are undertaken). After a while the relative increase in demand for consumer goods will increase profits in the late stages of production, which will attract more funds toward these sectors. As a result many early-stage projects have to be abandoned and the factors of production are shifted back to the late stages of production. As Bagus (2008, p. 285) explains: 'The recession ends when the investment projects again align with the preferred consumption–savings ratio of the market participants' (see also Garrison, 2001; Huerta de Soto, 2006; Mises, 1996; Rothbard, 1996).[5]

The overall perception of risk becomes disturbed as central banks ensure that they will act as liquidity providers in the case of a downturn (Cowen, 1998; Goodhart, 2008, pp. 332–4). Moral hazard develops in light of this decreased concern for illiquidity. The high injection of liquidity into the European financial markets by the ECB contributed to an underestimation of the underlying risks of investments (Issing, 2006, p. 2).[6]

The trigger for the unfolding crisis was the crash of Lehman Brothers in mid-September 2008. As a result, and under the impression of a feared financial meltdown, the German government followed other nations around the globe in aiding the domestic bank industry. The Finanzmarktstabilisierungsgesetz (financial market stability law) provided the government with the necessary political and economic power to intervene in favor of the banking system. A fund of €480 billion was created to guarantee the solvency of the troubled banks and to stimulate interbank lending. Furthermore, the so called Finanzmarktstabilisierungsfortentwicklungsgesetz (a law amending the financial market stability law) allowed for the possibility of creating 'bad banks'. A bad bank is an institution that purchases and holds distressed (often toxic) assets of the banking sector at face value and is backed by government guarantees (Ilgmann and Suntum, 2009, p. 9). In addition, the German government launched two stimulus packages worth €50 billion and €14 billion, as well as tax reductions in the form of a third package as part of the Wachstumsbeschleunigungsgesetz (law for an accelerated growth policy).

All these efforts seemed to have achieved their desired effects, as a meltdown of the financial system was largely prevented, at least for the time being. If we are dealing with a true Austrian business cycle, however, the remedy for such a crisis is not further monetary or fiscal intervention but a quick and unhampered liquidation of the bad assets through market forces. As Rothbard explains:

> The sooner the depression-readjustment is gotten over with, the better. This means, also, that the government must never try to prop up unsound business situations; it must never bail out or lend money to business firms in trouble. Doing this will simply prolong the agony and convert a sharp and quick depression phase into a lingering and chronic disease. (Rothbard, 1996, p. 77)

As information is distorted, or in some cases lost, as to the sustainable preferences of the market, a readjustment process must realign the market's structure to these preferences. Although stock market losses, bank insolvencies or increasing yields on debt issuances are painful, they represent important signals to entrepreneurs concerning the allocation of resources. During the boom, capital has been moved to areas of the economy where it is not needed.[7] Disruptions to the process of the bust serve to prolong the unnecessary imbalances from correcting. Indeed, as Howden (2010b, p. 180) explains, any action which prohibits these erroneous prices and capital allocations to correct will delay the learning process that entrepreneurs must undertake to return the economy to sustainability.

In the view of ABCT, government intervention merely shifts the problem from the bank's balance sheets to the government's, as their financial situation has now weakened due to their efforts to save the banking system from collapse.[8] By 2009, not a single country of the EMU fulfilled the stabilization criteria outlined in the Maastricht Treaty. Concerns have grown about the effectiveness of the stability criteria of the Eurozone and even about the future of the Euro itself. It now seems that 'the sovereign debt crisis that is unfolding . . . is a fiscal crisis of the western world' (Ferguson, 2010, p. 1).

The theory that the banking crisis was actually not cured by the stimulus and expansive monetary policy is backed by the view that Austrian theorists have always held, namely, that standard macroeconomic variables such as gross domestic product (GDP) do not accurately describe the underlying condition of the economy.[9] A short period of growth or recovery, as depicted by GDP figures, does not properly reflect the underlying imbalances. These economists (Huerta de Soto, 2006, pp. 305–12; Skousen, 1990, pp. 184–214) explain that macroeconomic aggregates hide data about the economic activity in the productive stages while focusing attention merely on net investment and consumption. In order to maintain the production structure, gross investment is constantly taking place, especially in intermediate goods. GDP figures neglect this important part of the nation's capital stock, and focus instead on final consumption.

At present, Europe dives deeper into debt and seems to abandon the self-imposed rules of stability that were originally created to ensure a strong Euro. As a result, interest rate spreads on government bonds of the so-called PIIGS nations (Portugal, Ireland, Italy, Greece and Spain) rose in early 2009 and then again in March 2010. The situation culminated when Greece was at the verge of default that could only be prevented by a rescue package by the other members of the European Union.[10] Yet, promising financial aid to the troubled countries means not only breaking the very principles upon which the Eurozone was founded but also the opening of a Pandora's Box. It constitutes a major moral hazard for the remaining PIIGS states that are more likely to ask for an equal treatment (i.e. receiving guarantees) by the members as well as setting a legal precedent to provide them with such funds (Howden, 2010a).

Unsatisfied with the course of political events, a group of economists, joined by a former professor of law at the University of Erlangen-Nürnberg, Karl Albrecht Schachtschneider, have questioned the legitimacy of the bailout in front of the German Federal Court, the Bundesverfassungsgericht. These individuals had already fought and lost one case against the German adoption of the Euro in 1998. This time, however, they insisted on their position that the Greek bailout would turn the 'European Union into an inflationary union' (Starbatty, 2010). Indeed, financial aid to Greece seems to constitute a breach of European Law. Article 125 of the Treaty on the Functioning of the European Union clearly states that the Union shall not be liable for or assume the commitments of central governments of any member state. Guarantees by the member states for Greek bonds constitute a breach of that rule.

Even ignoring the more explicit bailouts, a tacit bailout was already undertaken in recent years. As Bagus (2010) points out, the ECB has long accepted Greek bonds as collateral for new loans. Since the interest rate at which banks borrow money from the central bank is lower than the interest received from the government bonds, demand for Greek bonds was induced. Had the ECB not accepted Greek bonds as collateral, Greece would have had to pay even higher interest rates than they did. Hence, Greece and other troubled states were already being bailed out by the rest of the Eurozone before the sovereign debt crisis even emerged, as their debt was effectively monetized. In November 2010, every second Euro that the ECB lent to banks went to the 'financially weak countries' (FAZ, 2010).

In a crisis of this magnitude, the conduct of the ECB to act as a lender of last resort for the unstable domestic banking systems of its member states conflicts with its mandate laid down in Article 105 of the Treaty of the European Union. This article states the goal of price stability and obliges the ECB – albeit in vague terms – not to interfere with the functioning of the free market. As the banking crisis widens into a sovereign debt crisis, the ECB has departed from the rule-based policy approach it was designed for and intervened with greater discretion in the market.

RULES VS. DISCRETION IN MONETARY POLICY

The question of how the monetary policy of a central bank should be designed has a long tradition in economic thinking. Simons (1936) raised the issue, referring to two opposite paradigms as a choice between rules and authorities. In the context of monetary policy discussed here, a rule means a 'restriction on the monetary authority's discretion' (Dwyer, 1993, p. 4). Simons favored rules or legal guidelines for central banks, such as a strict commitment to price stability, over the authority to intervene discretionally. He argued that a 'definite, stable, legislative rules of the game as to money are of paramount importance to the survival of a system based on freedom of enterprise' (Simons, 1936, p. 339).

On the other hand authority or discretion 'means that the monetary authority is free to act in accordance with its own judgment' (Dwyer, 1993, p. 4). Advocates of discretionary-based monetary policy such as Modigliani (1977) point to the enhanced economic performance that an expert-guided central bank could contribute to with its wise macroeconomic policies. More recently, however, economists tend to discount the possibility of exploiting a tradeoff between inflation and employment that underlies the discretionary paradigm: 'The economic profession now generally agrees that in the end, increasing the money supply will result in a similar rise in the rate of increase of the general price level and will have no systematic effect on the real economy' (Schwartz and Castañeda, 2009, p. 9). Therefore, the ECB was deliberately designed under the influence of the rule-base-paradigm, preventing the monetary authority to please political objectives instead of ensuring a functioning, stable and predictable framework for the agents in the market economy. More precisely, the ECB is considered 'goal independent' (Schwartz and Castañeda, 2009, p. 10), as its day-to-day action is executed by the Governing Council that makes its decisions according to the mandate, that is keeping the rate of price inflation below but very close to 2 percent over the medium term (ECB, 2004, p. 51).

The actual content of those guiding rules that the monetary authority is obliged to pursue are still subject to discussion. The extreme positions reach from dynamic rules such as the Taylor rule (1993) to a strict fixation of the monetary base (e.g. Wallace, 1977), which would entirely eliminate any discretion of the central bank.

Yet Hayek ([1928] 1984) argued as early as 1928 that even the goal of price stability is not sufficient to prevent the trade cycle with its accompanying destabilizing effects on the banking sector. In a market economy, money and its interest rate serve to coordinate the intra and intertemporal decisions of economic agents. With a constant money supply, Hayek explains, a growth in productivity of the economic system would lead to an overall drop in the general price level. Any policy preventing this smooth price deflation from occurring will induce expectations of stable consumer prices when these prices actually need to fall. As Selgin reckons, in economies marked by increasing levels of productivity (such as the European Union has been), monetary policy should allow for 'secular deflation interrupted by occasional negative supply shocks' (1997, p. 70). By not allowing for the general price level to decline with increases in productivity, monetary policy will be too lenient – real, inflation-adjusted interest rates will be set too low. In relative terms, the production structure will be lengthened by these expectations in the same way as by any inflationary policy. Eventually, even rules that aim at price stability will cause recessions. Hence, as Hayek concludes: 'There is no basis in economic theory for the view that the quantity of money must be adjusted to changes in the economy if economic equilibrium is to be maintained or – what signifies the same – if monetary disturbances to the economy are to be prevented' ([1928] 1984, p. 106).

Certainly, the adoption of an independent central bank, as in the case of the ECB, is a major advantage over discretionary monetary authorities. But taking into account the insights from ABCT, it seems that an approach to monetary policy which only aims at price stability is not enough. In his discussion of the causes for the economic crisis of 2007 and 2008, Goodhart (2008, p. 332) points to the relatively low and stable inflation during the recent decade despite the ongoing monetary expansion. His reference to the growth in productivity that limited the effects of the increased money supply on the price level seems to back the Austrian proposition that inflation targeting is not a sufficient way of preserving financial stability.

Additionally, the recent crisis revealed that another important issue needs to be addressed. Although general rules for sound monetary policy have been implemented, the question of how best to deal with the central bank's function as a lender of last resort in our current fractional reserve banking system 'is not properly reflected in central bank statutes' (Schwartz and Castañeda, 2009, p. 12). When they contain systemic risks, the monetary authorities are in danger of becoming subject to political pressure and taking actions that result in unwanted effects with respect to their principal rules. From 2008 onward the ECB board members seemed to have used official interest rates not only as a macropolicy tool, but also as a provider of additionally liquidity to the banking sector as a result of political pressure (Schwartz and Castañeda, 2009, p. 13).[11] Such pressure arises periodically, but especially in these financially fragile situations.

There is a danger that the current European monetary regime will be abused by fiscally imprudent governments to finance their deficits. Bagus (2009a) compares that situation to the 'tragedy of the commons'.[12] The more recent discussion about the Eurobond (a government bond jointly issued by Eurozone members) (Matussek 2010, p. 1) indicates that this worry has already become more than just a mere scientific debate. As the ECB began to buy bonds of the troubled countries again in November 2010 (Atkins et al., 2010), warning voices were heard, fearing that the Eurozone, which once was based on the premise of price stability and budgetary discipline, could ultimately become a 'transfer- and liability-union' (*Transfer- und Haftungsunion*) (Neuerer, 2010).

Yet, a generalized fiscal transfer between members of the Eurozone by the means of jointly issued bonds and purchases of those bonds by the ECB would not only count as a severe departure from the rule-based monetary regime that lay at the foundations of the ECB. It would also put an end to the separation between fiscal and monetary policies in a way that the ECB would become an instrument for domestic fiscal issues. In order to maintain macroeconomic stability, these policies need to be addressed and managed in a strictly separate manner (Levy, 2001). Otherwise, the credibility of a central bank's commitment to price stability suffers, and with it the issued currency.[13]

CONCLUSION

During recent decades, and with the experience of the inflationary crisis of the 1970s, a shift can be observed, from discretionary to rule-based monetary policy with the task of safeguarding the purchasing power of the currencies. The German Bundesbank adopted this approach early, and built a reputation of sound monetary policy that later served as a role model for the newly established ESCB. The rules of the ESCB focused on overall price stability, but were insufficient to avert the financial crisis of 2007. Furthermore the framework of rules did not deal properly with the central bank's function of serving as a lender of last resort in a severe sovereign debt crisis.

Economists have long warned that recurring boom and bust cycles are caused by a centrally managed monetary system and will prevail until monetary authorities cease to interfere with the market interest rate. In this view, a monetary rule fosters the market economy in a better way than a discretionary central bank does. Yet, as the crisis has shown, the financial sector is subject to systemic risks that become apparent at the same critical moment in which a rule-based approach is most needed: in the moment of crisis. During times of economic growth, political pressure on the board of the ECB is likely to have less effect than in times when governments face substantial budgetary problems. The sovereign debt crisis unfolding after the largely evaded financial meltdown shows the importance of addressing the issue of discretion and rules with regards to the central bank's function as a lender of last resort. This debate and its practical outcome in the institutional framework will be crucial for the survival of the Euro as a common currency and thus for the larger peaceful European project.

NOTES

1. These goals are established in the German law for stability and growth (§1 in the Gesetz zur Förderung der Stabilität und des Wachstums der Wirtschaft from 1967).
2. Ottmar Issing, a former member of the executive board of the European Central Bank remarks: 'The Bundesbank missed its target roughly half of the time . . . This does not mean, however, that the Bundesbank did not take monetary targets seriously. On the contrary, money growth targets were regarded as constituting the basis for a rules-oriented approach to monetary policy. Announcing a monetary target implied a commitment by the Bundesbank towards the public. Deviations of money growth from the target had always to be justified. Even if it is true that the reputation of the Bundesbank ultimately was achieved by its success in fulfilling its mandate to safeguard the stability of its currency, its final goal, current policy continuously had to be justified in the context of its pre-announced strategy. In this sense, the strategy contributed to the transparency, the accountability and the credibility of Bundesbank's policy' (Issing et al., 2005, pp. 50–52).

3. The natural rate of interest is that rate that equilibrates the intertemporal plans of savers and investors in real terms (Huerta de Soto, 2006, pp. 284–91).
4. This lowering of the interest rate need not rely on the absolute level of prevailing interest rates. Even seemingly high interest rates may be too low compared to the market's needs. Any expansion in credit on the part of the central bank will reduce interest rates lower than they *would have been*, thus setting in motion a boom-bust cycle (see Mises, 1943; [1949] 1998, p. 442 fn. 17).
5. More recently, Howden (2010b) has looked at a secondary effect of the traditional Austrian business cycle: as credit enters through the banking system, a relative shift of capital and entrepreneurial ability exits the real, productive sector of the economy, and into the newly and increasingly profitable financial sector. A financial bubble results, with a crash necessary to realign profit rates with the production-based economy, and reallocate entrepreneurial efforts.
6. The ECB also recognizes that a 'broad consensus exists among participants that financial markets have been *exceptionally liquid* in recent years and that this has fostered *higher leverage and greater risk-taking*' (ECB, 2007, p. 10; emphases added).
7. Philipp Bagus and Antonio Zanella's chapters in the current volume focus on one particularly egregious misallocation of capital during the boom. As the ECB and the insurance industry's regulatory Solvency Accords promoted European sovereign debt to be held by financial companies at lower regulatory capital requirements, a reduction in borrowing interest rates for European governments occurred, with a corresponding increase in public sector spending and debt levels. The ramifications of these artificially increased public debt levels are only now becoming recognized.
8. In one particularly devastating recent case, Iceland's parliament would have been forced into insolvency if there was no international aid package after bailing out its own banking sector (Bagus and Howden, 2011).
9. Jörg Guido Hülsmann's chapter in the present volume focuses on one such aspect of the error of incomplete GDP calculations, and how in particular a lack of attention to capital depreciation has made the current recession deeper than is commonly reckoned.
10. As these pages are written (December 2010), Ireland and Portugal have joined Greece in asking the European Union to rescue them from default.
11. Bagus and Howden (2009a; 2009b) delve into the fresh credit programs instituted by the ECB after 2008, finding a significant tendency for not only lower-quality collateral to be accepted in its refinancing operations, but also a tendency to lower the acceptable range of credit ratings on collateral when politically significant counterparties were in danger of exclusion.
12. A tragedy of the commons is a dilemma in which the actions of a group of individuals based on self-interest will eventually lead to a situation that is not in anyone's long-term interest. The famous example by Garrett Hardin (1968) deals with a group of herders sharing a common parcel of land. Each herder will try to exploit the parcel of land as much as possible, although this conduct, if shared by the whole group, will not be sustainable.
13. Howden (2009) discusses the convergence of these two kinds of policies in the United States.

REFERENCES

Atkins, R., D. Oakley and P. Wise (2010), 'ECB forced to act as crisis fears rise', *Financial Times*, www.ft.com/cms/s/0/a272b8d8-eb64-11df-b482-00144feab49a. html#axzz16n64812h, 8 November.
Bagus, P. (2008), 'Monetary policy as bad medicine: the volatile relationship between business cycles and asset prices', *Review of Austrian Economics*, **21**, 283–300.

Bagus, P. (2010), 'The bailout of Greece and the end of the Euro', Ludwig von Mises Institute daily article, http://mises.org/daily/4091.

Bagus, P. and D. Howden (2009a), 'Qualitative easing in support of a tumbling financial system: a look at the Eurosystem's recent balance sheet policies', *Economic Affairs*, **29** (4), 60–65.

Bagus, P. and D. Howden (2009b), 'The Federal Reserve system and Eurosystem's balance sheet policies during the financial crisis: a comparative analysis', *Romanian Economic and Business Review*, **4** (3), 165–85.

Bagus, P. and D. Howden (2011), *Deep Freeze: Iceland's Economic Collapse*, Auburn, AL: Ludwig von Mises Institute.

Baylis, J. and S. Smith (2001), *The Globalization of World Politics. An Introduction to International Relations*, Oxford: Oxford University Press.

Beyer, A., G. Vitor, C. Gerberding and O. Issing (2009), 'Opting out of the great inflation: German monetary policy after the breakdown of Bretton Woods', Deutsche Bundesbank Eurosystem discussion paper series 1: Economic Studies 12/2009.

Clarida, R. and M. Gertler (1996), 'How the Bundesbank conducts monetary policy', New York University economic research reports, http://econ.as.nyu.edu/docs/IO/9383/RR96-14.PDF.

Cowen, T. (1998), *Risk and Business Cycles: New and Old Austrian Perspectives*, London: Routledge.

Dwyer, G.P. (1993), 'Rules and discretion in monetary policy', *Federal Reserve Bank of St Louis Review*, **75**, 3–13.

ECB (2004), 'The monetary policy of the ECB', www.ecb.int/pub/pdf/other/monetarypolicy2004en.pdf.

ECB (2007), 'European Central Bank financial stability review', www.ecb.int/pub/pdf/other/financialstabilityreview200706en.pdf, June.

FAZ (2010), 'EZB kauftirische Staatsanleihen. Bankentrauen sich auf den Verbriefungsmarkt', www.faz.net/s/Rub09A305833B12405A808EF01024D15375/Doc~EE6041517751D40D98B2EBAFB9F3EF1A8~ATpl~Ecommon~Scontent.html.

Ferguson, N. (2010), 'A Greek crisis is coming to America', *Financial Times*, 10 February.

Fischer, S. (2010), 'Euro in Gefahr. Wie Horst dem Köhler widerspricht', *Spiegel* online, www.spiegel.de/politik/deutschland/0,1518,692086,00.html.

Goodhart, C.A.E. (2008), 'The background to the 2007 financial crisis', *International Economics and Economic Policy*, **4**, 331–46.

Hardin, G. (1968), 'The tragedy of the commons', *Science*, **162** (3859), 1243–8.

Hayek, F.A. ([1928] 1984), 'Intertemporal price equilibrium and movements in the value of money', in R. McCloughry (ed.), *Money, Capital and Fluctuations: Early Essays*, Chicago, IL: University of Chicago Press, pp. 71–118.

Hayek, F.A. (1990), *Denationalisation of Money: The Argument Refined (An Analysis of the Theory and Practice of Concurrent Currencies)*, London: Institute of Economic Affairs.

Howden, D. (2009), 'Is monetary policy the new fiscal policy?', working paper, St Louis University, Madrid Campus.

Howden, D. (2010a), 'Greece: the next ashes to be spread across Europe?', Institute of Economic Affairs blog, www.blog.iea.org.uk/?p=2437.

Howden, D. (2010b), 'Knowledge shifts and the business cycle: when boom turns to bust', *Review of Austrian Economics*, **23** (2), 165–82.

Huerta de Soto, J. (2006), *Money, Bank Credit, and Economic Cycles*, Auburn, AL: Ludwig von Mises Institute.

Ilgmann, C. and U. von Suntum (2009), 'Bad banks: the case of Germany', CAWM discussion paper 22, www.wiwi.uni-muenster.de/cawm/forschen/ Download/Diskbeitraege/DP_22-Ilgmann-Van-Suntum-Bad-banks.pdf, Münster.

Issing, O. (2006), 'Der Euro hat ein langes Leben', *Handelsblatt*, 29 May.

Issing, O., V. Gaspar, O. Tristani and D. Vestin (2005), *Imperfect Knowledge and Monetary Policy*, Stone Lectures in Economics, Cambridge: Cambridge University Press.

Kohler-Koch, B., T. Conzelmann and M. Knodt (2004), *Europäische Integration – Europäisches Regieren*, Wiesbaden: VS Verlag.

Levy, M.D. (2010), 'Don't mix monetary and fiscal policy: why return to an old, flawed framework?' *Cato Journal*, **21** (2), 277–83.

Matussek, K. (2010), 'Germany considers accepting joint sale of Eurobonds, focus says', Bloomberg, www.bloomberg.com/news/2010-11-27/germany-considers-accepting-joint-sale-of-eurobonds-focus-says.html.

Mises, L. von (1943), '"Elastic expectations" and the Austrian theory of the trade cycle', *Economica*, new series, **10** (39), 251–2.

Mises, L. von. (1976), *A Critique of Interventionism*, New York: Foundation for Economic Education.

Mises, L. von (1996), 'The Austrian theory of the trade cycle', reprinted in R.M. Ebeling (ed.), *The Austrian Theory of the Trade Cycle and Other Essays*, Auburn, AL: Ludwig von Mises Institute, pp. 25–36.

Mises, L. von (1998 [1949]), *Human Action*, Auburn, AL: Ludwig von Mises Institute.

Modigliani, F. (1977), 'The monetarist controversy, or, should we forsake stabilization policy?', *American Economic Review*, **67** (2), 1–19.

Moravcsik, A. (1993), 'Preferences and power in the european community: a liberal intergovernmentalist approach', *Journal of Common Market Studies*, **31** (4), 473–524.

Neuerer, D. (2010), 'Angst vor der Transferunion. Schuldenkrise wird zur Dauerbelastung für Europa', *Handelsblatt*, www.handelsblatt.com/politik/international/angst-vor-der-transferunion-schuldenkrise-wird-zur-dauerbelastung-fuer-europa;2697425, 22 November.

Rothbard, M.N. (1996), 'Economic depressions: their cause and cure', in R.M. Ebeling (ed.), *The Austrian Theory of the Trade Cycle and Other Essays*, Auburn, AL: Ludwig von Mises Institute, pp. 58–81.

Rothbard, M.N. (2001), *Man, Economy, and State*, Auburn, AL: Ludwig von Mises Institute.

Sachverständigenrat (2008), 'Die Finanzkrise meistern – Wachstumskräfte stärken. Jahresgutachten des Sachverständigenrates zur Begutachtung des gesamtwirtschaftlichen Entwicklung', Wiesbaden, http://www.sachverstaendigenrat-wirtschaft.de/fileadmin/dateiablage/download/gutachten/ga08_ges.pdf.

Schwartz, P. and J. Castañeda (2009), 'Central banks: from politically independent to market-dependent institutions', *Economic Affairs*, **29** (3), 9–16.

Selgin, G. (1997), *Less than Zero: The Case for a Falling Price Level in a Growing Economy*, London: Institute of Economic Affairs.

Simons, H.C. (1936), 'Rules vs. authorities in monetary policy', *Journal of Political Economy*, **44** (1), 1–30.

Skousen, M. (1990), *The Structure of Production*, New York: New York University Press.
Starbatty, J. (2010), 'Aus der Währungsunion wird eine Inflationsunion', *Frankfurter Allgemeine Zeitung* online, www.faz.net.
Taylor, J.B. (1993), 'Discretion versus policy rules in practice', *Carnegie-Rochester Conference Series on Public Policy* **39**, 195–214.
Wallace, N. (1977), 'Why the Fed should consider holding M0 constant', *Federal Reserve Bank of Minneapolis Quarterly Review* (summer), 2–10.

10. The Euro as a hindrance to recovery? A comparative analysis of the Czech Republic and Slovakia

Jiří Schwarz and Josef Šíma

Czechoslovakia emerged as an independent state after the collapse of the Austro-Hungarian Empire in the aftermath of World War I in 1918. Rather than creating a decentralized multi-ethnic federal state, the newly formed body epitomized the idea of 'Czechoslovakism': one (non-existent in reality) nation of 'Czechoslovaks' made up of two branches, 'Czechs' and 'Slovaks'. This event – a source of heated historical and political debates between defenders and opponents of Czechoslovakism – made both Czechs and Slovaks the subjects of the same institutions and created a basis for exposing them for decades to the same set of policies. Despite the breakup of the country during the events around World War II, the situation lasted in principle until the early 1990s. Both nations shared the same currency (Czechoslovak koruna) and despite the 'federalization' of the country in 1968 (under the communist regime), all key decisions were done centrally, from Prague, the country's capital. Communism ended with the 'Velvet Revolution' in the two 'countries' in November 1989 and both went through the early stages of economic and social transition together; a process of dismantling central economic planning and political oppression and replacing them with market- and rule-of-law-based social order.

The first stages of economic transition were undertaken identically in both republics under the reform strategy adopted by the federal Czechoslovak government. The main pillars were price liberalization and internal currency convertibility (in January 1991); small-scale privatization (1990–93 when tens of thousands of small businesses were auctioned off); restitution (in which nationalized assets were returned to the original, true, owners); and large-scale privatization of state-owned enterprises (since 1991) through different methods, including the 'voucher scheme' in which shares (of some 1500 companies) were handed over to the adult population for free (minus a small handling fee) and turned Czechs and Slovaks into nation of stockholders.

After the parliamentary elections in June 1992 with the success of pro-reform coalition in the Czech Republic and of nationalist-leaning party in Slovakia, it became clear that there was no way to continue a joint reform strategy.[1] The impact of reforms on the Czech Republic and Slovakia started to be dramatically different and hence Slovak public opinion was not willing to tolerate the federal approach any longer, and called for a slowing of the pace of reform in Slovakia. As a result of the breakup of the Soviet bloc, heavy and military industry in Slovakia – a large chunk of Slovak industrial production – collapsed and consequently Slovak unemployment increased from a negligible 1.5 percent in 1990 to over 10 percent in 1991 and 1992 (compared to an increase from 0.8 to 2.6 percent in the Czech Republic). This development produced the prescient political decision to split the federation peacefully, which happened as of 1 January 1993. The countries kept close economic ties through a customs union and common labor market, but the shape of reform strategies started to differ. Monetary policies also began to diverge as the agreed-upon monetary union proved to be unsustainable, for both political and economic reasons (Fidrmuc et al., 1999). The decisions was made to separate the currency, with a date set for 8 February 1993.

In 1993 the era of a single Czechoslovak state that originated in 1918 definitively ended. Joint political, legal and monetary institutions that had formed the framework for development of both states were replaced by new political regimes, independent legislative processes and separate currencies. More effort to transform the economy (such as the second wave of voucher privatization) or an explicit plan to open up and join the European Union characterized the early development of the young and independent Czech Republic; whereas voucher privatization had no continuation in independent Slovakia as an era epitomized with a high level of political corruption ensued.

THE PATHS DIVERGE

To sum up, the starting institutional position of both countries in 1993 was practically identical. That is only true in terms of formal institutions; for numerous reasons the informal institutions were slightly different in the two countries. First, there never were any 'Czechoslovaks', but only Czechs and Slovaks with slightly different cultural and social norms and habits. Second, the structure of the economies was and still is slightly different, partly due to historical reasons but partly also as a result of socialist planning that took place during the whole of the communist era. Third, the structure of interest groups is quite different, due in large part to a substantial Hungarian minority in southern parts of Slovakia. As a consequence, the resulting institutional equilibria diverged over time.[2]

Whereas the Czech government largely continued in pro-market reforms in the first half of the 1990s, a pro-reformist government in Slovakia did not appear until the end of that decade. Then, however, the situation changed. Both countries published their strategy of Euro area accession prior to their EU entrance, planning to enter the monetary union in 2008–10 (Czech National Bank, 2003; National Bank of Slovakia, 2003). The pro-reformist Slovak government at that time had been able to lay the firm foundations of successful institutional development by, among other things, the introduction of a flat-tax regime and pension system reform. Some of the reform steps were reversed or adjusted by the following government but the general trend of positive institutional development did not change. This allowed the Slovaks to join the Euro area exactly as planned in 2009.

On the other hand, development in the Czech Republic was in the exact opposite direction. After the reform era of the 1990s came several years of social-democratic governments which were not willing to carry out any profound changes in the institutional framework. This situation changed slightly only recently. Primarily due to the financial crisis, attention was drawn again to the high levels of structural deficit, low labor market flexibility, pension system problems and so on. As a consequence of the inability of Czech governments to introduce necessary reforms, the deficit level does not yet fulfill Maastricht criteria and Euro adoption is therefore out of the question.

The Euro area accession and the process leading up to that event therefore constitute one of the biggest differences in the Czech and Slovak institutional development. Adoption of a common currency is usually expected to have a number of both positive and negative direct effects on the economy. Some of them might have even played an important role during the financial and subsequent economic crisis. It is, however, hard to evaluate the impact of the Euro's adoption in Slovakia compared to the economic development in the Czech Republic for two reasons. The first difficulty stems from the fact that it is still too soon to observe many of the expected effects as Slovakia introduced the Euro only in 2009. Second, it is sometimes nearly impossible to discover causality, and the only way of finding some impacts of Eurozone accession is to use econometrics to derive general correlations from a larger sample of countries.

Existing literature dealing with the Euro is mostly focused on the optimal currency area indicators, on the degree of economic alignment of respective candidate states with the rest of the Eurozone and finally on the direct or indirect impact of Euro adoption on the national economy or various types of subjects – always solely in economic terms, ignoring the less quantifiable consequences. We would, though, state a hypothesis that the pursuit of European Monetary Union (EMU) entrance worked also as a commitment device for the Slovak public and fiscal policy reforms. The reasoning is that to achieve higher economic alignment with the Euro area, higher flexibility of the economy is needed, which could only be reached through an improvement of the institutional environment. Similarities between the Czech Republic and Slovakia allow us to address this hypothesis by looking at the development of various measures of institutional quality for these two countries in the last years.

POSITIVE EFFECTS OF THE EURO

Exchange Rate Risk

Among the benefits of Euro area accession is traditionally listed a decrease in exchange rate risk. It is unquestionable that exchange rate volatility imposes costs on all subjects that have financial links to countries already included in the Euro area: citizens who have to keep or buy Euros whenever they travel to or trade with the Eurozone, investors and firms importing from or exporting to the Eurozone. Of course both investors and firms have the option of hedging against the exchange rate risk using some of the available financial instruments. This induces additional costs to the producers and inevitably increases the price of the final product. Adopting a common currency should therefore save some resources that would otherwise be devoted to hedging against the risk. Moreover in the longer term this should lead to an increase in the intensity of international trade, a larger inflow of foreign capital and deeper financial markets integration.

It has been estimated that, given that the exchange rate volatility of the Slovak koruna in 2004 and 2005 amounted to 1.6 percent and based on an estimate of exchange rate risk and the volume of resources exposed to risk, the elimination of the exchange rate risk by joining the Euro area would save approximately 0.02 percent GDP (Suster et al., 2006, p. 10). In light of the openness of the Slovak economy and its relatively high orientation towards Eurozone countries, it is unlikely that the effect of the elimination of exchange rate risk would be significantly higher in other countries.[3]

Regarding the longer-term effects of risk elimination, the empirical evidence is to a large degree mixed. Rose (2000) was among the first to estimate the effect currency unions have on trade. Using an empirical analysis of 186 countries over the period 1970–1990, Rose identified that joining a currency union boosts trade with other members of the union by more than 200 percent. A large stream of literature followed Rose, recently focusing especially on the impact of the Eurozone entrance. The findings are that the so-called Rose effect of the Euro is very different to that of other the currency unions included in his pioneering paper. For example Frankel (2008) reviews the existing literature and finds the Euro Rose effect to lie between 10 and 15 percent; other authors report different estimates, both smaller and larger. As a consequence it is very hard to reach some definite conclusion. Havránek (2010) uses a meta-regression analysis with 28 empirical papers analysing the impact of adopting the Euro to account for possible publication bias and find the 'true' underlying effect. He finds that there is no trace of the Rose effect in the Euro beyond the publication bias. On the other hand Havránek (2010) finds a sizable Rose effect (a trade boost of over 60 percent) of currency unions other than the Eurozone. To sum up, there seems to be no convincing evidence that adopting the Euro has any significant impact on the amount of trade between members of the Euro area.

Researchers from the National Bank of Slovakia expected that after the integration of Slovakia and other new members into the Euro area, foreign trade with the Euro area would increase by 60 percent. Given the degree of trade orientation towards the EU, this would lead to an overall increase of foreign trade by 50 percent (Suster et al., 2006, p. 18). It is usually assumed that an increase in international trade by 1 percent leads to an increase of GDP of 0.3 percent. It is therefore expected that in the long term the effect of trade growth due to Euro adoption in Slovakia will increase the level of GDP in the next 20 years by 7–20 percent. However, in light of the abovementioned recent study, this estimate seems to be highly exaggerated and the final long-term impact on foreign trade would be very modest, if any at all.

Regarding the prospects of larger foreign direct investment inflow, quantitative empirical evidence of the Euro impact is even less informative than for the foreign trade. The majority opinion is that joining a currency union has a sizable and positive effect on FDI. As Havránek and Iršová (2010) uncover using meta-regression methods, a 10 percentage point increase in foreign presence is associated with an increase in the productivity of domestic firms in supplier sectors of 11 percent. This spillover effect increases even if the respective countries are more open to international trade, which should be one of the impacts of Euro adoption. Given the structure of the origin of FDI in Slovakia, where 88 percent comes from EU countries, out of which 67 percent comes directly from the Euro area countries (Suster et al., 2006, p. 20), the adoption of a common currency is expected to increase further the proportion of FDI from Eurozone members.

Transaction Costs and Transparency

Another category of savings following the adoption of a common currency is connected to the existence of transaction costs stemming from the need to use various currencies. It has been estimated that adopting the Euro in Slovakia would lead to savings of 0.36 percent of GDP (Suster et al., 2006, p. 8). The governor of the Czech National Bank, Miroslav Singer, in 2006 expected the savings in the Czech Republic to reach 0.5 percent of GDP a year due to a reduction in transaction costs. However the national banks of both Hungary and Poland estimated the savings to be significantly lower, at around 0.2–0.3 percent of GDP (Borowski 2004; Csajbók and Csermely, 2002). It was also expected that joining the Euro area would lead to a decrease of capital costs. In Slovakia the expected effect on real interest rates on corporate loans was almost 1 percentage point. The interest rates on deposits decreased as well, but Suster et al. (2006, p. 15) expect the overall effect to be positive, especially over a longer horizon through higher rates of return on investments.

Finally, the introduction of a common currency is often expected to have a direct impact on cross-border deviations from the law of one price. Apart from the already-mentioned reduction of exchange rate volatility, the adoption of the Euro could be perceived as a signal that a country's representatives are willing to commit to an even deeper integration, including tariff reduction or elimination, decreased technical barriers and more collaborative policy ventures. Higher confidence that the markets will stay open and that the environment will be trade friendly in the future may motivate the producers and traders to invest more into international infrastructure.

The forces of arbitrage, which tend to decrease price dispersion, could also be tricked by a sort of money illusion as prices expressed in different currencies are more complex and discourage businesses to trade. A single currency reduces this complexity and boosts travel and trade. Lastly, the stickiness of nominal prices could, due to nominal exchange rate movements in the situation of more currencies, lead to real price misalignments. Empirical evidence, however, reveals that even though there was a significant decrease of price dispersion in Europe over the period 1990–2003, it has to be attributed to changes in the first half of 1990s (Engel and Rogers, 2004) – that is, before the introduction of the Euro. Also utilizing a difference-in-differences method and comparing development in countries that became members of the EMU in 1999 or 2002 to a control group of Sweden, Denmark and the UK, Wolszczak-Derlacz (2010) does not observe any decrease in price dispersion due to Euro introduction after 1999 either. The evidence therefore seems to suggest that the European region is already so interconnected that the adoption of a common currency does not have any significant impact.

NEGATIVE EFFECTS OF THE EURO

One-off Costs

The most obvious category of costs connected with the adoption of the Euro is one-off costs stemming from the needs of businesses, financial institutions and public sector institutions to adjust their information systems to be compatible with the new currency. It is common to modify all important documents to show the amounts in both currencies after joining the Eurozone and adopting the Euro. Moreover both currencies will circulate in a transient period in order to make the transition from one currency to the other as smooth as possible. This would further increase the costs as in this period businesses are required to accept payments in both currencies. Personnel training constitutes another source of additional costs.

In addition to the costs borne directly by the users of money, taxpayers will be forced to cover the costs of information campaigns organized by the government. In the case of Slovakia the costs of the information campaign alone were expected to be around €6 million. The total sum of these one-off costs can differ due to differences in the methodology of their computation. Estimates calculated by central banks of the Euro area countries range from 0.3 to 0.8 percent of each country's GDP. However, it is not only the total sum but also the distribution of costs among individual sectors that is important. The biggest part of these costs in absolute terms is usually borne by banks and large enterprises, but when recalculated to annual turnover, the highest burden lies on small and medium-size enterprises, which constitute 99.1 percent of all enterprises in Slovakia (Suster et al., 2006, p. 32).

Medium- to Long-term Effects

A Flash Eurobarometer survey (European Commission, 2008) among trade and hotel sector businesses revealed that only 47 percent of enterprises expected the Euro to have positive consequences for them in the medium to long term. Twenty-two percent did not know, 16 percent did not expect any consequences at all and 16 percent expected a negative effect of after the Euro's introduction. If we take a look at the distribution according to the annual turnover, out of the smallest trade and hotel enterprises 39 percent expected positive and 21 percent negative consequences.

According to the Slovak National Agency for Development of Small and Medium Enterprises survey (NADSME, 2008) conducted in 2008 among almost 1000 enterprises of various sizes from 0 to 249 employees, 48.7 percent of the surveyed enterprises saw the adoption of the Euro as a circumstance that would not have a significant impact on the firm; 33.1 percent expected the introduction of the Euro to have a negative impact on them; only 18 percent thought that the Euro would bring them more benefits than costs. Again, the smaller the enterprise, the bigger the costs and the lower the benefits that were expected. Almost two-thirds of questioned firms did not expect any cost reduction after the introduction of the Euro. About 20 percent did expected some costs reduction, but almost 40 percent of them expected these reductions to be only up to 0.1 percent of their turnover. What exactly was the expected positive impact of the Euro? Of the firms questioned, 28.6 percent answered they expected simplification of trade with their Eurozone partners, 21.9 percent saw the main benefit of the Euro in larger price transparency, and 10 percent hoped that the Euro would help them to penetrate new markets. Over 5 percent expected that the Euro would lead to an increase in the number of customers and finally 3.9 percent of businesses hoped that Euro adoption would allow them to import more from the Eurozone.

Loss of Independent Monetary Policy

It seems as if the Slovakian entrepreneurs doubted the longer-term positive effects that the Euro should bring them. Perhaps they feared the costs of losing independent monetary policy, which is especially detrimental where an economy is not exposed to similar shocks to the rest of the currency union. The larger the differences in the structure of economic activity, the larger will be the risks stemming from the inability to react independently to shocks. In this context we must mention that Slovakia and the Czech Republic have economic structures that are most different to the Eurozone average. In 2008, the share of industry in Slovakia was 31 percent (33 percent in the Czech Republic), whereas the average share of industrial sector in the Eurozone was only 20 percent. The opposite situation exists in the service sector, which made up 33 percent in Slovakia (34 percent in the Czech Republic) but 50 percent in the Eurozone (Czech National Bank, 2009, p. 41).

Slovak GDP per capita in 2008, expressed in purchasing power parity, was 67 percent of the Eurozone average. The price level reached 64 percent of the Eurozone average. In the period 1998–2008, the real exchange rate of the Slovak koruna against the Euro appreciated by 6.3 percent a year. To compare this pace with other countries, the Czech Republic appreciated by 4.2 percent a year, Hungary by 3.9 percent, Poland by 2.7 percent, Slovenia by 0.6 percent (Czech National Bank, 2009, p. 26). As a consequence, substantive real convergence of Slovakia is expected to continue, the equilibrium real appreciation trend of the Slovak koruna is expected to be 1.6–2.7 percent over the next five years (Czech National Bank, 2009, p. 18). Without the possibility of altering the exchange rate, the appreciation will turn into equally higher inflation vis-à-vis the Eurozone average.

Another serious implication of the loss of independent monetary policy due to Euro adoption was a significant loss of international competitiveness due to the fixing of the exchange rate between the Slovak koruna and the Euro at a markedly stronger value relative to the long-term appreciation trend. The Czech National Bank simulated the evolution of exports and imports using a hypothetically devalued exchange rate path for the Slovak koruna, calculated from the average depreciation of the exchange rates of Slovakia's neighboring countries' currencies in the period 2008Q3–2009Q1. The results suggest that net exports could increase by 0.2 percent of GDP (exports up by 2.4 percent of GDP, imports up by 2.2 percent of GDP) in 2008Q4. The biggest impact was in 2009Q1, when net exports would rise by 0.7 percent of GDP (exports by 6.6 percent of GDP, imports by 6.0 percent of GDP). The Czech National Bank also simulated the effects of hypothetically fixing the Czech koruna at the same time as Slovakia did. Using the Czech National Bank's core prediction DSGE model, the resulting impact on Czech growth in 2009 was a decrease of 1.5 percentage points (Czech National Bank, 2009, pp. 19–20).

The loss of its independent monetary policy does not only have negative consequences. We can in fact imagine two situations where fixing the exchange rate and importing monetary policy from abroad can be beneficial.

First is the case in which a country's own monetary policy is not sufficiently credible; that is, if it is not able to keep inflation low and inflation expectations anchored. This is mostly the case of countries at the beginning of the economic transition from central planning. In that situation, the central bank can be subjected to political pressures. Given the lack of reputation due to a short history of independent central banking in these countries, the central bank cannot be trusted to be able to repel these governmental influences. In that case, importing low inflation from abroad could be a viable choice.

Second, even if the central bank has sufficient credibility, it may lack the competence to carry out its own monetary policy. In other words, the central bank may not be able to predict the future development of economy correctly and therefore hit its inflation (or other) target. Holub (2003) thoroughly analyses the credibility of monetary policy and competence in the Czech Republic in the second half of 1990s. He concludes that the Czech National Bank does not suffer from a lack of anti-inflationary credibility or monetary policy competency. Inflation in Slovakia until 1999 was almost the same as in the Czech Republic. Only from 1999 to 2000 did inflation exceed single-digit values. However, this increase was caused by a gradual increase of regulated prices during the process of price liberalization, and was widely anticipated (National Bank of Slovakia, 2000).

By the end of 2000 inflation had returned to 8.4 percent. After the adoption of inflation targeting in 2005, inflation remained low (even though the target was overshot a few times). According to some, the credibility of Slovak monetary policy was slightly lower than in the Czech Republic (Arestis and Mouratidis, 2003; Ravenna, 2005). In terms of competency, Slovak monetary policy is of a relatively high quality – missing the inflation target (or inflation prediction in the years prior to the adoption of inflation targeting) was mostly caused by unexpected shocks to commodity prices or administrative and regulated prices.

To conclude this section: Slovakia was in no serious need to import monetary policy from the ECB. We could argue that the adoption of inflation targeting was only an instrument to keep inflation low in order to fulfill the corresponding Maastricht criterion. Its success shows that the National Bank of Slovakia was able to pursue credible and competent monetary policy independently. The most serious consequences for the crisis and recession developments in Slovakia is the impossibility of allowing the currency to depreciate in order to increase the competitiveness of Slovak businesses.

INSTITUTIONAL DEVELOPMENT

As we mentioned above, in addition to these costs and benefits in a narrow economic sense we assume that the commitment to adopt the Euro helped the Slovaks to improve their institutional environment. It is not possible to confirm the causal effect of Euro adoption rigorously or to quantify the degree of influence the Euro has had on Slovakian institutional development in the last years, but the differences between the development of Czech and Slovak institutions can shed some light on the effect.

First we will put forward a brief description of the political situation in the period after the break-up of Czechoslovakia. After the pro-reformist government of Václav Klaus and a short period of a technical government that led the country to an early general election, social democrats formed their first government in 1998 and held the position for two consecutive electoral terms until 2006. It is true that the social democrats were positively inclined toward adopting the Euro in the shortest possible time horizon. So the failure to adopt the common currency by 2009 as planned was not caused by a lack of enthusiasm towards the Euro, but rather by the government's inability to cope with growing structural problems of the Czech fiscal system. Driven mainly by the political cycle and the need to win over the majority of the electorate, social-democratic governments were not willing to face the risk of deeper public reforms. Some reforms were adopted only after 2006 by the government of Mirek Topolánek (2006–09).

By the end of 2002 and during the first half of 2003 it started to become clear that the Czech Republic and Slovakia would join the European Union in 2004. Upon EU accession both countries would also become members of the Economic and Monetary Union and their governments would agree to join the Eurozone as soon as their economic situations allowed for it. As a consequence, at that time the first official documents describing the accession strategy appeared. The Czech strategy states, 'the Czech Republic's large public budget deficits, together with the built-in trends towards a further structural widening of those deficits and inadequate conditions for the symmetrical functioning of automatic stabilisers, represent a serious barrier to effective fiscal stabilisation policy' (Czech National Bank, 2003, p. 5). Also emphasized is the problem of the Czech labor market's low flexibility. The government was unable to tackle any of these issues successfully.

In a similar manner, the Slovak strategy document states, 'it is . . . necessary to consolidate the budget situation in a sustainable manner' (National Bank of Slovakia, 2003, p. 9). Whereas the Czech document focuses mainly on the deficit problem and apart from labor market flexibility only vaguely mentions the need to support economic growth, maintain stability, ensure corporate competitiveness and raise employment, the Slovak strategy directly mentions that 'the reform of public finances and pension reform, as well as healthcare and education reforms are of key importance' (National Bank of Slovakia, 2003, p. 10). The main difference between the two countries is that while there was a non-reformist social-democratic government in the Czech Republic, the Slovak government was led by a pro-reformist Mikuláš Dzurinda at that time. His first four-year term in office started in 1998, but practically all significant reforms were only carried out after 2002. Strong opposition to these reform steps led to a significant growth in the popularity of the newly emerged Slovak social-democratic party (SMER) that won the general election in 2006 and formed a coalition with Slovak nationalists.

It was expected that based on pre-election promises and rhetoric, the social democrats with Robert Fico as a prime minister would aim to roll back many reforms. Surprisingly this did not happen, at least not on a large scale, probably to a large degree thanks to the determination to adopt the Euro as planned. In this way, the adoption of the Euro first served as an argument for the need of profound reforms of various aspects of public policy; it then created a constraint for possible populist measures which could have been adopted by the coalition of social democrats and nationalists.

EMPIRICAL ANALYSIS OF INSTITUTIONS: WORLDWIDE GOVERNANCE INDICATORS

The analysis of institutions poses one large difficulty: in order to correctly address the development of institutional environment, one cannot be satisfied with the intended consequences of adopted reform laws. The reasons are primarily twofold. First, the authors of government documents are not necessarily correct as the process of regulatory impact assessment is still not very mature. Second, the unintended consequences can be strong enough to outweigh the planned effects.

There are two ways to tackle this issue, both based on ex post evaluations of the existing environment. The first one is to use some kind of index of institutional quality. To our knowledge the most suitable dataset for cross-country comparison for the last years is the Worldwide Governance Indicators (WGI) by Kaufmann et al. (2010), which covers six dimensions of governance over the period 1996–2009 in 213 economies. The advantage over other similar indices is that the values are calculated from 31 different sources, including surveys of firms and households, and subjective assessments of various commercial business information providers, nongovernmental organizations and other public sector bodies. Figure 10.1 shows the development of all six indicators during the period 1996–2009 for the Czech Republic, Slovakia, and the average for the Eurozone (EU-16). Note that prior to 2002, the WGI were calculated only every other year. As a consequence, the values for 1997, 1999 and 2001 are always averages of the value in the previous and the following year. The values can range from −2.5 to +2.5.

The first two dimensions describe the process by which governments are selected, monitored and replaced.[4] Verbal and accountability

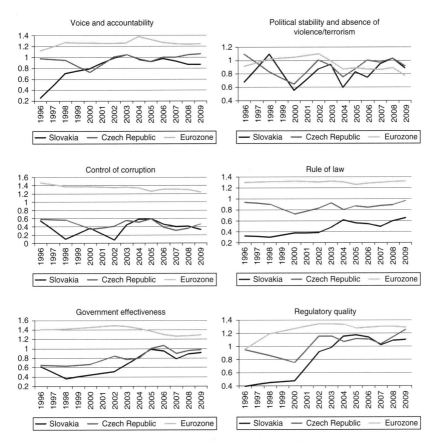

Source: Kaufmann et al. (2010).

Figure 10.1   Worldwide Governance Indicators

measures capture the perceptions of how far a country's citizens are able to participate in selecting their government, as well as freedom of expression, freedom of association and a free media. A simpler way to describe this indicator in the context of our analysis would be to say that it measures the maturity of democracy. We see that after the transitional period in 1990s, both countries converged to almost the same level. The second indicator, political stability and absence of violence/terrorism captures the likelihood that the government will be destabilized or overthrown by unconstitutional or violent means, including politically motivated violence or terrorism, and shows a very similar development.

More likely to be affected by Euro adoption is the second group of indicators, which measure the respect of both citizens and the state for the institutions that govern economic and social interactions among them. The rule of law indicator captures perceptions of the extent to which agents have confidence in and abide by the rule of society, and in particular the quality of contract enforcement, property rights, the police and the courts, as well as the likelihood of crime and violence. Here we observe the gap between the Czech Republic and Slovakia closing after 1998, with the smallest difference between the two series in 2004 after a sizable improvement in Slovakia between 2002 and 2004.

Control of corruption captures the perception of the extent to which public power is exercised for private gain, including both petty and grand forms of corruption, as well as 'capture' of the state by elites and private interests. This measure shows a story consistent with the development of the political situations in both countries. Economic theory predicts that the more the state interferes with the free market and voluntary contracts and transactions between individuals, the larger is the involvement of private interests in the public matters. The graph reveals that the biggest improvement in Slovakia took place between 2002 and 2004 – in that year Slovakia actually surpassed the Czech Republic and had better scores until 2008. However, it is worth mentioning that these two measures show the biggest difference between the Czech and Slovak Republic on one side, and the Eurozone on the other.

The most relevant indicators in our investigation should be the last two, assessing the capacity of the government to formulate and implement sound policies effectively: government effectiveness and regulatory quality. The government effectiveness measure captures perceptions of the quality of public services, the quality of the civil service and the degree of its independence from political pressures, the quality of policy formulation and implementation, and the credibility of the government's commitment to such policies. Given the political story described above, we would expect this measure to improve slightly after 1998, then more quickly between 2002 and 2006 and not deteriorate significantly after 2006. The data confirm these expectations.

Development of regulatory quality, which shows the perceptions of the ability of the government to formulate and implement sound policies and regulations that permit and promote private sector development, reveals a very similar story. Rapid improvement started in 2000 and was observable in both countries. But while the Czech Republic reached its peak in 2002, the situation in Slovakia improved further, until 2005.

EMPIRICAL ANALYSIS OF INSTITUTIONS: BUSINESS ENVIRONMENT AND ENTERPRISE PERFORMANCE SURVEY

Even though the WGI data reveal the general trends in the development of institutional environment, their shortcoming is their high level of aggregation. In order to be able to follow the development of various aspects of the institutional environment, another source of information is needed. For this purpose we use the data from the EBRD-World Bank Business Environment and Enterprise Performance Survey (BEEPS), which provides detailed information on how managers perceive various aspects of the business environment in 29 mostly developing countries in Central and Eastern Europe. The survey was first conducted in 1999 and repeated approximately every three years, with the last round in 2008–09. We made a selection of 11 questions dealing with topics connected to the quality of institutional environment and built a unique panel of data from all four rounds of the survey.

The questions are:

1. Are customs and trade regulations No Obstacle, a Minor Obstacle, a Moderate obstacle, a Major Obstacle, or a Very Severe Obstacle to the current operations of this establishment? (0–4, lower is better)
2. As I list some factors that can affect the current operations of a business, please look at this card and tell me if you think that each factor is No Obstacle, a Minor Obstacle, a Moderate Obstacle, a Major Obstacle, or a Very Severe Obstacle to the current operations of this establishment: tax rates. (0–4, lower is better)
3. As I list some factors that can affect the current operations of a business, please look at this card and tell me if you think that each factor is No Obstacle, a Minor Obstacle, a Moderate Obstacle, a Major Obstacle, or a Very Severe Obstacle to the current operations of this establishment: tax administration. (0–4, lower is better)
4. As I list some factors that can affect the current operations of a business, please look at this card and tell me if you think that each factor is No Obstacle, a Minor Obstacle, a Moderate Obstacle, a Major Obstacle, or a Very Severe Obstacle to the current operations of this establishment: business licensing and permits. (0–4, lower is better)
5. It is common for firms in my line of business to have to pay some irregular 'additional payments or gifts' to get things done with regard to customs, taxes, licenses, regulations, services etc. Never, Seldom, Sometimes, Frequently, Usually, Always. (0–5, lower is better)

6. As I list some factors that can affect the current operations of a business, please look at this card and tell me if you think that each factor is No Obstacle, a Minor Obstacle, a Moderate Obstacle, a Major Obstacle, or a Very Severe Obstacle to the current operations of this establishment: courts. (0–4, lower is better)
7. As I list some factors that can affect the current operations of a business, please look at this card and tell me if you think that each factor is No Obstacle, a Minor Obstacle, a Moderate Obstacle, a Major Obstacle, or a Very Severe Obstacle to the current operations of this establishment: corruption. (0–4, lower is better)
8. Are labor regulations No Obstacle, a Minor Obstacle, a Moderate Obstacle, a Major Obstacle, or a Very Severe Obstacle to the current operations of this establishment? (0–4, lower is better)
9. I am going to read some statements that describe the court system and how it could affect business. For each statement, please tell me if you Strongly Disagree, Tend to Disagree, Tend to Agree, or Strongly Agree: 'The court system is fair, impartial and uncorrupted.' (1–4, higher is better)
10. I am going to read some statements that describe the court system and how it could affect business. For each statement, please tell me if you Strongly Disagree, Tend to Disagree, Tend to Agree, or Strongly Agree: 'The court system is quick.' (1–4, higher is better)
11. I am going to read some statements that describe the court system and how it could affect business. For each statement, please tell me if you Strongly Disagree, Tend to Disagree, Tend to Agree, or Strongly Agree: 'The court system is able to enforce its decisions.' (1–4, higher is better)

Figure 10.2 plots the average responses to these questions. The number of responses is usually above 100, with the exception of question 1, where the number of Czech responders is 96, 59 and 99 in 2002, 2005 and 2009 respectively. The number of responses to other questions varies from 110 to 341. In addition to the responses, all graphs include differences between the average response in the Czech Republic and the average response in Slovakia in the given year. The orientation of the different graphs is the same as the orientation of responses. That it, if a lower response is better (as in question 1), then a downward movement of the difference means a relative improvement of Slovakia vis-à-vis the Czech Republic. If a higher value of the response is better (as in question 9), then a relative improvement of Slovakia is shown by moving the difference to the north.

The graphs reveal that there was an improvement in the perceived quality of all questioned areas between 2002 and 2005, which is consistent with

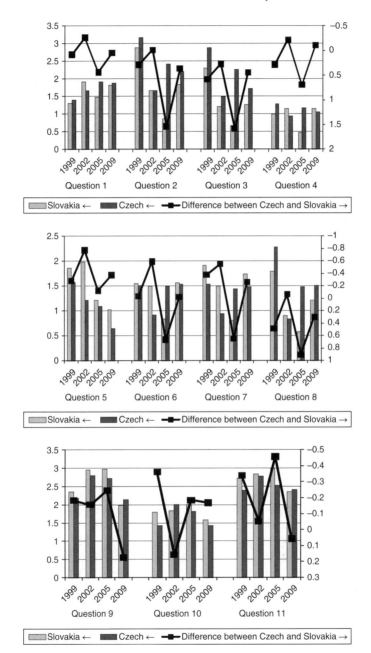

Figure 10.2   EBRD-World Bank Business Environment and Enterprise Performance survey responses

our earlier findings. Moreover the line displaying the differences between the Czech Republic and Slovakia shows a marked relative improvement of Slovakia in 2005. In contrast to the WGI data, the BEEPS data show a considerable worsening of the perceived situation between 2005 and 2009 in the majority of questions, with a drop larger in Slovakia than in the Czech Republic. This suggests that businesses perceived developments after 2005 in Slovakia very negatively relative to those respondents in the Czech Republic. It also indicates that, according to the BEEPS data, the constraint created by the plan to adopt the Euro probably was not strong enough to preserve the institutional improvements made by the pro-reformist Slovak government in the previous period.

None of the above proves the causal link between Eurozone accession and institutional improvement in Slovakia. However, both the absolute improvement and the relative improvement of Slovakia vis-à-vis the Czech Republic just in the period 2002–05 suggest that the hypothesis cannot be easily rejected.

THE EURO AND THE CRISIS

We have tried to describe various consequences of Euro adoption in Slovakia. We have done this not only in the usual narrow economic sense, but have also presented evidence in favor of the hypothesis that the Euro, among other effects, operated as a commitment device for institutional reforms. One question still remains to be answered: what was the impact of the Euro adoption on the course of the financial and subsequent economic crisis and post-crisis development? Was Slovakia better off with the Euro than it would have been with its own currency?

The economic effects of entering the Eurozone made the crisis, which usually creates more volatility, less costly by lowering the exchange rate risk. But the savings for the Slovak economy are only a fraction of a percent of GDP. The impact of the Euro adoption on trade with the Eurozone was proven to be insignificant. On the other hand, it is expected that the Euro adoption would produce a significant effect on foreign direct investments inflow, which also generates spillover effects on the productivity of domestic firms. This can be expected only in the longer term and therefore has no direct implication for the crisis. As a consequence, while in most cases the positive effects are expected to kick in later on, the one-off costs specified above have had to be borne by the businesses during the least favorable times.

In the light of the relatively high credibility and high competency of the National Bank of Slovakia, there is no reason to expect that independent monetary policy during the crisis could have led to the financial and economic situation being worse in Slovakia. It is true that until the Greek crisis in the first months of 2010, the Eurozone had been perceived as a low-risk environment without giving much care to the situation in the individual member states. During 2009, Slovakia could have therefore benefitted from being a part of this group of countries. On the other hand, the fixing of the exchange rate between the Slovak koruna and the Euro at a stronger value relative to the long-term appreciation trend led to a loss of international competitiveness which has been particularly painful during the global economic slowdown.

To sum up, despite the common expectations and a number of predictions, the introduction of the Euro in Slovakia did not lead to sizable positive effects in a narrow economic sense. Even in the longer run, considering the recent problems of the Euro caused by the events in Greece and Ireland, the balance of benefits, costs and risks would be approximately balanced.[5]

The effort to adopt the Euro and the adoption itself had other consequences as well. Since the break-up of Czechoslovakia, Slovakia had serious difficulties dealing with the structural problems of the economy because of strong opposition to any radical changes. Only after 1998 did a debate start discussing reforming the Slovak economic and institutional environment. Practically all significant reforms were passed after 2002 as a part of the Euro-area accession strategy and, contrary to pre-election rhetoric, most of the reforms were kept in place even after the social democrats together with the nationalists formed a new government coalition in 2006. The improvement of the institutional environment in Slovakia played an important role during the crisis too. Smaller structural problems meant more space for fiscal policy to deal with cyclical developments; larger flexibility of the economy helped to recover from the crisis more smoothly than most other economies.

Countries with serious imperfections in their institutional setup and which suffer from a lack of determination to introduce necessary reforms can benefit from adopting the Euro. The reason is simple: in order to improve the economic alignment with the Eurozone and fulfill the Maastricht criteria, a country must introduce reforms improving the flexibility and various structural deficiencies of the economy. This does not mean that it would not be possible to do so without the Euro. The Euro-area accession only creates a valuable incentive. When dealing with the impacts of the financial and economic crisis, the Euro is neither a big advantage nor a significant drawback.

To conclude, we have showed that the dissimilar reaction of the Czech and the Slovak economies to the crisis was to no great degree caused by the fact that Slovakia introduced the Euro and the Czech Republic kept its koruna. The only exceptions were caused by the fact that the exchange rate between the Slovak koruna and the Euro were fixed at an overly strong value, and that the Euro helped Slovakia to introduce a number of important reforms before the onset of the crisis. The main reasons that the 2008–10 recession hit both countries in different ways stems from the structural diversity of the economies, their different level of alignment with their main trading partners, and from the fact that they are exposed to slightly different shocks. However, given the high degree of openness of both countries and their high level of interconnection with the Eurozone countries, any potential crisis of the Euro would hit the Czech Republic, regardless of the currency it uses.

NOTES

1. For more on the ideological background to Czech reform see Šíma (2006).
2. For an equilibrium approach to institutions see Aoki (2001).
3. As far as we know, no estimates of exchange rate risk from joining the common currency by the Czech Republic are available.
4. Descriptions of all measures are taken from Kaufmann et al. (2010, p. 4).
5. It is noteworthy, to say at least, that the Slovakian minister of finance, Ivan Mikloš, who has been a leading advocate of Euro introduction in Slovakia and who was also in that role when the final decision was taken, has made it explicit that if the decision about the Euro had to be taken now, the force of the arguments against adoption of the Euro would be dramatically different, and that he personally would be against it.

REFERENCES

Aoki, M. (2001), *Toward a Comparative Institutional Analysis*, Cambridge, MA: MIT Press.
Arestis, P. and Mouratidis, K. (2003), 'Credibility of monetary policy in four accession countries: a markov regime-switching approach', Levy Economics Institute working paper 371, http://ssrn.com/paper=382421
Borowski, J. (ed.) (2004), 'A report on the costs and benefits of Poland's adoption of the Euro', Warsaw: National Bank of Poland.
Csajbók, A. and Csermely, Á. (eds) (2002), 'Adopting the Euro in Hungary: expected costs, benefits and timing', National Bank of Hungary occasional paper 24.
Czech National Bank (2003), 'The Czech Republic's Euro-area accession strategy', www.cnb.cz/en/monetary_policy/strategic_documents/emu_accession.html, 13 October.
Czech National Bank (2009), 'Analyses of the Czech Republic's current economic alignment with the euro area', www.cnb.cz/en/monetary_policy/strategic_documents/download/analyses_of_alignment_2009.pdf.

Engel, C. and J.H. Rogers (2004), 'European product market integration after the Euro', *Economic Policy*, **19** (39), 347–84.

European Commission (2008), 'Preparing for the Euro: survey among Slovak enterprises', Flash Eurobarometer 240.

Fidrmuc, J., J. Horvath and J. Fidrmuc (1999), 'The stability of monetary unions: lessons from the breakup of Czechoslovakia', *Journal of Comparative Economics*, **27** (4), 753–81.

Frankel, J.A. (2008), 'The estimated effects of the Euro on trade: why are they below historical effects of monetary unions among smaller countries?', National Bureau of Economic Research working paper 14542, www.nber.org/papers/w14542.

Havránek, T. (2010), 'Rose effect and the Euro: is the magic gone?', *Review of World Economics*, **146** (2), 241–61.

Havránek, T. and Z. Iršová (2010), 'Which foreigners are worth wooing? A meta-analysis of vertical spillovers from FDI', Czech National Bank working paper 3/2010, http://econpapers.repec.org/paper/cnbwpaper/2010_2f03.htm.

Holub, T. (2003), 'Importing low inflation via pegged exchange rates, currency boards and monetary unions', ICEG European Center working paper 21.

Kaufmann, D., A. Kraay and M. Mastruzzi (2010), 'The Worldwide Governance Indicators: methodology and analytical issues', World Bank Policy Research working paper 5430.

NADSME. (2008). 'Pripravenosť malých a stredných podnikov na zavedenie eura v SR', Slovak National Agency for Development of Small and Medium Enterprises, www.nadsme.sk/content/prieskumy.

National Bank of Slovakia (2000), 'Menový program Národnej banky Slovenska na rok 2000', *BIATEC Banking Journal*, **8** (1), 29–30.

National Bank of Slovakia (2003), 'Strategy of the Slovak Republic for adoption of the Euro', www.nbs.sk/en/publications-issued-by-the-nbs/nbs-publications/publications-about-the-euro-introduction.

Ravenna, F. (2005), 'The European Monetary Union as a commitment device for new EU member states', ECB working paper 516.

Rose, A.K. (2000), 'One money, one market: the effect of common currencies on trade', *Economic Policy*, **15** (30), 7–46.

Šíma, J. (2006), 'Les Tcheques et les idées "autrichiennes"', in P. Nemo and J. Petitot (eds), *Histoire du libéralisme en Europe*, Paris: Quadrige/PUF, pp. 1269–78.

Suster, M., M. Arendas, M. Bencik, P. Gertler, F. Hajnovic, Z. Kominkova and T. Lalinsky (2006), 'The effects of Euro adoption on the Slovak economy', National Bank of Slovakia policy paper 1/2006.

Wolszczak-Derlacz, J. (2010), 'Does one currency mean one price?', *Eastern European Economics*, **48** (2), 87–114.

11. Compounding agricultural poverty: how the EU's Common Agricultural Policy is strangling European recovery

Brian Ó Caithnia

The Common Agricultural Policy (CAP) has been the pride of European integrationism since its inception. It has been the crowning glory of technocracy and the ultimate statement of unity in post-war Europe. Founded as part of the Treaty of Rome[1] in 1957, the CAP has consumed at times up to 70 percent of the EU budget[2] and has embodied the European Union's (EU) desire to maintain economic self-sufficiency. The integrity of the CAP has been equated by some with the integrity of the essential political fabric of the EU itself (Hasha, 1999). For decades, however, the CAP has also come under a significant amount of criticism from economists for consuming a disproportionate share of the EU budget, introducing market distortions, wasting government funds and contributing to rural inequities. Nevertheless, it has survived many attempts to abolish it, and has acquired a reputation for being virtually impossible to reform in any meaningful way.

There are few EU programs where one finds such broad political consensus among the member states. In 2005, Jacques Chirac the French president said, 'I am not willing to make the slightest concession on the common agricultural policy . . . The CAP is the future' (Open Europe, 2005, p. 3). José Zapatero, the Spanish prime minister, said, 'On reform of the CAP, France and Spain have a common position' (Open Europe, 2005, p. 3). Bertie Ahern, the Irish prime minister, said, 'I believe that calls for CAP reform are misplaced because they are based on a misunderstanding of the role of the CAP in European society and the world economy' (Ahern, 2005).

The recent global economic crisis has shattered the financial stability of the Euro and raised questions about the long-term viability of an 'ever closer Union'.[3] In this chapter I shall briefly bring the reader up to speed on how the CAP got to where it is today, how it has exacerbated the tumbling edifice of European dynamism on a dying continent and why an educated electorate is essential if we wish to bring the CAP's wealth-destroying capabilities to an end.

THE CAP (CREATE AGRICULTURAL POVERTY?) ESTABLISHED

The aims as laid out by the Treaty of Rome rendered the Common Agricultural Policy an incoherent policy that from the very beginning could never be realized in reality. The aims, as outlined in article 39 of the Treaty of Rome, were as follows:

1. to increase productivity
2. to ensure fair living standards for the agricultural community
3. to stabilize markets
4. to ensure availability of food
5. to provide food at reasonable prices.

A layman will instantly recognize that the goals of the CAP are vague and contradictory. Goals such as stabilizing markets and increasing productivity are irreconcilable, for example. Increased agricultural productivity, by its essence, destabilizes markets by driving down the price of food and, as a consequence, the income of farmers. Since both policies cannot be fully pursued simultaneously, it soon became evident that productivity was to be sacrificed at the altar of farmers' paychecks. Among the multiple goals originally proclaimed for the CAP, stable and politically acceptable farm incomes have proven to be the paramount concern of EU policymakers. The political sensitivity of farm incomes results from the reality that Europe has a long history of protectionism in farming and the share of the EU civilian workforce employed in agriculture has always been far larger than the share of gross domestic product (GDP) attributable to gross value added in the agricultural sector.

By 1962, the details of the CAP had been hammered out and it was decided that the CAP would operate on three fundamental principles: 1) free trade within the Community based on common prices; 2) a preference for Community produce in Community markets; and 3) joint financial responsibility. By employing a variety of mechanisms, the original CAP provided support generally by maintaining stabilized internal prices well above world prices for unlimited quantities of most products. The CAP insulated domestic markets from world market forces, exempting EC producers from the adjustments that otherwise would have been required. When the EU was a net importer of most agricultural goods in the earliest years of the CAP, the EU budget benefited from substantial import levy revenues while the cost of agricultural support provided through high internal prices fell mostly on consumers. As Bryan Caplan explains in *The Myth of the Rational Voter*, there appears to be a 'make-work bias' among the voting population where there is a 'tendency to underestimate the economic benefits from conserving labor' (Caplan, 2007, p. 40). He takes farm subsidies in the United States as an example, which are equally popular in farm and non-farm states. Polls suggest that people agree with the statement that farm subsidies are necessary to guarantee a secure food supply; economists, on the other hand, see farm subsidies as wasteful and unnecessary for these ends. He then asks, 'Why are economists not listened to?' One might think that people just have not thought about it, but even when explained well, economists' analyses are not persuasive or interesting to many people. Thus, consumers become increasingly 'rationally ignorant' that they are paying elevated prices for their food – it is not worth the effort of becoming informed, protesting or caring.

Blame is normally laid at the feet of the French for the CAP (Zobbe, 2002). Many see Germany as being the poor soul that was dragged into accepting the CAP as the price for a free market in industrial goods.[4] It should be noted, however, that German agriculture opposed the policy even more so because it feared the CAP would reduce its protections, which were the highest in Europe at the time. The farm lobby in Germany had held the country captive since the tariff-wall days of Otto von Bismarck. With the highest support prices in the EEC, Germany feared that harmonization would bring painful price cuts for its politically influential arable farmers.

THE DISSOLUTION OF AGRICULTURAL TRADE IN EUROPE

By 1968, quotas for refined sugar were introduced to combat the excessive 'food mountains' that were already accumulating, just as the US economists had earlier predicted.[5] As early as 1969, one-sixth of the EU wheat crop had to be denatured, rendering it unfit for human consumption but still suitable for animal consumption, and was thus subsidized as animal feed in an attempt to balance supply and demand. Fears grew in the 1970s that the CAP was going to destabilize the EU in its entirety and 'structural' surpluses, rising budget costs, disparate inequalities among farmers in terms of CAP benefits and endangered international relations contributed to an attempt at reform. This led to a principle being adopted in 1982 that producers should accept less support beyond some threshold production level. 'Guarantee thresholds' were adopted for milk, sugar, cereals, rape seed and processing tomatoes. Further reforms in 1984 and 1986 saw the imposition of milk delivery quotas and the introduction of price supports. In 1988, the EU Commission, known for its truth telling, announced to the world that 'for most products, open-ended buying-in (unlimited government support purchases) is a thing of the past'. As we shall see, a leopard does not change its spots.

THE CAP: THE HYDRA-HEADED BEAST

Much like the mythical hydra that spawned new heads when one head was cut off, when the economic justifications for the CAP ceased to be effective in holding off any meaningful reform, a whole plethora of new reasons arose from the ashes to replace them. Aided by a series of disease outbreaks such as BSE (1997) and foot-and-mouth disease (2001) and the growth in climate change as a political justification for the expansion of government power, CAP policy has shifted away from traditional reasons defending it. This culminated in a declaration on the future by leading agricultural economists entitled 'A Common Agricultural Policy for European public goods' (ECIPE, 2009) to propose a shift in CAP objectives. It argued that the current key aims – enhancing the efficiency of agriculture, changing incomes distribution in the EU and encouraging rural development – should no longer play a prominent role. The pursuit of quantity, demanded by the CAP price supports, compromised quality, safety and the environment. Instead it championed environmental reasons. This includes contributions to the fight against climate change, the protection of biodiversity, and water management that tackles pollution, water scarcity and flooding. The economists concluded that the future CAP should differ fundamentally from the current one. Interventions in agricultural markets – for instance through export subsidies – and the Single Farm Payment that gives farms income support without asking for production in return – should be progressively abolished.

In 2010 the EU agricultural commissioner Dacian Cioloş called for a 'greening of the CAP'. EU environment commissioner Janez Potočnik even went as far as saying that he saw 'somewhere in the future' an EU policy called the 'Common Agricultural and Environmental Policy' (Potočnik, 2010). He wrote, 'We need nothing less than a CAP that respects [soil and water] and promotes practices that use them in a sustainable and resource-efficient way. We also need a CAP that can invest in protecting and restoring them when they have been degraded, contaminated or polluted.' Franz Fischler, a former EU agriculture commissioner and current chairman of the RISE Foundation for rural development, lamented that when the CAP was first introduced farming was intensified as a result of the unlimited purchases made available at artificially high prices.[6] Now, he says, CAP reform should 'supersede food security' by making EU farm policy deliver green public goods and services (Fischler, 2010).

What does he mean by public goods? Public goods mean different things to different stakeholders. In the literature, Samuelson (1954) and others have argued that a shortfall in the provision of public goods, compared to the scale of public demand, underpins the case for public intervention, and that securing the provision of public goods is a valid reason for public intervention. This rationale for public intervention underpins a number of sectors or realms of public policy such as clean water, 'biodiversity' and 'a stable climate'.

Using public good theory and amalgamating it with environmentalism and climate change, the farming lobby has managed to hijack the economies of Europe. Biofuels, for example, have made rapid inroads in recent years into the market for transport fuel. According to the UN Environmental Program, world ethanol production for transport fuel tripled between 2000 and 2007 from 17 billion to more than 52 billion liters worldwide, while biodiesel production expanded eleven-fold from less than 1 billion to almost 11 billion liters (UNEP, 2009, p. 33). A period of high oil prices further boosted production of ethanol and biodiesel in 2008. The main producing countries for transport biofuels are of course the US, Brazil and the EU. Brazil and the US subsidized 55 and 35 percent, respectively, of the world's ethanol production in 2009 and the EU subsidized 60 percent of the total biodiesel output. US production consists mostly of ethanol from corn; in Brazil the main product is ethanol from sugar cane; in the EU most of the biofuel is biodiesel from rapeseed (UNEP, 2009, p. 15).

The main stimulus to this extraordinary growth in the use of biofuels has been the introduction of policies to encourage a switch away from fossil fuels for road transportation. EU biofuels policy has evolved over the years from modest support for ethanol production as an agricultural byproduct to the elaboration of mandates for renewable fuels. Surplus wine was taken off the market for decades and used mostly as bioethanol. The EU even passed legislation in 2008 that mandated the use of biofuels in the transport sector. As a part of its 'climate change package', the EU adopted the Directive for Renewable Energy (DRE) in 2009, which established an EU-wide binding target of 10 percent of transport energy from renewable sources by 2020 (European Commission, 2008), along with a requirement that 20 percent of all energy come from renewable sources (up from 8 percent in 2009). Biofuel mandates, tax concessions and supporting border measures intensify the linkage between markets for agricultural products and energy. Instead of bringing about greater stability, these biofuel policies increased agricultural price variability by rendering agricultural markets dependent on both the level and stability of petroleum prices too.

While farmers may simply want a more stable income for themselves, supporters of 'greening' the CAP are more ideological. As Franz Fischler lamented:

> Overall, I see Europe's agriculture and rural development suffering from market failures, public budget cuts and public neglect. Food and feed, the environment and climate change are on an unsustainable path. In expanding production, Europe's land managers have been providing insufficient environmental 'goods', such as habitats, species and cultural landscapes, and too many environmental 'bads', such as pollution of the atmosphere, soil and water. This is a sign of market failure. (Fischler, 2010, p. 1)

By generously rewarding production at any cost, the CAP has driven the intensification of agriculture in Europe. Paolo Bruni, president of EU farmers' lobby Copa-Cogeca, which is the European umbrella body for agri co-ops, noted that by lumping costly regulations and obligations on farmers while not vastly expanding subsidization simultaneously, EU farming becomes artificially squeezed into intensive farming. In particular, it is often ignored that farming also has negative side-effects for society: water is extracted from rivers and polluted with fertilizers and pesticides. When this happens it is normally called a 'market externality' and is used to justify an expansion of government power into the monitoring and allocation of resources and property rights. The externalities that economists such as Samuelson refer to arise from a lack of clearly defined property rights (Mises, [1949] 1998, pp. 599–605).

This is all idle chatter however, for even now talk of new eco-conditionality of direct subsidies for farmers does not really make sense, because cross-compliance requirements already exist and farmers are already expected to respect EU environmental law. The EU has up until recently not had the 'polluter gets paid not to pollute' principle; the EU has had the 'polluter pays principle' (PPP). If you pollute, you should be getting a criminal civil action anyway, not just having your subsidies removed.

Paolo Bruni points out that 'If production was not economically viable, many regions of the EU would face land abandonment. This could destroy huge investments that farmers and their co-operatives have put into the sector' (in Ryan, 2010). Here we see the incoherent mess that is the environmental justification of the CAP. On the one hand they advocate regulations to protect the environment, but this accelerates pollution and farming intensification. On the other hand they advocate the subsidization of farmers to maintain 'Europe's agrarian heritage', but this keeps more land in production and puts farmers back into the first situation of intensive farming to survive.

THE CAP: THE GREAT ANNIHILATOR OF THE FARMING COMMUNITY

As well as keeping prices artificially high, punishing EU consumers and blocking imports from the developing world and bankrupting third-world farmers, the CAP has also failed in its objective to protect farmers' jobs and stabilize incomes. Farm incomes fell 70 percent between 1995 and 2000 alone (Open Europe, 2005, p. 11). This decline occurred at the same time as the share of small farms in the total number of dairy farms was estimated to decrease from 70 percent in 1990 to less than 10 percent in 2009 while the share of large farms increases from 3 percent to 45 percent by 2020 (Jongeneel, 2010). Despite CAP propaganda telling us that it is implemented in the name of the small poor farmer, the overwhelming majority of the benefits accrue to input suppliers and big landowners (Open Europe, 2005, p. 11). The OECD estimates that only 25 percent of the total value of producer subsidies is actually gained by farmers. Benefits to farmers have also increased much less than budget increases, since direct payments mostly offset reduced prices. In the UK for example, it has been the case that 20 percent of farms and agribusinesses take 82 percent of all CAP subsidies, while the bottom 20 percent receive just 0.05 percent. As Jack Thurston, co-founder of FarmSubsidy.org, has said, 'The bigger you are, the more subsidies you get . . . It is the reverse of what you think a subsidy is' (in Walt, 2010). The absurdity is also seen where the EU spends just under €1 billion a year (about 2 percent on the total CAP budget) on tobacco subsidies while simultaneously promoting anti-smoking programs. The CAP is the world's largest system of agricultural subsidies, spending $55 billion in 2010 (European Commission, 2010).

As we can see in Figure 11.1, the EU uses export subsidies on a scale vastly greater than all other countries combined.

Figure 11.1 summarizes total levels of export subsidy use (converted into $US) for all member countries that notified for any year, 1995–2002. The reporting of export subsidy notifications by states participating in the Uruguay round of the General Agreement on Tariffs and Trade (GATT) negotiations led initially to full compliance in reporting. However, there

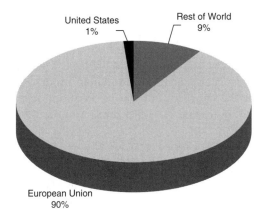

United States
1%

Rest of World
9%

European Union
90%

Source: Economic Research Service, USDA (2010).

Figure 11.1   Percentage of world domestic support subsidies, 1998–2003

has essentially been a breakdown of the current Doha round hosted by the World Trade Organization (WTO), which began in 2001 as a result of the EU and the US refusing to compromise on their agricultural policies. Compliance with the reporting of export subsidies had almost entirely ceased two years into negotiations by 2003, rendering it difficult to determine where the current percentages of world export subsidies lie. It is reasonable to estimate Figure 11.1 would look similar to a present-day account of current subsidies.

It is worth noting that Eurostat data 'showed farmers as a group in most EU-15 countries (at the turn of the millennium) to have average incomes broadly on a par with those of households in general in the same country (except for Portugal)' (Ackrill, 2008). As one author noted, this finding did nothing to further political support for more such statistics at least among agricultural households (Hill, 2008). Other concerns that Hill notes include farming groups, in some countries, opposing the publication of data showing members' total incomes, as well as variations in farmers' total incomes across different countries, undermining the 'national interest' in political debates. As recently as November 2010, the CAP – which in the past published the amounts paid to farmers – ceased publishing this information, describing it as 'an obligation to publish personal data' and thus an attack on individual freedoms (Thurston et al., 2010). This is a startling development, especially considering that earlier in the year, former Bulgarian vice minister of agriculture, Dimitar Peychev, was arrested after it was discovered that his 27-year old-daughter received

€781 456 in CAP subsidies in 2009, mainly from the Rural Development Program. In total, his wife and daughter received €1.5 million from the CAP while he was responsible for distributing money meant for general EU policies (Vaglenov and Balabanova, 2010). A wealth redistribution program that costs each European household around €1000 a year yet denies the public the knowledge of who is benefiting from it is an affront to justice and common sense. As Valentin Zahrnt puts it:

> The burden of proof for agricultural subsidies has been misallocated in the past. Those who defended the status quo of the CAP referred broadly to low agricultural incomes and endangered food security. But they never produced sufficient hard evidence on poverty incidence among farm households and the transfer efficiency of CAP payments to poor households, or credible scenarios under which EU food security could not be maintained. (Zahrnt 2010a, p. 57)

THE SCRAMBLE FOR JUSTIFICATION

With the collapse of the Soviet Union and the mood swinging against central planning in the early 1990s, the CAP appeared out-moded and archaic. Aware of this, the European Commission ceased using economic reasons to justify the CAP and sought out new, vague and more subjective defenses. These are best summarized by Franz Fischler:

> Without a strong CAP a nature oriented and sustainable agriculture will hardly be achievable. The trend of industrial farming would be enforced at the expense of animal welfare and environmental services on the one hand. On the other hand, less favored regions would be abandoned leading to a variety of negative consequences for rural and urban areas and their inhabitants. Rural areas form an important and beautiful part of European culture. The CAP must play its part in safeguarding this cultural and natural heritage. (Fischler, 2008, pp. 22–7)

Another manifestation of propaganda nurtured by the farm lobby to defend subsidization is the propagation of romantic agrarian myths, which include the confusion of modern commercial agriculture with rural heritage and the suggestion that current agricultural policies serve to uphold fundamental social values. Agricultural interests can exploit these myths to generate public support for farm programs. As we shall see, placing the entire agricultural sector on welfare has in reality contributed to the depopulation and breakdown of rural Europe.

In recent years, attempts at reform have focused primarily on generating significant direct payments to farmers, regardless of ancillary impacts. Principal among the proposals was a claim for the 'multifunctional nature of agriculture' that requires remuneration to farmers for their role as 'stewards of the environment' and the rural landscape. The Commission has declared:

> The fundamental difference between the European model and that of our major competitors lies in the multifunctional nature of Europe's agriculture and the part it plays in the economy and the environment, in society and in preserving the landscape, whence the need to maintain farming throughout Europe and to safeguard farmers' incomes. (Commission of the European Communities, 1998)

Even if we accept such a goal as genuine, such programs do not promote the stated policy objectives of protecting landscapes and biological diversity in an intelligent fashion. For example, how could anyone have suggested that the policy of set-aside, where farmers are paid to not work their land, would be soothing to the eye? It is also the case that inflated product prices help maintain higher farm-level profits and thereby keep more land in use. In this way, the EU simultaneously pays farmers not to farm certain fields and subsidizes the farming of other fields that would otherwise have remained fallow, all in the name of a beautiful environment. This is reminiscent of the policies that the US implemented as part of the 'New Deal' of the 1930s:

> The FFB (Federal Farm Board) programs had thus inadvertently encouraged greater wheat production, only to find by spring that prices were falling rapidly; greater surpluses threatened the market and spurred greater declines. It became clear, in the impeccable logic of government intervention, that the farmers would have to reduce their wheat production, if they were to raise prices effectively. The FFB was learning the lesson of every cartel – production must be reduced in order to raise prices. And the logic of the government's farm monopoly also drove the FFB to conclude that farmers had been 'overproducing.' (Rothbard, [1963] 2004, p. 269)

Rothbard then proceeded to explain:

> And so the grandiose stabilization effort of the FFB failed ignominiously. Its loans encouraged greater production, adding to its farm surpluses, which overhung the market, driving prices down both on direct and on psychological grounds. The FFB thus aggravated the very farm depression that it was supposed to solve. With the FFB generally acknowledged a failure, President Hoover began to pursue the inexorable logic of government intervention to the next step: recommending that productive land be withdrawn from cultivation, that crops be plowed under, and that immature farm animals be slaughtered – all to reduce the very surpluses that government's prior intervention had brought into being. (Rothbard, [1963] 2004, p. 273)

The EU commissioners are not stupid people. They are fully aware how embarrassing it is to have year-on-year food surpluses that must be destroyed or disposed of in some way. Realizing that they cannot continue to maintain such an obviously backwards policy forever, the latest reforms have been in the direction of shameless welfare for farmers. In the 2003 reforms, known as the Fischler Reforms, direct subsidies were replaced with a Single Farm Payment (SFP) scheme that would be based on area and historic subsidy allocations detached totally from production. Franz Fischler was accused of trying to kill the CAP, but today it is widely recognized by farm unions that it was he who in fact saved it.[7] Fischler created a new monster that the advocates of free market reform must contend with, the green monster and the entire theory of public goods and pseudo-scientific evidence that it is founded upon that has captivated the public's imagination.

HOW DOES THE CAP OPERATE TODAY?

In recent years the EU has shifted focus away from explicitly aggressive economic protectionism. Lobbyists have guided protectionism into an increasingly sophisticated and hard to measure form. 'Quality standards' have become the new trade barriers. For example, EU standards to protect consumers against aflatoxin cost African exporters of nuts, cereals and dried fruits $650 million a year and reduced their exports by 64 percent. The World Bank estimates that the policy, which is exceedingly costly for many Africans, *may* prevent one death per billion people in Europe per year (Open Europe, 2005, p. 15).

The sheer size of the European farm lobby has always ensured that there has been substantial resistance to CAP reform. Nonetheless, despite the privileged position lobbyists have won for the farming community as a whole, the share of agricultural labor in total employment has shrunk in all EU countries, thus rendering its privileged position increasingly less secure. The role of agriculture in total EU income and employment has declined dramatically since the inception of the CAP. The EU farm population has declined an average of 3 percent annually since 1968, although the decline has been gaining speed: 4.5 percent annually from 1986 to 1996 and falling in the EU-15 by 18 percent between 1995 and 2005. However, agriculture's contribution to GDP also has continued to decline, by more than employment in percentage terms. EU agriculture employed just over 5.1 percent of the EU-15 workforce in 1996, but accounted for only 1.7 percent of GDP. Farm household incomes also have improved dramatically, equaling or surpassing non-farm incomes

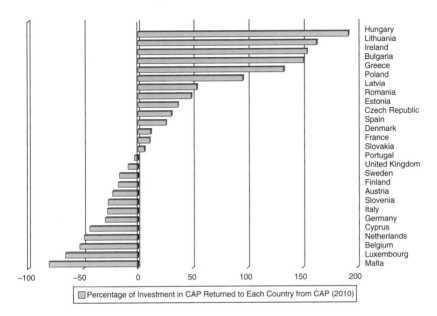

Source: European Parliament (2010).

Figure 11.2 *Percentage of investment in CAP returned to each country from CAP, 2010*

in most EU countries (European Commission, 1997). Today average EU farm household incomes, including agricultural subsidies and income from non-agricultural activities, have been raised to parity or better in relation to non-farm incomes in almost all EU countries.

Even though the EU agricultural population has declined, the farm population still constitutes a critical 'agricultural' vote in many EU countries and the large benefits accruing to farm interests have made them active political partisans. CAP benefits have become progressively more concentrated in a smaller percentage of farmers that are relatively wealthy, reducing public support for the CAP as a source of assistance to needy farmers (Open Europe, 2005). The relatively smaller benefits accruing to a larger number of small farmers remain important to those farmers, however, sustaining important political support for the CAP. The Mediterranean countries and Ireland have been the principal beneficiaries of CAP and other EU programs. A farmer in Greece gets more than €500 per hectare, whereas his Latvian colleague obtains less than €100 per hectare. The winners and losers of the CAP may be seen in Figure 11.2.

Germany, and, to a lesser extent, the United Kingdom have been the principal net contributors to the EU budget. Germany's political position as principal EU paymaster has been complicated by its particularly strong political need for high prices that result because German farms are relatively small and German non-farm incomes are relatively high, while the UK has received a rebate to compensate for contributing significantly more to the EU while receiving significantly less than other countries from the CAP. The Benelux countries also appear to be dealt a raw deal with regards the CAP, but one must also remember that the monolithic edifice of EU bureaucracy has its seat centered in these countries, so that, while they might not benefit directly from the CAP, there are certainly indirect benefits. In comparing Figures 11.3 and 11.4 it becomes clearer who is doing the heavy lifting for the CAP and who the free-riders are.

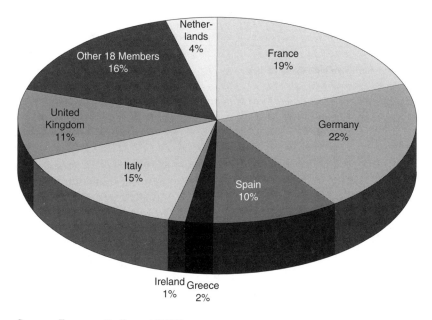

Source: European Parliament (2010).

Figure 11.3   National percentage of contributions to CAP direct income supports, 2010

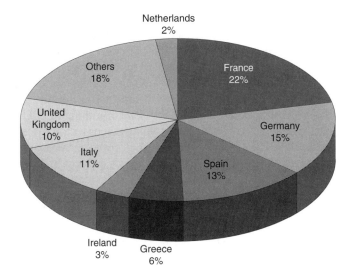

Source: European Parliament (2010).

*Figure 11.4   National percentage of receipts from CAP direct income
            supports, 2010*

WHAT HAPPENS WHEN SUBSIDIES ARE REMOVED?

New Zealand unilaterally abolished its agricultural subsidies in the mid-
1980s. While the EU has lost about 40 percent of its agricultural jobs since
1986, farm employment in New Zealand has remained stable. Farm output
in New Zealand actually rose by 150 percent compared to 20 percent in the
EU in the same period. Without subsidies, many farmers concentrated
more on value than volume, so there are more imports, but also more
value-added exports. Output and net incomes for the New Zealand dairy
industry are higher now than before subsidies ended – and the cost of milk
production is among the lowest in the world (Rodale Institute, 2002).
    The Swedes in 1990 also rejected the idea that high market support
could be justified because of any 'non-economic' objectives of agriculture.
Instead, any positive environmental externalities were to be paid by direct
payments. The underlying philosophy was that compensations/adjustment
measures should be paid not because past policies automatically created
an entitlement for future support but because society had an obligation,
in agriculture and elsewhere, to abolish past policies under socially acceptable conditions.

In 1990, all internal market regulations in Sweden were abolished, which propelled the country forward as having one of the most deregulated agricultural sectors in the world. Farmers were offered only a modest and temporary compensation and, contrary to the reforms of the CAP, the reform was not caused by external pressures or a budgetary crisis. Sadly, in the end, almost everything had to be reversed after Sweden joined the Common Agricultural Policy as a pre-requisite to joining the EU in 1995. Agricultural policy in Sweden was predominantly based on price support (Rabinowicz, 2004). Total level of support in Sweden, measured by the Producer Subsidy Estimate (PSE), in 1990 was 57 percent and food prices were very high in comparison to international standards. Purchasing power adjusted comparisons indicated that Swedish food prices were 60 percent above the EU level, while prices in general only 35–40 percent (Bolin and Swedenborg, 1992). Moreover, food prices were also rising in real terms during most of the 1980s. In 2007, the poster-boy of the European socialist elite, Sweden, became the first country in the EU to call for the total abandonment of all subsidies and regulations in the farming sector, apart from the small amount allotted to environmental subsidies. Having experienced the sweet taste of market freedom, the Swedes naturally reject the bureaucratic waste of Brussels.

DID THE CAP STABILIZE MARKETS?

In following the spirit of the age, the technocratic ideologues who designed the CAP were deluded enough to still believe that they could micro-manage the complex super-system of European agriculture. Nobel prize winning economist Frederich Hayek spent his life fighting what he called 'the fatal conceit'. Hayek considered the idea that governments could more efficiently and rationally allocate the resources of society than individuals themselves as being the greatest danger to mankind in the 20th century. In reality, he saw that there is a debilitating problem of the division of knowledge in society which confronts governments in their endeavors (Hayek, 1948, p. 77).

It is sometimes suggested that the increase in productivity arising from superior technology was a result of the genius of the CAP that the market could not provide. It has been claimed that a technological revolution took place as a result of higher prices brought about by the CAP price fixing.[8] However, the real explosion in agricultural growth occurred outside the protected fortresses of Europe and the US in the developing countries of the third world where there were no subsidies at all. This became what in 1968 USAID director William Gaud called the 'Green

Revolution' and referred specifically to countries such as India, where agricultural production in items such as cereal doubled in merely 20 years between 1961 and 1985 (Conway, 1998). Furthermore, the CAP subsidies prevented the consolidation of small farms into larger farms and allowed the continued existence of inefficient farms. This would indicate that any technological advancement that occurred happened despite, rather than as a result of the CAP.

Global changes in agriculture were largely in a polar opposite direction to that of the policies pursued by the CAP. For example, the farm population in the US in 1900 was 29 million; by the year 2000 it had decreased to just less than 5 million. In 1900 farmers constituted 39 percent of the population; by the year 2000 they constituted just over 1.5 percent. Schumpeter (1942) best described the very process that took place as one of 'creative destruction'. As weak and inefficient farmers are driven into bankruptcy new opportunities appear and resources are released for a more appropriate allocation of resources brought about by alert entrepreneurs. If anything, because weak and inefficient farmers were supported by the CAP, technological progress was greatly retarded. Furthermore, since the CAP certainly seeks to avoid surpluses, it would appear that the technological improvement of agriculture would necessarily have had to coincide with an ever more restrictive and costly CAP policy (which has indeed been the case).

Furthermore, contrary to the plans for self-sufficiency in agricultural produce, the food trade deficit of the EU-27 is huge and increasing, having jumped from €10.9 billion in 2000 to €24.4 billion in 2008 (of which €13.3 billion comes under the EU classification of 'fish') and in agriculture alone having been of €6.6 billion on average from 2000 to 2008. The most obvious new trend is the recent evolution of agricultural prices on world markets with the world food crisis of 2008. After decades of assault by governments on world food markets, the interventions finally began to bear fruit as global food prices started to rise rapidly in 2007–08. As one author exclaimed:

> Nobody in his right mind believed that the secular downwards price trend could be reversed. This is not true anymore. We do not really know what future agricultural prices will be but they may remain high, by historical standards, for the foreseeable future. And if that happens, we know that the future of agriculture will be profoundly affected. (Petit, 2008, p. 55)

Many have accused the agricultural devastation of the CAP of being a main participant in the deterioration of world food markets. In establishing what has become known as 'Fortress Europe' (Spoerer, forthcoming), Europe is today still a land surrounded by protectionist walls. It aggressively dumps countless millions of tonnes of food at subsidized prices upon third-world economies, annihilating third-world producers. As the United Nations Development Programme's annual report for 2005 put it:

> When it comes to world agricultural trade, market success is determined not by comparative advantage, but by comparative access to subsidies – an area in which producers in poor countries are unable to compete. High levels of agricultural support translate into higher output, fewer imports and more exports than would otherwise be the case. That support helps to explain why industrial countries continue to dominate world agricultural trade. (Human Development Reports, 2005, p. 130)

An unreformed European agriculture policy will continue to hamper the EU's and other donors' efforts to eradicate poverty and will perpetuate human suffering. Having participated in the problem, they are now congratulating themselves that the CAP is in fact the solution, since they can now expand their quotas since world food stocks have become so low (Barnier, 2008).

Despite all of this, the EU remains the world's biggest importer of farm products from developing countries and European farming remains in a strategically weak position overall. As a comparison, one US farmer produces six times more value added than his or her European counterpart (Csaki, 2008). On average, over the period 2006–08, the EU has imported €53 billion worth of goods. This is more than the US, Japan, Canada, Australia and New Zealand combined. The Producer Subsidy Estimate (PSE), calculated by the Organisation for Economic Co-operation and Development (OECD), is an indicator of the annual monetary value of gross transfers from consumers and taxpayers to agricultural producers. In 2009 the total PSE for all products in the EU-27 was valued at almost US$120 billion compared to just US$30 billion for the US itself (OECD, 2010). As Figure 11.5 indicates, the EU is the world's primary contributor to OECD producer supports.

When food prices surged in 2007–08, food security hit the headlines and global governance machinery such as the G-8, the World Bank and the FAO (Food and Agriculture Organization of the United Nations) quickly rushed forward with summits and declarations. As Zahrnt put it:

> Concerns over low farm incomes, the decline of rural communities and the landscaping benefits of farming all looked like dispensable luxuries when compared to this potential threat to our survival. So food security became maybe the most pervasive and powerful argument of those who call for the protection of European agriculture. (Zahrnt, 2010b)

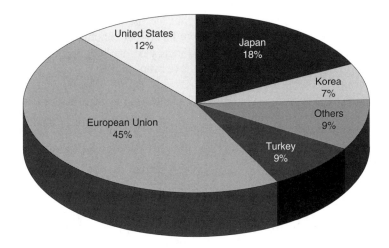

Source: OECD (2010).

*Figure 11.5   Contributors to total OECD agriculture support policies,
          2010*

The world food crisis of 2006–08, which saw food stocks empty out and
the prices of essential foods such as rice and wheat increase by 217 percent
and 136 percent respectively, has shaken the economics profession to the
bone. In 2007 the food price index calculated by the FAO rose by nearly 40
percent, compared with 9 percent the year before. For decades it was simply
assumed that there would always be a secular decreasing downward trend
in food prices. This view has now been shattered. Out of the ashes of this
food crisis, the EU has predictably championed the CAP as the solution to
any future food crises by building upon its food stockpiles and strategically
releasing them onto the market at times of need. In 2010, the European
Commission announced its intention to sell out of its cereal stocks in order
to stabilize the situation after a Russian grain export ban had stung world
markets (EU Business Ltd., 2010). In 2007 in response to a parliamentary
written question, the UK government revealed that over the preceding
year the EU public stock had amassed '13 476 812 tonnes of cereal, rice,
sugar and milk products and 3 529 002 hectoliters of alcohol/wine', which
will either be destroyed or given an export subsidy. Globally, an estimated
100 million tonnes of grain per year are being redirected from food to fuel
(Toepfer International, 2007). Total worldwide grain production for 2007
was just over 2000 million tonnes. Even a World Bank policy report released
in July 2008 concluded that '. . . large increases in biofuels production in the
United States and Europe are the main reason behind the steep rise in global

food prices', and went on to estimate that the rise in food prices caused by biofuels was 75 percent (Mitchell, 2008). The paper concluded by admitting that without the artificially stimulated increased production of biofuels in the US and EU price increases would have been smaller.

Of course, for all the disingenuous 'poor mouth' chatter of the need to ensure food security, what the EU has in fact done is make the food security of billions of humans increasingly precarious. Al Gore himself, the global champion of biofuel subsidies, has been the latest to realize the error of his ways. Speaking in November 2010 at a green energy business conference in Athens, he said, 'it is not good policy to have subsidies for [US] first-generation ethanol . . . First generation ethanol I think was a mistake. The energy conversion ratios are at best very small . . . It's hard once such a program is put in place to deal with the lobbies that keep it going' (Reuters, 2010). He continued, 'The size, the percentage of corn particularly, which is now being [used for] first generation ethanol definitely has an impact on food prices' (ibid.). One must ask with such testimony, how are these programs still in place?

It is estimated that public support for farmers in OECD countries costs a family of four on average nearly US$1000 per year in higher prices and taxes. Even according to the 2003 Human Development Report the average dairy cow in the year 2000 under the EU received $913 in subsidies annually, while an average of $8 per human being was sent in aid to sub-Saharan Africa. While the CAP has changed significantly in the last 10 years and a special subsidy for cows no longer exists, it has merely been a rearranging of the deck chairs on the *Titanic* as the total budget allocated to farmers has not changed.

WHAT TRULY DRIVES THE CAP?

As Valentin Zahrnt has pointed out, 'Food security is not threatened in the EU. The EU has the purchasing power to source supplies from the world market' (2009, p. 15). Nonetheless, Michel Barnier, the French agriculture minister from 2007 to 2009, ex-EU commissioner and member of the governing centre-right UMP party, has called on Europe to establish a food security plan and to resist further cuts in Europe's agriculture budget: 'This is about ensuring that future generations don't pay a price too.' With deft political timing, the French agriculture minister assailed the market, raging that 'What we are now witnessing in the world is the consequence of too much free-market liberalism . . . We can't leave feeding people to the mercy of the market. We need a public policy, a means of intervention and stabilization' (in Hall, 2008).

American economists such as Tuinman (1963) in the early 1960s were extraordinarily prescient in seeing that the CAP would seek to export its problems overseas. France's Michael Barnier has also called for Africa and Latin America to adopt their own versions of Europe's Common Agricultural Policy as a response to rising demand for food, saying: 'I think [the CAP] is a good model. It is a policy that allows us to produce to feed ourselves. We pool our resources to support production. West Africa, East Africa, Latin America and the southern shore of the Mediterranean all need regional common agricultural policies' (in Hall, 2008).

While critics of the CAP prepare to use surging food prices and threats of shortages to seek freer trade in agriculture, Barnier has remained adamant that he would not allow Europe's system of subsidies and barriers to trade take the blame for the 'disorder' surrounding the spike in commodity prices and associated unrest in some countries (Mortished and Webster, 2008).

IS THERE ANY RESISTANCE?

There exists palpable fury with the CAP, however. In the year 2000 one journal reviewing the CAP published the following commentary:

> It is, perhaps, even more interesting that the current rationale for the continued existence, if not further health and prosperity of the CAP – multifunctional agriculture – does not appear in any of these commentaries. If it did, perhaps at least one might have been written as an obituary, or at least as a valedictory. Surely the title – Common Agricultural Policy – has now become as anachronistic as the USSR, a contradiction, if not an actual lie in every word. (Harvey, 2008, p. 54)

It continues, stating:

> If the only sustainable rationale for any sort of policy towards agriculture (and/ or rural land use) is that of market failure (as implied by the multifunctional arguments), then it follows that the reasons for intervention (and hence for policy design and objectives) must also differ, in both quantity and kind, across space and territory and, therefore, between countries. The notion and concept of a common policy is inherently contradictory, if not meaningless (and thus a lie). Even if the rationale continues to be supported and protected, as [Csaki, 2008] points out, the current members of the EU have very different requirements at least in terms of quantity, if not also of the kind of policy. (Harvey, 2008, p. 54)

The current plans for the CAP are that spending for market and income support policies under Pillar 1 of the CAP will eventually fall to 32 percent of the total EU budget in 2013 from more than 70 percent in the early 1980s. Also, there will be tremendous pressure on the financing of the CAP from 2013 onwards because the 10 new EU member states that were previously receiving only 25 percent of the full EU rate in 2004 will receive 100 percent of the CAP support level applicable in the current EU.

The intellectual defensibility of the CAP is waning among the public, however, and the economics profession is becoming ever braver in attacking the CAP. As one author recently put it, 'the costs borne by taxpayers and consumers were larger than the farmers' benefits because high prices crowded out consumer demand and the subsidized expansion of European agriculture bound labor and capital resources that might have been used more productively in other parts of the economy. Hence the CAP was not just a zero-sum game' (Spoerer, forthcoming).

In the world of postmodernist economics we see chatter defending the CAP such as 'the CAP [is] an integral part of the European welfare state and its "moral' economy" . . . it has a *political* rationale' (Rieger, 2005, p. 166). The justification for the CAP is becoming increasingly absurd and much of the concrete philanthropic language that surrounded its creation is being dropped. As Rieger proudly puts it, 'The CAP is an inward looking policy *par excellence*. Its task was never to improve the welfare of the world, but rather to see that European farmers were safe within it' (2005, p. 167).

We can agree with Rieger that the CAP has not improved the welfare of the world. But he is wrong about seeing European farmers as being safe in Europe. What the CAP has done is neuter European agriculture and castrate entrepreneurship in farming. The European farmer has gone from being a vital lynchpin in a previously fecund European agriculture industry, to an impotent cog in the political machine. The CAP has been the protagonist in the depletion of world food supplies, in the process nurturing a new era of food shortages; ironically the supposed reason that was used to justify the CAP in the first place.

AFTER ALL THE REFORMS, HAS THE CAP NOT BEEN IMPROVED?

Dairy became the only sector to experience a sustained fall in the absolute level of nominal spending through the reforms of Franz Fischler's 2003 'Health Check' the mid-term review of the Agenda 2000 reforms. Milk quotas were set to be abolished by 2013. As Zahrnt put it, 'Quotas are used to protect natural resources, such as fish, but not to create a rent for producers. Why should milk producers be privileged over other sectors of the farm and non-farm economy?' (Reform the CAP, 2010). However, in 2009, due mostly to over-production, European milk prices for farmers were extremely low (less than €0.20 ($0.29) per liter from €0.40 two years earlier. Instead of reducing the production to stabilize prices, the EU reintroduced subsidies for milk in 2009 to support producers. 'As [a] consequence, the EU is again exporting milk to the whole developing world, especially towards Africa, at 'dumping' prices . . . By so doing, the EU is destroying the livelihoods of farmers in the poorest countries of the world while artificially maintaining a too high level of production' (Godoy, 2010).

EU agricultural policies have increased agricultural prices by 12 percent in 2008, transferring €36 billion from consumers to producers. This is particularly damaging to low-income households that spend a relatively high proportion of their income on food. According to Eurostat in 2010, food, beverages and tobacco constitute approximately 25 percent of the expenditures of the bottom quintile of EU household incomes, whereas this share is at only 15 percent for the quintile with the highest incomes (Eurostat, 2010). Therefore, poor consumers foot a disproportional share of the bill.

The EU spends about $75 billion on subsidies for agriculture, even though the sector represents only about 2 percent of the total gross domestic product of the EU. Recently it has been revealed that agricultural subsidies rose by 22 percent in 2009, up from 21 per cent in 2008 (OECD, 2010). Some 90 percent of EU produce is protected in some way by the CAP, with some 70 percent in receipt of support prices.

It has also been noted that the CAP is a contributing factor to the decline in European health in recent decades. Artificially cheap sugar, used as a bulking agent as well as a sweetener in a wide variety of both savory and sweet food and drink, has led to increased consumption and contributes to rising levels of overweight and obesity. By heavily subsidizing milk and beef, they ensure that foods with high saturated fat content are comparatively more affordable for people on low incomes than they otherwise would have been. By contrast, fruit and vegetables, which receive little support from the CAP, are relatively expensive. Cheap fatty and sugary foods, and expensive fruit and vegetables, contribute to food poverty – the inability to afford or have access to food that comprises a healthy diet. This inequality in diet predisposes to inequality in diet-related disease – people on lower incomes have higher rates of coronary heart disease, obesity and diabetes. One study summed it up well:

In conclusion this study indicates that, since its creation, CAP subsidies and withdrawals could have been responsible for hundreds of thousands of premature deaths across the EU. The true figures are likely to be much higher than the conservative estimates above. Reform of current CAP policies, as outlined in this report could therefore prevent a great many further deaths. (Birt, 2007, p. 15)

IS THERE ANY HOPE FOR THE FUTURE?

The EU is facing long-term relative decline because of the interaction of aging populations, unfunded pension systems, falling competitiveness, and over-indebted and bankrupt governments. The proportion of inter-EU trade peaked in 1992, and has been declining ever since (Open Europe, 2005). Rigid labor markets, rigid input price markets, excessive regulation, high taxation, and declining workforces are a stark contrast to the low-tax, low-regulation, baby-booming and open trade Europe of the 1950s and 1960s which rapidly caught up with the US after the Second World War. As the French Institute of International Affairs wrote in 2002, 'The enlargement of the European Union won't suffice to guarantee parity with the United States. The EU will weigh less heavily on the process of globalization and a slow but inexorable movement onto history's exit ramp is foreseeable' (Institut Français des Relations Internationales, 2002, p. 3).

Europe's deep clientalism will always hinder any real reform. After 50 years of propaganda the truth about why the CAP continues to exist is best summed up by Pascal Lamy, the French EU trade commissioner, who states: 'The EU has taken a deliberate decision to keep its farmers on the land, whether or not they are internationally competitive . . . If we are fully competitive, employment in the farm sector will drop from 7 million farmers to just one million. This is politically unacceptable' (quoted in Legum, 2002, p. 147).

And this is the truth. There are no economic or scientific or environmental or sociological reasons to support the CAP. When all the arguments are distilled we are left with a grain of truth: the CAP exists so that some politically connected elites may gain at the expense of everyone else. The concentration of special interest groups renders the dispersed unorganized masses impotent in the face of these vast special privileges the EU has copper-fastened. Intellectually, the CAP is in tatters. It has failed on all of its intended objectives. The one area it did nominally succeed in was increasing the income of some farmers. As we have seen, the vast majority of farmers were, in fact, driven off their lands. When we brush away the pseudo-science and fake concern for one's fellow man we are left with a huge payout of taxpayers' money, regressively hammering the poor, being directed to a handful of rich farmers. This is the way the CAP has always been, since the beginning.

I shall finish with two quotes that will give us a guide as to what we may expect from the CAP in the future; one of these viewpoints shall win, and the lives of many depends on which one.

The first is from Dominique de Villepin, French premier 2005–07: 'We must invent new methods of intervention . . . we need protection, to defend national and European products in the face of foreign competition . . . It is time for a real European economic patriotism to be born' (Villepin, 2005).

In contrast, when Frédéric Bastiat the intellectual knight of classical liberal France decried in 1850 the tyrants of his day he spoke in solidarity with the poor and disposed of his country. He wrote:

> To rob the public, it is necessary to deceive it. To deceive it is to persuade it that it is being robbed for its own benefit, and to induce it to accept, in exchange for its property, services that are fictitious or often even worse. This is the purpose of sophistry, whether it be theocratic, economic, political, or monetary. . . . When plunder becomes a way of life for a group of men living together in society, they create for themselves in the course of time a legal system that authorizes it and a moral code that glorifies it. (Bastiat, [1845] 1996, p. 308)

NOTES

1. The Treaties of Rome are two treaties that were both signed on 25 March 1957 by Belgium, France, Italy, Luxembourg, the Netherlands and West Germany. The first Treaty established the European Atomic Energy Community (the EAEC Treaty; often referred to as the Euratom Treaty) while the second Treaty established the European Economic Community (the EEC Treaty; often referred specifically to as the Treaty of Rome).
2. CAP budget was almost 75 percent of EU budget in 1985 (Directorate-Generale for Agriculture and Rural Development, 2008).
3. An 'ever-closer union among the peoples of Europe' is one of the stated aims of the Treaty of Rome, 1957.
4. The radical French agriculture minister '. . . led the fight for the first CAP. The Germans tried to block every step. Adenauer [the German prime minister] was under tremendous pressure from farmers, a large majority of his own coalition, and even business interests to reject any CAP . . . In subsequent rounds of bargaining, de Gaulle faced Erhard, not Adenauer. Political cooperation had also failed. Now he took a harder line. He told his cabinet in early 1963 that if the CAP was not completed soon, "there will be no Common Market at all"' (Parsons, 2003, p. 137).
5. 'It would appear that output can easily be increased at a minimum rate of 2 per cent or more annually – almost double the anticipated rate of rise in demand. If this should take place, European net demand for imported non-tropical foods and feeds would be halved by sometime in the late 1960s and would virtually disappear over the following decade' (Coppock, 1963, p. 173).
6. Rural Investment Support for Europe (RISE) is a CAP lobby group founded in 2006.
7. 'The farm organisations in Europe today admit that the Fischler reforms saved the CAP for the time being, and recognise that if Fischler had given in to Chirac's request

to postpone reforms until after the WTO round, this could have meant the end of the CAP as we know it. Without reforms, not only would the EU have lacked a solid, credible base in order to actively participate in the Doha development round talks, but also the Brussels European Council agreement of 2002 would not have held up against the pressures of the "one percenters" in connection with the 2007–13 financial perspectives' (Pirzio-Biroli, 2008, p. 108).
8. 'The encouragement that high prices give to the agricultural sector leads to greater investment in plant and equipment, and more frequent replacement of this equipment. Technological change is thus likely to be adopted more rapidly than otherwise, since much of the new technology is embodied in new equipment, and is adopted so as to increase output rather than reduce costs, since the output price is supported' (Harvey, 1988).

REFERENCES

Ackrill, R. (2005), 'Common Agricultural Policy', in P. van der Hoek (ed.), *Handbook of Public Administration and Policy in the European Union*, Boca Raton, FL: CRC Press, pp. 435–87.
Ackrill, R. (2008), 'The CAP and its reform: half a century of change?', *EuroChoices*, **7** (2), 13–21.
Ackrill, R., R.C. Hine and A. Rayner (1998), 'CAP reform and implications of member states: budget and trade effects', in A. Rayner and R.C. Hine (eds), *The Reform of the Common Agricultural Policy*, Basingstoke: Macmillan, pp. 104–31.
Ahern, B. (2005), 'Taoiseach defends funding of the Common Agricultural Policy (CAP)', Department of the Taoiseach, http://www.taoiseach. gov.ie/eng/Government_Press_Office/Taoiseach's_Press_Releases_2005/Taois each_defends_funding_of_the_Common_Agricultural_Policy_CAP_.html, 9 September.
Bagus, P. (2010), *The Tragedy of the Euro*, Auburn, AL: Ludwig von Mises Institute.
Barnier, M. (2008), 'How Europe should tackle the global food crisis', Europe's World, www.europesworld.org/NewEnglish/Home_old/Article/tabid/191/ ArticleType/articleview/ArticleID/21209/language/en-US/Default.aspx.
Bastiat, F. ([1845] 1996), *Economic Sophisms Parts One & Two*, trans. A. Goddard, Irvington-on-Hudson, NY: Foundation for Economic Education.
Birt, C. (2007), *A CAP on Health? The Impact of the Common Agricultural Policy on Public Health*, London: Faculty of Public Health.
Bolin, O. and B. Swedenborg (eds) (1992), *Mat till EG-pris*, Stockholm: SNS Förlag.
Brooks, J. (2003), 'Agriculture: why is it still so difficult to reform?', OECD Observer, http://oecdobserver.org/news/fullstory.php/aid/1177/Agriculture:_ Why_is_it_still_so_difficult_to_reform_.html.
Caplan, B. (2007), *The Myth of the Rational Voter*, Princeton, NJ: Princeton University Press.
Collins, N.R. (1963), 'Discussion: the European Common Market and agriculture', *Journal of Farm Economics*, **45** (5), 993–6.
Commission of the European Communities (1998), 'Proposals for council regulations (EC) concerning reform of the Common Agricultural Policy', COM (98) 158 final, http://aei.pitt.edu/13186/, 18 March.

Conway, G. (1998), *The Doubly Green Revolution: Food for All in the Twenty-First Century*, Ithaca, NY: Comstock Publishing.

Cooper, T., K. Hart and D. Baldock (2009), *Provision of Public Goods through Agriculture in the European Union*, Brussels: Institute for European Environmental Policy.

Coppock, J.O. (1963), *The North Atlantic Policy: The Agricultural Gap*, New York: Twentieth-Century Fund.

Csaki, C. (2008), 'The CAP at fifty', *EuroChoices*, **7** (2), 4–5.

Directorate-Generale for Agriculture and Rural Development (2008), *From 1980 to 2006: CAP Expenditure – European Commission, DG Agriculture and Rural Development (Financial Reports)*, Brussels: European Commission.

ECIPE (European Centre for International Political Economy) (2009), 'A common agricultural policy for European public goods', ECIPE, www.ecipe. org/archived-events/a-common-agricultural-policy-for-european-public-goods-declaration-by-a-group-of-leading-agricultural-economists.

EU Business Ltd (2010), 'EU to put cereal stocks on market by end of year', www. eubusiness.com/news-eu/farm-food.6ao, 27 September.

European Commission (1997), 'Towards a common agricultural and rural policy for Europe', report of an Expert Group, Brussels.

European Commission (2008), 'Proposal for a directive of the European Parliament and of the Council on the promotion of the use of energy from renewable sources', EUR-Lex.europa.eu, http://eur-lex.europa.eu/LexUriServ/ LexUriServ.do?uri=COM:2008:0019:FIN:EN:HTML, 23 January.

European Commission (2010), 'The EU's Common Agricultural Policy (CAP): on the move in a changing world: how the EU's agriculture and development policies fit together', *EU Agriculture and Rural Development*, http://ec.europa.eu/ agriculture/developing-countries/publi/brochure2010/text_en.pdf.

Eurostat (2010), 'Key figures on Europe', *Eurostat pocketbooks*, http://epp.euro-stat.ec.europa.eu/cache/ITY_OFFPUB/KS-EI-10-001/EN/KS-EI-10-001-EN. PDF.

Fischler, F. (2008), 'Europe's CAP: changes and challenges', *EuroChoices*, **7** (2), 22–7.

Fischler, F. (2010), 'Foreword from the Chairman Dr. Franz Fischler', Rise Foundation, www.risefoundation.eu/index.php?option=com_content&view=ar ticle&id=48&Itemid=64, 24 November.

Godoy, J. (2010), 'Farm subsidies on increase', *Asia Times*, www.atimes.com/ atimes/Global_Economy/LH10Dj05.html, 10 August.

Hall, B. (2008), The rising cost of food: Europe's CAP the "answer" to food crisis', *Financial Times*, www.ft.com/cms/s/0/939ee094-148d-11dd-a741-0000779fd2ac. html?nclick_check=1, 27 April.

Harvey, D. (1988), 'Food mountains and famines: the economics of agricultural policies', inaugural lecture at the University of Newcastle upon Tyne, Newcastle, 3 March.

Harvey, D. (2008), 'Happy birthday to the CAP: comment on the CAP's 50th birthday', *EuroChoices*, **7** (2), 54.

Hasha, G. (1999), 'The European Union's Common Agricultural Policy: pressures for change – an overview', United States Department of Agriculture, Economic Research Service.

Hayek, F. (1948), 'The use of knowledge in society', *American Economic Review*, **35**, 519–30.

Hayek, F. (1989), *The Fatal Conceit: The Errors of Socialism*, Chicago: University of Chicago Press.
Hill, B. (2008), 'Using the Wye Group Handbook to develop EU statistics on the incomes of agricultural households', *Journal of Agricultural Economics*, **59** (3), 387–420.
Human Development Reports (2005), *International Cooperation at a Crossroads: Aid, Trade and Security in an Unequal World*, New York: United Nations Development Program.
Institut Français des Relations Internationales (2002), *World Trade in the 21st Century*, Brussels: European Commission.
Jongeneel, R (2010), 'European dairy policy in the years to come: quota abolition and competitiveness', LEI report.
Learn, E.W. (1963), 'The impact of European integration on American agriculture', *Journal of Farm Economics*, **45** (5), 983–91.
Legum, M. (2002), *It Doesn't Have to be Like This: Global Economics a New Way Forward*, Glasgow: Wild Goose Publications.
Ludlow, N.P. (2005), 'The making of the CAP: towards a historical analysis of the EU's first major common policy', *Contemporary European History*, **14** (3), 347–371.
Mises, L. von ([1949] 1998), *Human Action: A Treatise on Economics*, Auburn, AL: Ludwig von Mises Institute.
Mitchell, D. (2008), *A Report on Rising Food Prices*, Washington, DC: World Bank.
Mortished, C. and P. Webster (2008), 'France's answer to global food crisis is EU Protectionism', *Times Online*, www.timesonline.co.uk/tol/news/world/europe/article3746899.ece, 15 April.
OECD (2003), 'Agricultural Policies in OECD Countries: A Positive Reform Agenda', OECD policy brief, www.oecd.org/dataoecd/27/43/2955711.pdf, June.
OECD (2010), 'Agricultural policies in OECD countries at a glance', OECD, www.oecd.org/document/47/0,3343,en_2649_33773_45538523_1_1_1_37401,00.html.
Open Europe (2005), 'Open Europe: why the EU must reform to survive', http://www.openeurope.org.uk/research/factsheet.pdf.
Paarlberg, D. (1964), 'Reviewed works: "North Atlantic policy: the agricultural gap" by John O. Coppock', *American Economic Review*, **54** (4), 508–10.
Paarlberg, D. and P. Paarlberg (2000), *The Agricultural Revolution of the 20th Century*, Ames, IO: Iowa State University Press.
Parsons, C. (2003), *A Certain Idea of Europe*, Ithaca, NY: Cornell University Press.
Peeters, K. (2008), 'A competitive, sustainable and diverse agriculture: a view of the CAP beyond 2013', *EuroChoices*, **9**, 4–9.
Petit, M. (2008), 'The CAP after fifty years: a never-ending reform process', *EuroChoices*, **7** (2), 55.
Pirzio-Biroli, C. (2008), 'An insider's perspective on the political economy of the Fischler reforms', in J. Swinnen (ed.), *The Perfect Storm*, Brussels: Centre for European Policy Studies, pp. 102–14.
Potočnik, J. (2010), 'Can the CAP bring considerable benefits to our environment?', 3rd Forum for the Future of Agriculture: The Economics and Politics of Food Security vs. Climate Change, Brussels.
Rabinowicz, E. (2004), 'The Swedish agricultural policy reform of 1990 – a window of opportunity for structural change in policy preferences', paper of the symposium Adjusting to Domestic and International Agricultural Policy

Reform in Industrial Countries, Philadelphia, International Agricultural Trade Research Consortium.

Reform the CAP (2010), 'Milk quota', www.reformthecap.eu.

Reuters (2010), 'U.S. corn ethanol "was not a good policy" – Gore', Reuters, http://af.reuters.com/article/energyOilNews/idAFLDE6AL0YT20101122?page Number=2&virtualBrandChannel=0&sp=true, 22 November.

Rieger, E. (2005), 'Agricultural policy: constrained reforms', in W. Wallace and M.A. Pollack (eds), *Policy-Making in the European Union*, Oxford: Oxford University Press, pp. 161–90.

Rodale Institute (2002), 'Farming without subsidies? Some lessons from New Zealand', http://newfarm.rodaleinstitute.org/features/0303/newzealand_subsidies.shtml.

Rothbard, M.N. ([1963] 2004), *America's Great Depression*, Alabama, AL: Ludwig von Mises Institute.

Rothbard, M.N. (1973), *For a New Liberty: The Libertarian Manifesto*, New York: Collier Macmillan.

Rothbard, M.N. (1982), *The Ethics of Liberty*, New Jersey: Humanities Press.

Ryan, R. (2010), 'Strong CAP needed to help farmers cope with regulations, says Walshe', *Irish Examiner*, www.irishexaminer.com/business/kfcwojgbgboj/rss2/#ixzz15d4jtq53, 21 July.

Samuelson, P.A. (1954), 'The pure theory of public expenditure', *Review of Economics and Statistics*, **36** (4), 387–9.

Schumpeter, J.A. (1942), *Capitalism, Socialism and Democracy*, London: Unwin.

Spoerer, M. (forthcoming), 'Fortress Europe in long-term perspective: agricultural protection in the European Community, 1957–2003', *Journal of European Integration History*.

Stead, D.R. (2008), 'The birth of the CAP', *EuroChoices*, **7** (2), 6–12.

Swinnen, J. and H. de Gorter (2002), 'On government credibility, compensation, and underinvestment in public research', *European Review of Agricultural Economics*, **29** (4), 501–22.

Thurston, J., N. Mulvad and B. Alfter (2010), 'Reaction to ECJ ruling', *Farm Subsidy*, http://farmsubsidy.org/news/features/ecj-reaction/, 9 November.

Toepfer International (2007), 'Biofuels to keep global grain prices high', Reuters, www.reuters.com/article/idUSL309054420070730, July 30.

Tuinman, Abe S. (1963), 'The European Economic Community and its agricultural policy', *Journal of Farm Economics*, 974–82.

UK Taxpayers' Alliance (2009), *Food for Thought: How the Common Agricultural Policy Costs Families over £400 a Year*, London: Taxpayers' Alliance.

UNEP (2009), *Towards Sustainable Production and Use of Resources: Assessing Biofuels*, New York: United Nations Environment Program.

Vaglenov, S. and T. Balabanova (2010), 'A family affair: Bulgarian farming minister distributes EU money among his family', *Farm Subsidy*, http://farmsubsidy.org/news/features/family-affair/, 16 September.

Villepin, D. de (2005), *L'Homme européen*, Paris: Plon.

Walt, V. (2010), 'Even in hard times, E.U. farm subsidies roll on', *Time*, www.time com/time/business/article/0,8599,1989196,00.html#ixzz161g83cuA, 14 May.

Zahrnt, V. (2009), 'Public money for public goods: winners and losers from CAP reform', *ECIPE working paper* 08/2009.

Zahrnt, V. (2010a), 'Declaration on CAP reform', *EuroChoices*, **9** (1), 57.

Zahrnt, V. (2010b), 'Greening the CAP, and pruning it too', *Europe's World*, summer, http://www.europesworld.org/NewEnglish/Home_old/Article/tabid/191/ArticleType/ArticleView/ArticleID/21663/language/en-US/GreeningtheCAP andpruningittoo.aspx.

Zobbe, H. (2002), 'The economic and historical foundation of the Common Agricultural Policy in Europe', paper from the Xth EAAE Congress Exploring Diversity in the European Agri-Food System, Zaragoza, Spain, European Association of Agricultural Economists.

Index